King of the Castle

A Biography of William Larnach

King of the Castle

A Biography of William Larnach

Fleur Snedden

David Bateman

Photographs and illustrations are from the collections of Hardwicke Knight, Otago Settlers Museum, Robinson family collection, W W Stewart family and the Larnach family collection.

ARTS COUNCIL OF NEW ZEALAND *TOI AOTEAROA*

First published in 1997 by David Bateman Ltd, 30 Tarndale Grove, Albany, Auckland, New Zealand

Copyright © Fleur Snedden, 1997
Copyright © David Bateman Ltd, 1997

ISBN 1 86953 353 4

Cover design by Sue Reidy Design
Book design by Claire Preen
Printed in Hong Kong by Colorcraft Ltd

Dedicated to the memories of my father Ivan Larnach Hjorring, and my stepfather John Francis Mangos.

CONTENTS

THE LARNACH FAMILY

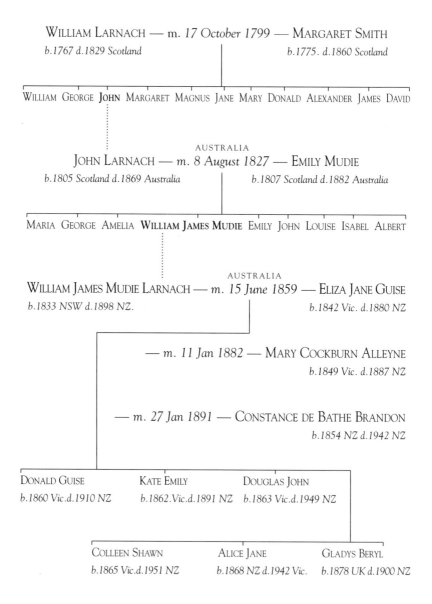

WILLIAM LARNACH — m. *17 October 1799* — MARGARET SMITH
b.1767 d.1829 Scotland — *b.1775. d.1860 Scotland*

WILLIAM GEORGE **JOHN** MARGARET MAGNUS JANE MARY DONALD ALEXANDER JAMES DAVID

AUSTRALIA
JOHN LARNACH — m. *8 August 1827* — EMILY MUDIE
b.1805 Scotland d.1869 Australia — *b.1807 Scotland d.1882 Australia*

MARIA GEORGE AMELIA **WILLIAM JAMES MUDIE** EMILY JOHN LOUISE ISABEL ALBERT

AUSTRALIA
WILLIAM JAMES MUDIE LARNACH — m. *15 June 1859* — ELIZA JANE GUISE
b.1833 NSW d.1898 NZ. — *b.1842 Vic. d.1880 NZ*

— m. *11 Jan 1882* — MARY COCKBURN ALLEYNE
b.1849 Vic. d.1887 NZ

— m. *27 Jan 1891* — CONSTANCE DE BATHE BRANDON
b.1854 NZ d.1942 NZ

DONALD GUISE — KATE EMILY — DOUGLAS JOHN
b.1860 Vic.d.1910 NZ — *b.1862.Vic.d.1891 NZ* — *b.1863 Vic.d.1949 NZ*

COLLEEN SHAWN — ALICE JANE — GLADYS BERYL
b.1865 Vic.d.1951 NZ — *b.1868 NZ d.1942 Vic.* — *b.1878 UK d.1900 NZ*

PROLOGUE

For many years boxes of papers and letters belonging to William Larnach had lain stacked in a cupboard, and I had made a half-hearted promise to myself that one day I would sort them into some kind of order. It was the arrival of a letter from the playwright Michelanne Forster that forced me into action. Michelanne had heard that the Larnach papers had been passed down to me by Larnach's granddaughter, Gretchen Guise (Larnach) Hjorring, my grandmother, and Michelanne was eager to see them to help in her research for her play *Larnach, Castle of Lies*. Together, over several days, we sorted through Larnach's scrapbooks of letters and newspaper cuttings, which recorded events in the lives of himself and his family from their arrival in the very early days of Australian colonisation, until their later settlement in New Zealand.

When I first met Michelanne she had already done considerable research on the Larnach family. She was so immersed in their lives that, through her enthusiasm, I also became bewitched with the family. They became real people. We read their letters, looked at their photos, discussed their foibles, their fortunes and their woes, and it was Michelanne who persuaded me to write this biography of William Larnach, his wives, family and the many interesting people whose lives crossed his.

Without the help of many people, this first attempt at writing would not have progressed very far. Special thanks are due to my lifelong friend Jenifer Curnow, whose encouragement and practical advice gave me the determination to persevere; to my youngest daughter Alexandra for her many pages of typing before I mastered the word processor; to my son Charles for pushing me into the twentieth century and insisting I become computer literate; to my eldest daughter Kate who read the manuscripts; to my other daughter Victoria, who was on call to visit the Mitchell Library in Sydney; and to my daughter-in-law Sally Tagg for her professional photographic assistance. The prize for patience must go to my husband Jim, who has had to live in the shadow of Larnach for three years and can now recite this book by heart.

I also owe a debt of gratitude to Hardwicke Knight, the author of *The Ordeal of William Larnach*, for his permission to freely quote from his book, and to Wayne Goodall for sending me his thesis, *William J.M. Larnach, 1833-1898, New Zealand Politician*, both most helpful works. That debt of gratitude extends to the trustees of the Alfred and Isobel Reed Trust, in assisting me with a grant towards my research.

I want to record my thanks to the many librarians and archivists who have answered my letters, and steered me through the research labyrinth. Mrs Tania Connelly and Sean Brosnahan of the Otago Settlers Museum, Mrs Val Laing of the McNab Dunedin Public Library, Claire Wood of the National Archives in Dunedin, and Beverley Booth of the Hocken Library deserve special mention, as does Doris Gardiner, archivist of the National Bank Archives in Wellington, who even stirred Lloyds Bank of London into researching for me.

The staff of the Alexander Turnbull Library in Wellington, the Auckland Institute and Museum Library, the Auckland Public Library, the Mitchell Library in Sydney, La Trobe Library in Melbourne, the Battye Library in Perth, the smaller libraries of Singleton, Geelong, Ararat, Wagga Wagga, and Riverina in Australia, Des Archives de France, the Wick Library in Scotland, the NZ Railway and Locomotive Society and the Postal History Society of NZ all contributed to the information in this book.

Many people took the trouble to write in answer to my queries, others contributed in a material way: Mrs Margaret Barker of Larnach Castle with documents and photographs; Mrs Kath Martin of Nelson with a suitcase of photos and letters relating to the Larnachs; Mrs Sylvia Howden by allowing me to view her great-aunt's (Constance Larnach, née de Bathe Brandon) wedding dress and by sharing family reminiscences with me; Mr John Larnach Hume for sending me letters of Eliza Larnach's; the Robinson Family of Singleton, who permitted me to reproduce the photo of Rosemount from their collection; the family of W.W. Stewart, who gave permission to photograph the painting by their father from his book *When Steam was King*; and to Maria Jungoswka of Scope Publishing Services who provided helpful advice. To all, my heartfelt thanks.

Larnach is generally dismissed as the man who built a castle-like residence, and later committed suicide in Parliament House. As my research progressed, I found a man quite unlike my previous idea of him, which had been based on the unhappy memories of the several years my grandmother had spent in Larnach's company. My grandmother had portrayed to me the image of an aloof, short-tempered Victorian patriarch, but I found some endearing qualities as well. He was generous and soft-hearted, and at the same time ambitious, bossy, vain and gregarious; a man who accepted life's blows philosophically, showed great loyalty to his friends, and whose ideas and contributions to the country received little recognition. He was not afraid to risk his money or his time. His years as a young banker on the Australian goldfields, his entrepreneurial ideas of opening up unexplored Australian land, and his business and political career in New Zealand show him to be overall an honest, enterprising and adventurous man. Certain aspects of his business dealings in New Zealand in association with many well known figures of the time were considered by some to be questionable, although most of his associates went on to collect knighthoods and premierships. New Zealand needed men of his calibre, and his life is a good study of the way our colonial forefathers contributed, for better or for worse, to the country we enjoy today. Their aspirations, their speculations and their political machinations show that little has changed since the last century.

Michelanne Forster's play, *Larnach, Castle of Lies*, covers a fairly short period in William Larnach's life. A playwright has the luxury of artistic licence, and I feel she has captured his personality at that stage in his life with credibility. My task, as a narrator of historical facts, leaves little room for the imagination, but requires pernickety insistence on authenticity. In delving into the history of Larnach, this constraint was not a hindrance, it only highlighted the fact that his life was as full of drama as any fictional saga written today. The tale is a tangled web spun among the branches of the family tree; a tale of cruelty, tragedy, intrigue, success and ultimately failure.

Chapter I

A SCOTTISH HERITAGE

On 11 January 1972 Mr Peter Malcolm Entwistle, a young man with a macabre sense of interior decoration, stood before the magistrate in the Dunedin Court and pleaded guilty to improperly interfering with human remains. A few days earlier, Entwistle had been confronted at his home by the police, who had presented a search warrant, and the twenty-three-year-old post-graduate student had told them the skull they found had been given to him at a party a year previously, by a friend who "had no further use for it", and he had kept it as an interesting reminder of a man of some local fame who had died violently. The skull had been kept polished and in good condition. It was easily recognized by the bullet hole in the side of the forehead as that of William James Mudie Larnach.

Entwisle was initially convicted but the conviction was set aside and the charge against him dismissed. The magistrate was satisfied there had been no "interference" with the remains which were later returned to the once beautiful mausoleum in Dunedin's Northern Cemetery.

Exhuming skeletal remains of the dead was an action the early Christians sometimes took, but only when they felt the deceased, by his exemplary life, should be canonised — a category in which William Larnach, like most of us, would not be listed. For the majority of people, Larnach is just a name attached to a castle, a name that has been remembered in Dunedin long after those of his less flamboyant contemporaries, who may well have deserved greater recognition but who did not invest so heavily in a fantasy of stone that has captured people's interest. Today, Larnach Castle, on the heights of the Otago Peninsula, is a popular tourist attraction that has been artistically restored to its former glory.

While William Larnach's name has survived because of his home, little is remembered of the man himself. Yet nothing reveals a man's personality more than his home; it is a blueprint of his character. Larnach's flamboyance is evident in the design of the house and the scale of the grounds. Further study of the design of the castle shows that he was an ingenious innovator, and a meticulous organiser. He was a popular employer, generous, gregarious, ebullient, and an hospitable party-giver. He could be arrogant, yet mixed easily with people from all walks of life. He was a forceful master in his own home, yet had a sense of humour and was a doting father. What forces moulded this man, and where did it all go awry?

Vindicating himself, Peter Entwistle told the magistrate that he was not aware that William Larnach had any living relatives who would be upset by his actions. He overlooked the fact that Larnach was a family man. He had grandchildren and great-grandchildren, who in turn have continued to produce even more generations. More relevant to this narrative, however, is that Larnach, like all of us, had parents and grandparents, and some of his hereditary characteristics can be traced back to his Scottish grandfather, after whom he was named but never met. The Dunedin poet Charles Brasch wrote "the balanced man . . . is he who lives in the present, yet does not cease to live with and relive his past too, his personal past and that of his family, and his town and his country . . . In these pasts he would find the threads of his being." [1]

Larnachs have lived in the north of Scotland for many generations, mostly in the windswept town of Wick, situated about 24 km down the rocky coast from John o'Groats, in the County of Caithness. It was here in 1767 that Grandfather William was born. As a capable young lad of eleven, with an aptitude for accounting, William Larnach from Wick entered the Royal Navy as a cabin boy and quickly scrambled up the promotional ropes to become a naval purser. During the Napoleonic Wars, Purser Larnach sailed on a large flagship carrying 100 guns and the 800 men needed to man them. As purser he was also required to organise huge quantities of ammunition and provisions for long periods at sea, from cannon balls to ship's biscuits, from powder barrels to kegs of rum for the crew of these crowded wooden ships.

Purser Larnach married Margaret Smith at Wick on 17 October 1799, on the same day that their firstborn son was christened. Cricket may have been on the minds of the newly weds when they started their family of eleven children, but it was a football team comprised entirely of Larnachs that years later brought some small fame to the town of Wick. It was a town noted for its love of football, and 100 years before the wedding of William and Margaret, the Kirk Sessions record how the young people had to stand before the Elders for "playing at the football and danseing [sic] on the Sabbath." They were described as a "jolly pagan lot". [2]

During the long periods that William spent at sea, Margaret Larnach lived with her young family on her widowed mother's farm at Achingall, in the Strath of Watten — a wide valley west of Wick, where in summer "the cornfields shewed a rich uninterrupted verdure for several miles around." [3] In 1804, in the slate-blue stone cottage at Achingall, where the thatched roof tied down with rope told of wild winter winds, John Larnach, the third son of Purser William and Margaret Larnach, was born. In years to come he would have a son whom he would name William, after his father.

When Purser Larnach retired from the navy, he returned to the fertile farm of his mother-in-law — but not as a farmer, his interests were far too commercial for that. Land to him was a profitable commodity, to be used to advantage by buying, selling or leasing it. Purser Larnach became a "tacksman" — a middle man who leases land directly from the owner of a large estate, which he then sublets into small farms. William's holdings were quite substantial, extending from Achingall to Newton, a distance of 16 km; but they were not large enough to employ all his seven sons, should they wish to farm.

Back around the ninth century, when the marauding Vikings were drawn to "Vik", (their word for bay), they discovered not only the shelter of a bay at the mouth of a river, but also rich farmland that beckoned from the west. Thus had begun a long and prosperous history of agriculture in the area. At an early age young John Larnach developed farming skills which would stand by him for the rest of his life. Unlike his father, land speculation did not interest John. His six brothers all reflected some facet of their father's background, becoming farmers, bankers and shipbrokers.

Four years before the death of Purser Larnach in 1829, his wife Margaret, aged 50, bore their eleventh and last child. Margaret survived her husband by over thirty years. On her tombstone is the inscription "Many of her family in distant parts of the world."

The average Scottish farmer of that time was "a canny professional farmer, who added the use of basic scientific and commercial principles to traditional hard work and sobriety, all of which was seen as a living out of one's Christian vocation."[4] In rural Scotland in the early 1800s, from laird to lowly shepherd, these ethics were almost instinctive. But John Larnach's character was also shaped by the community in which he was raised.

The picture that the rest of Scotland presented was of rather grim dour people, their spirits quelled by the poverty that a stern Presbyterian God had sent them to atone for their sins. But this was not so in the County of Caithness. Many centuries of prosperous farming meant that they suffered not the plight of poverty, but the evils of plenty. Even in bad times there was always enough barley for the distillation of whisky, and the inns drew a much larger congregation than the church. In Kirk records, a zealous minister defaced the statue of Saint Fergus, the patron saint of Wick, in an attempt to wipe out any traces of Catholicism. The good people of Wick had venerated Saint Fergus for centuries, and each year his feast day was devoted not to prayer, but to mirth, jollity and drunken brawls. The fact that their patron saint was now the wrong denomination worried them not one iota. In their fury at the vandalism of their icon, they bundled the hapless Presbyterian minister down to the beach, halting their religious festivities just long enough to drown the reverend gentleman in the waters of Wick Bay. These people were used to taking the law into their own hands; petty authority was disregarded. Such was the environment that John Larnach grew up in.

During John Larnach's early years, one of the fastest growths in population for many centuries took place in Britain. This, coupled with antiquated land laws and a scarcity of arable land, promoted the idea of emigration to many a young man eager to have his own farm. Younger sons, tenant farmers, skilled agricultural workers, shepherds, all hoped to find land in the Antipodes. Hope alone was not enough to succeed in the colonies, these

4

young people also needed a strong determination to make the most of the opportunities there. A writer to the *Sydney Morning Herald* noted: "People come here to better their conditions, many with limited means, their tempers a little soured with privations and disappointed expectations (for all expect too much), cut off from the ties of kindred, old friendships, and endearing associations, all struggling in the road of advancement, and no one who reflects will be surprised that they jostle one another."[5]

Given the conditions in Scotland in 1823, it is not surprising that John Larnach joined the army without a commission. He was assigned as a cadet to Major Archibald Clune Innes to serve in Australia. He farewelled his grieving parents, brothers and sisters, and set off in pursuit of success, the first of several Larnachs who would leave for Australia. His five-year-old brother Donald, while proud to relate stories at school of John in the Antipodes, was broken-hearted by his departure and resolved to follow him in the future, a resolution he kept. William and Margaret had produced a close-knit family who kept in touch with one another in spite of great distances.

In 1788 when the first fleet of prison hulks arrived at Port Jackson, Sydney, many convicts had died because of appalling conditions on the journey. But improvements had taken place by the time John Larnach set sail thirty-five years later. The journey to Australia that had taken earlier vessels 252 days could now be done in 110 days. The vessels were faster and roomier. Passengers had about the same amount of space to themselves as present day travellers flying from Britain to Australia. In 1823 a wooden berth 2 m square, with less than 2 m of headroom was considered "ample space" for four convicts, and passengers were not much better off. The route the vessels took depended on the supply of fresh food and water. By 1820, most captains sailed down to Rio then "ran down their easting" straight to the southern coast of Australia, then north to Sydney.

In July 1823, the vessel *Andromeda*, a barque of 408 tonnes, arrived in Port Jackson, Sydney. On board was John Larnach. At nineteen years of age, the young cadet saw from the deck of the ship the country he would live in for the rest of his life. The mild winter temperatures of July were in great contrast to the eye-watering winter winds of Wick, and the town, encircled by bush, presented a picture of neat stone cottages with pretty gardens, vegetable plots and flourishing orchards. Governor Macquarie's handsome hospital, designed mainly by his wife, had been completed, as had later buildings designed by the convict architect Francis Howard Greenway. One of his most notable buildings, which still stands today, was the Hyde Park Barracks, housing 800 convicts. This is where John would be stationed.

Walking up Pitt Street, John would have passed

an Eligible, Capital and very commodious dwelling house, well shingled and glazed throughout, containing four spacious Rooms, with detached kitchen and wash house. A large garden capable of an abundant supply for a large family, with some choice fruit trees; a capital well with good water, good Stock and Poultry yards fenced in, eligibly and undeniably situate for Business or Residence in the most desirable part of Pitt's Row. The former residence of the late Sergeant Richard Guise. [6]

Thirty-six years later, John Larnach's son would marry Sergeant Richard Guise's great-granddaughter.

Next to the barracks, Hyde Park was slowly being transformed from a dusty wasteland to a horse-racing track, with the winning post at the Market Street end. There was also an area of fine open spaces where the colonists could play cricket, promenade along the newly formed paths and admire the substantial houses now being built on the western side of Elizabeth Street.

Marring this sense of happy progress in a town so magnificently sited were gangs of convicts with leg-irons jangling. These men were quarrying rocks, digging holes, sawing logs, and, due to a shortage of draught animals, carting rubble, and were accompanied by the crack of lashing whips, applied to any convict who should falter for one moment.

Under the command of Major Innes, a cheerful man of great panache, John Larnach was initiated into the harsh rudiments of convict supervision, where "physical brutality had only one place in that ordered world, as the fit corrective for the disorderly, vulgar, brutal, barbarian habits of the lower orders."[7] Within six months of John's arrival in Sydney, popular Major Innes was transferred to administer a penal colony in Van Diemen's Land (Tasmania). With his departure, John, having taken stock of the opportunities of acquiring land in the colony, resigned from his cadetship, and, through the influence of Major Innes, obtained a position in the country on the Hunter Valley property Ravensworth, owned by the surgeon general, Dr James Bowman.

In the country John soon found another form of torture — the armed wariness and nervous calm that existed between Aborigines and settlers. Each side watched the other from the shadows, waiting to pounce when a victim would unwittingly find himself isolated, and become a quarry for spear or musket. If an Aboriginal was the aggressor and killed a white man, all hell would break loose until he paid for his crime, but in the reverse situation "the Aborigine were seen as a society that had failed to emerge from a primitive state, and their deaths were of no consequence."[8]

John Larnach became the overseer for Dr Bowman. The Bowmans had arrived as free settlers from Scotland in 1798. It was not unusual for these early settlers, once established in Sydney, to acquire land. Rather than undergo the hardships of isolation, they then employed overseers to run their estates, enabling these affluent settlers to continue practising their profession or trade in the comfort and safety of Sydney.

An overseer had to measure up to rigid standards. He had to be a tough disciplinarian to control the convict labourers who worked on the land and the female convicts (often hardened viragos) who looked after the cook house and laundry. To extract the best from the land he had to be a competent farmer, but most of all he had to be able to cope with the ever-silent threat of an Aboriginal spear in the back, or the reprisals wrought by escaped convicts in surprise raids. All this had to be done single-handedly and in isolation. It was a well paid, demanding job for the implacable young man from Wick.

In 1825, the first hint of John Larnach's tough character emerged.

While John was still overseeing the Bowman property, he employed a few friendly Aborigines. Unfortunately, two convict fencers were speared to death by Aborigines, and John joined a party of mounted police to track the offenders. When the search was unsuccessful, an Aboriginal guide, who had offered his assistance to help find the killers, was brutally treated and shot on suspicion of being involved with the murderers. In spite of royal instructions to every governor of Australia "that the Aborigine must not be molested", they were still classed as a pest to be exterminated; and although many were shot by remote settlers, this produced no outrage.

On this occasion, however, even the cold-blooded governor, Sir Ralph Darling, had some doubts as to the guilt of the "naked savages". He hinted in a letter to the Earl of Bathurst that John Larnach may have been just a little over zealous in his efforts to promote law and order. "I fear the conduct of the Natives in this case has not been altogether unprovoked, and being strict observers of the Law of Retaliation, I have been informed they never fail to exact blood for blood." [9] But that was as far as the matter went.

A year after that incident John Larnach achieved his ambition. He had saved enough money to acquire a land holding of his own, on Patrick Plains in the Hunter Valley near Singleton. This made him eligible to serve as a juror for the Hunter River District, together with James Mudie, his neighbour and a father of three daughters.

*   *   *

In spite of great distances between neighbours in remote areas of Australia, lavish balls were held by the increasing number of pastoral families. Guests, starved of company, were happy to travel up to 320 km to attend. Many marriages resulted from these gatherings, and it is likely that John Larnach became acquainted with his future wife, Emily Mudie, at such an event.

*   *   *

In a time when unbridled cruelty was commonplace, Emily's father, James Mudie, stands out as one of the more ruthless members of society in New South Wales in the 1830s. Born in Aberdeen, he retired from his position of 1st Lieutenant in the 69th Company of Marines under a cloud. He had been charged with offences that have never been revealed, and for which he should have been dismissed from the Marines, but the Admiralty, worn down by his many persistent appeals, indulgently let him retire.

Faced with a shortage of money and no employment, he compiled a book entitled *An Historical and Critical Account of a Grand Series of Medals Covering the Reign of George III*. Even acquiring that poor deranged king's patronage did not make the book a seller, and Mudie and his publisher found themselves in the Insolvent Court, Portugal Street, London, having lost £10,000 on the venture. He was nicknamed Major Medallion, eventually becoming known as Major Mudie, a moniker he was happy to acknowledge, but slow to reveal its phoney origin.

Then bankrupt, James Mudie, a widower with three daughters and no prospects, had cast his scheming eye in the direction of his wealthy cousin, Sir Charles Forbes. Through his connections with the Colonial Office, Forbes had arranged for land grants in New South Wales to be given to Mudie, paid for his passage and those of his daughters to Australia and, hoping never to see Mudie again, provided him with a regular remittance.

The convict ship *Asia*, flying the red and white pennant denoting its shackled convict cargo, dropped anchor in Sydney Cove in July 1822. Only one out of 190 male convicts had died on the voyage, and James Mudie and his daughters were among the few settlers who made up the ship's complement. The voyage had been tedious. Apart from watching the sailors fishing for bonitos and sharks, the only other entertainment was provided by the convicts, a grotesque charm bracelet of chained men — pimps, poachers, murderers, forgers, shoplifters, highway robbers, cattle thieves and fraudsters — who emerged each day from a hatchway for a brief period of fresh air and exercise, often dancing round the deck to the clanging beat of leg irons. Not that James Mudie was upset by the sight of these fettered wretches. It appealed to his sense of righteousness, his Calvinistic views of Divine Orderliness, and his strong opinion that all wrongdoers (except himself, of course) should pay in full for their sins — a view held by a great many of his contemporaries.

With the sizeable financial backing of Sir Charles Forbes, James Mudie received a land grant of 4150 well selected acres (1701 ha) at what was then known as Patrick Plains in the Hunter Valley. The family left Sydney for the Hunter Valley "in a fine little cutter-packet, named the Lord Liverpool, which sails weekly between Sydney and Newcastle, a distance of 78 miles [125 km]. Only twelve hours easy sail, cabin fare, including provisions, wine and spirits, 1/6d., and the accommodation excellent, the vessel having formerly been a pleasure yacht in India." [10]

From Newcastle, the hard part of the journey began. Mudie, his family and his sixty assigned convicts, plus the many heavily laden drays packed with all the stores and equipment needed to start life in the outback, had to be barged 112 km up the Hunter River to Maitland. From there bullock teams pulled the drays overland through thinly timbered country. As each gully was approached, the drays were let down by rope, unloaded, hauled up the banks and reloaded by the convicts.

Emily Mudie was fifteen years old when she and her two younger sisters and father reached the spot that was to be their home in this strange vast continent. They were quite unused to the summer heat, the strange birdcalls of galahs and rosellas, the raucous laughter of kookaburras and cockatoos, and the earth-shaking bounding of kangaroos, sometimes up to 500 in number, thundering past them. Surrounded only by convicts, their isolation from congenial company presented a grim prospect for them all. Even James Mudie must have paused a moment to reflect on their changed circumstances, but he wasted little time on dwelling on the past. He quickly organised the building of a number of slab-sided huts for temporary accommodation. In recognition of his cousin's generosity, and dreaming of the impressive mansion he hoped to build in the future, he named the property Castle Forbes.

Mudie's land was of the richest alluvial soil, capable of producing heavy crops of wheat and maize, and at harvest time he needed the labour of up to 120 convicts who, for the slightest misdemeanour, were subjected to excessive floggings under Mudie's merciless gaze. The land was relatively clear of timber, although fine stands of cedar grew abundantly on various parts of the property. He built his home of timber, using cedar for joinery, but the house has not survived into the 1990s, the land having been swallowed up by a hungry suburbia. Mudie boasted that his "homestead was a fortress, guarded by Newfoundland dogs, and that my servants were severely disciplined under exacting rules. I kept the convicts in their proper place, and at their proper distance, and compelled them to wear the regular convict dress of mustard yellow, branded with a number and my own name as assignee master." [11] Shades of his naval training shine through the personality of James Mudie. To enforce discipline in the navy, fearsome punishments were provided by law — hanging from the yardarm, ceremonial floggings with the cat, running the gauntlet. There was endless scope for a sadist sheltered by the arm of the law.

Mudie's hard discipline, unrelieved by the softening influence of a wife, extended to the upbringing of his daughters. Girlish giggles rarely rang from the rafters of Castle Forbes, which was run like a battleship. Strive as he might to produce an atmosphere of high moral rectitude for the three girls, Mudie was thwarted by the female convicts he employed in his house. He complained that "with fearful oaths" the women would flatly refuse to obey his orders, in the hope of being sent back to "The Factory", as the female prison in Parramatta was called. Mudie regarded the prison as "an agreeable retreat that could not be regarded as a place of punishment. The females are well fed and, in addition to the abundance of food, they are further indulged with tea and sugar." [12] He refused to give in to the women's pleas, and continued to mete out his own punishments, such as that most resented form of punishment, the shaving of the women's heads, which increased their sense of outrage and desperation.

To the visitor, admitted at the gate by the porter, Castle Forbes presented a well-run establishment. According to the enthusiastic Rev.

John McGarvie, minister of St. Andrews Scots Church, Sydney, it was "pleasing, comfortable and British-like, and calculated to set a spirited example of enterprise to your less opulent neighbours." One of the less opulent, though enterprising, neighbours happened to be John Larnach.

*   *   *

Romance in the country conjures up visions of young lovers strolling through green fields, dotted with drifts of daffodils and spring lambs frolicking in the background. At Castle Forbes, the scene dissolves; the lambs remained, but the daffodils emerged as yellow-garbed, sullen-faced prisoners, dispiritedly toiling at their work to the whistling sound of the cat-o'-nine-tails. Yet even against such a background, love blossomed. Twenty-year-old Emily Mudie and twenty-three-year-old John Larnach were married on 8 August 1827.

James Mudie acquired not only a capable farmer in his new son-in-law, but one in tune with his own iron-heeled views of discipline. He was quick to use his son-in-law's ability, and made John Larnach not only his overseer, but his business partner as well. Under John's management Castle Forbes became "one of the finest agricultural establishments in the Colony, producing substantial quantities of wool, meat and wheat."[13]

Chapter II

JOHN AND EMILY LARNACH

Several miles south of what was known as Mr Singleton's Ford, at the head of Patrick Plains, is a hillside commanding sweeping views of the fertile Whittingham flats and the distant hills on the other side of the Hunter Valley. In 1827 a circuitous cart road from Sydney was forming into what would become the Main North Road. On the east side of the track stood Castle Forbes, and directly opposite the recently finished home of John and Emily Larnach, to be known as Rosemount. "A large windmill, with Dutch arms and a convict bell fixed to the roof, was built on the highest point of the land to provide power for gristing wheat grown on the property, and Rosemount was built immediately in front of it."[1]

The large substantially built two-storied house had stone walls 52 cm thick, and covered verandahs on both upper and lower floors. Attic windows in the roof looked out to the four points of the compass, and straying from the colonial style were two little Italianate balconies extending from French doors on the upper floor. The garden was surrounded by post and rail fences. It was a house of classical simplicity.

Rosemount (left), William Larnach's birthplace, was built by John Larnach in 1829. Rosemount became Baroona (right) after additions were made in 1870 by the new owner Albert Dangar.

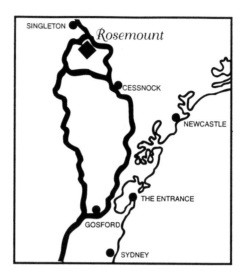

Map showing Rosemount's situation in the Hunter Valley, New South Wales, Australia.

Although the house still stands, the property is now known as Baroona. There have been extensive additions and the original house has been retained as the central square, although barely recognisable.

By the beginning of 1833 John and Emily had three children, and on 27 January their fourth child, William James Mudie Larnach, was born. He was named William after his grandfather in Wick, who had recently died, and was also saddled with the name of his maternal grandfather, James Mudie. By Australian standards at that time, it could be said William was born with a silver spoon in his mouth. His birth took place at the height of his father's prosperity. In a faded old photograph of Rosemount, the crino-lined figure of Emily, standing on the upper verandah, is barely discernible, but it is clear enough to notice that the apron-covered skirt and rolled up sleeves of the average pioneer women living in bark huts with dirt floors were not her lot. These pioneer women, mostly the wives of ex-convicts, constantly toiled under primitive conditions, their reddened and calloused hands testimony to their hard work. Emily's hardest job was organising an incompetent and mostly unwilling staff of convict women to help with the chores of the busy pastoral homestead: washing linen, turning the mangle, heating the flat iron, melting kangaroo fat for candles, cooking, cleaning, butter-making, child-minding, sewing and the many other things that kept pioneer women so busy.

There was an abundance of food from the property. Flour was milled from their own home-grown wheat, kangaroo soup simmered in cauldrons, and the hind legs of wallaby were stuffed with veal forcemeat, trussed like a hare and roasted on a spit over the open fire in the colonial kitchen. Or there was the Australian culinary delight of parrot pie, which required one dozen parakeets, some bacon rashers, hard-boiled eggs and a few slices of beef, all covered with puff pastry.

Henry Kingsley, brother of the author Charles, spent three years on the Australian goldfields, and describes life in an Australian country house:

> . . . where Kangaroos came skipping and staring and gandering past the dining-room window; where opossums held high jinx on the roof and murdered sleep every night; a house with a flower garden, at the bottom of which was a large pond which swarmed all through the burning summer's day with teal, widgeon, great cranes, pelicans, black swans and purple water hens; a house in which scorpions came tittle, tittle, tittle along the passage, looked in at the library door to see how you are getting on, and then packed themselves away under the doormat; where enormous centipedes came from under the fender at a terrific pace, eight inches long, twenty legs astride, struck with a sudden uncontrollable impulse to walk up the leg of your trousers! A house where your papers were old copies of the *Spectator* and *The Illustrated London News*, and one's drink weak claret and water. [2]

Emily, in common with all the other women in country districts, had more to fear than multi-legged insects. In the Hunter Valley marauding bushrangers, roaming singly or in gangs, were particularly prevalent. Many were only chicken stealers, but others were muggers or rapists, and the women, often alone all day, put on a brave front defending themselves, holding muskets they were inept at firing in their trembling hands. Arson-minded Aborigines were more easily deterred; they were suitably wary of the "magic fire stick that killed invisibly with a loud bang."

Although spiced with an element of danger, life at Rosemount was a comfortable one. James Mudie, now a magistrate on the Bench at Maitland, enjoyed entertaining, especially Presbyterian ministers. The formidable Rev. John Dunmore Lang and his wife Wilhemina, whose memorial statues, although under threat of demolition, are still to be seen in Scots Church, York Street, Sydney, were frequent visitors. Lang specifically mentions the names of Mudie and Larnach as settlers who would like a permanent minister in their area. Any minister visiting the estate was called upon to conduct a church service at Castle Forbes, and the convicts, spruce in yellow overalls covering lash-scarred backs, were, like Mudie's grandchildren, forced to attend.

Social activities of a more exciting nature centered around the neighbouring property, Neotsfield, a splendid manor house built by Henry and Grace Dangar, "with all the refinement of civilisation."[3] They set the tone for the district. It was to be more English than England, despite the predominance of Scottish settlers. Grace Dangar dreamt of transforming that area of the Hunter Valley into "Merrie England", complete with village green, church and school house, with cultivated parklands surrounding their "gentlemen's seat". Fox hunting was indulged in, *sans* fox; the men in their pink coats, riding to the hounds in full cry, flushed out dingoes. Horse racing and breeding were popular pastimes, particularly with the Larnachs, but the highlight of the year was in the autumn, when huge drays were loaded with wool bales. The women packed their finery and all proceeded along the new road to Sydney to sell the wool clip. There was the Agricultural Show to attend, Race Week to be enjoyed, and to round off the city visit, a large dinner party at Government House in the presence of the governor, followed by a ball in honour of the Queen's birthday.

Yet this idyllic country life had its dark side, and the two men most responsible for the misery in the district were James Mudie and John Larnach. The governor, Sir Ralph Darling, was a martinet in the mould of

Mudie, and shared with Mudie an extreme dislike of ordinary mercy where convicts were concerned. He appointed Mudie to the honorary and powerful position of magistrate. A magistrate's powers were wide; he could try a man in his employ, and convict and punish him, the proceedings taking place in the magistrate's own home. The appointment was seen as a reward for a man who had successfully established his land, and consequently many magistrates were completely unsuited to the position. They fell far short of the English squire who, when dealing with his labourers, was firm, kind but distant, "civil but strange". In this sparsely populated country, many magistrates lacked the checks and balances of a more civilised society to guide them.

Flogging was the usual punishment. The number of lashes was decided by the magistrate, and anything from twenty-five to 150 lashes could be handed out. Every stroke was noted and listed. Even twenty-five lashes was a draconian torture, able to skin a man's back and leave it a tangled web of criss-cross scars. Flogging was not a pretty sight. The convict was bound to a wooden triangular structure set in the ground. He was stripped of his shirt and flogged with a cat-o'-nine-tails, each tail having about ten knots in it. The tails were soaked in salt water, and when dry, they hardened like wire. The flogging area was a favourite haunt of dogs, eager to lick up the blood and pieces of flesh scattered on the ground.

As a magistrate, James Mudie became greatly feared for his excessive floggings, and under his direction and John Larnach's supervision, Castle Forbes became synonymous with hell. As sole controller of nearly one hundred convicts, and to make sure fear was instilled into them, John Larnach was not above having a convict given fifty lashes in the morning, then sending the felon back in the afternoon for another fifty for the same offence.

Perhaps because of the harsh conditions imposed on the workers at Castle Forbes, the place prospered. Thomas Barker, one of the largest purchasers of grain in the colony, wrote to Mudie, "My opinion of your agricultural exertions is formed from seeing the state of your farm, with the barnyard full of the largest wheat stacks I have ever witnessed . . . among the settlers in that respectable district, I do not know of any who cultivated so extensively, and brought so much wheat to the Sydney market."[4] For a short time John and Emily's life was lived in an atmosphere of affluence and contentment, heedless of the festering resentment growing among their convict assignees.

On a spring morning in November 1833, the pealing of the convict bell fixed to the top of the windmill at Rosemount called the convicts from their crude shanties to another day's toil. At that time Rosemount and Castle Forbes were run as one property, under the name of Castle Forbes. James Mudie was absent from the property, and his daughters were staying with their sister Emily. Early that morning, John Larnach drove his sheep to a stream about a mile away from the homestead. Scab, a highly infectious disease that could ruin a flock if they were not dipped properly, was rampant and, being meticulous, John had decided to do the job himself. Before the days of washing pens, the sheep were simply driven through a stream of running water to clean grass on the other bank.

A few days previously, six convicts had escaped from Castle Forbes and had joined up with some bushrangers who had recently overpowered a police party, tied the surprised constabulary to trees, and made off with their horses and guns. On this spring morning, this rebellious lot proceeded to Rosemount and turned Emily out of the house with her sisters and young children, including ten-month-old William. To the men's credit the women and children were unharmed, but they ransacked the house and then "coolly sat down and regaled themselves with the best of everything. Before leaving they destroyed and scattered about the yard what property they could not take away with them."[5] They stole food, clothes, guns, ammunition and horses, then continued on their way in search of their quarry, John Larnach.

They were led by a relatively trusted convict from Castle Forbes named John Poole, and, heedless of the dreadful consequences of their actions, these desperate men, debased by the pain inflicted on them, crept up on the unsuspecting John Larnach. Threatening to chop his head off and stick it on the chimney of their hut, they fired indiscriminately at him. They were unaccustomed to the use of firearms, and this was Larnach's salvation, as they truly meant to kill him. He managed to avoid the poorly aimed bullets by diving into the water and swimming to the other bank of the river, where he fled to the neighbouring property of Henry Dangar for refuge and help.

The convicts continued their rampage down the valley, plundered another property, then at a third farm took out their spleen on the master and flogged him mercilessly.

For about ten days, apprehension reigned in the district, no one knowing who would be the next victim. Larnach, with the police and other settlers, searched relentlessly until on the tenth day the escapees were captured, but only after Robert Scott, a farmer and magistrate from Patrick Plains, shot and killed one of the convicts who had been slow to throw down his gun. The others then submitted quietly and were remanded to Sydney for trial.

*   *   *

Young William James Mudie Larnach was just a year old when the trial of those who had rebelled at Castle Forbes took place, but the repercussions continued for about eight years. The trial, held in December 1833, strongly censured James Mudie and John Larnach. It became a test case for the Conservatives, who blamed the anarchy of the convicts on the newly appointed humane Governor Bourke and his Liberal followers. Bourke argued that the convicts had been driven to their actions by their ill-treatment. The problems in dealing with convict labour were highlighted, and the trial stirred up strong opposition to the dumping of more felons on Australian soil. The one good thing to come out of the trial was that the first step was taken towards the abolition of convict transportation, but this far-reaching result was of little satisfaction to the condemned men.

Convicts were not usually represented by a barrister, but an anonymous donor paid for the services of Roger Therry to defend them. He related that:

The trial presented a truly painful exhibition . . . The men repeatedly declared that they would prefer death to being returned to their employer. The only line of defence that I conceived in any way available to them was to show that their treatment had been such as to present some mitigatory features which might lead to a punishment short of death. [6]

But no such mercy was shown, and the men were tried and sentenced to death within twenty-four hours.

John Hitchcock, the most intelligent of the condemned men, said he had no grounds to offer for why the sentence of death should not be pronounced on them, but he implored the government to institute an enquiry into their past treatment, not only at Castle Forbes, but at other establishments in the Hunter Valley. He also asked that he and his fellow prisoners be allowed to uncover their lacerated backs to the public gaze in the court, but for reasons known only to the judge this request was refused.

The huge public interest in the trial was matched by the outrage people felt at the cruelty inflicted on the convicts. Mudie, undeterred by the outcry and unrepentant, with his wide powers as magistrate, sent two of the sentenced men back to Castle Forbes to be executed in full view of their companions as a gentle reminder of the fate of those who dared to contemplate escape. The other three men were hanged in Sydney, and the sixth, being too young to hang, was sent to the hell hole of Norfolk Island for life.

James T. Ryan, a settler, writes in 1835 of a trip to Patrick Plains in the Hunter Valley:

That was the first occasion on which I heard the name of Major Moody [sic], who received a terrible character. In conversation the men all saying how they would serve him if they had their will. The hanging of the five men for robbing his house was the chief topic of conversation. We had to pass by Moody's house on the right, and his windmill on the left hand side of the road; we had to pass under the limb which proceeded from a large gum tree like a yard arm from the main mast of a ship. This was the place where the men were hanged, under this immense limb, pinioned and placed on a dray on a platform, which raised them sufficiently to have a good fall as they were launched into eternity within view of Moody's house, and in close proximity to the mill. Just at the time the men swung off, a terrible hurricane burst out with great violence and blew the sails off the mill, which never worked again from that day to this. The mill sails were lying on the ground as we passed by, and it was said that the storm lasted to within an hour of the men being cut down. During its violence the men were wafting to and fro like a swing swang, being frequently entangled together.[7]

The Rosemount gristing mill, before being damaged when lightning struck at the moment two convicts were hanged on the property in 1833.

The old gristing mill was never repaired, and to all who passed by on the Great Northern Road it remained a constant reminder of man's inhumanity. It was not until John Larnach's death in 1869, when Henry Dangar's son bought Rosemount, that the mill was demolished.

After the trial, the criticism of Mudie and Larnach was intense, and the public felt Governor Bourke should honour the dead men's wishes for an inquiry. A commission was set up and presided over by the solicitor-general and the superintendent of police. They found that the food at Castle Forbes had been adequate and that, of the sixty convicts, half had never been flogged. In fact, they found Mudie and Larnach had not been overly harsh or oppressive, but they strongly censured Larnach for returning convicts for a second flogging for the same offence. Roger Therry, the convicts' counsel, believed Larnach was "really guiltless of the severities practised there", but blamed Mudie for his part in enforcing harsh punishments.

The results of the inquiry didn't please Mudie and Larnach at all. They wanted freedom from all blame and still maintained their actions had been justified, so they published a pamphlet, "Vindication of James Mudie and John Larnach . . . relative to the treatment of their Convict Servants." This they sent to the Colonial Office in London, but to no avail; the results of the inquiry were fully upheld by the Colonial Office. After the petition's lack of success, John Larnach, thoroughly tired of the whole affair, withdrew to his farm and hoped to disappear from the limelight. With a father-in-law like James Mudie, this proved almost impossible.

Within the family the aftermath resulted in endless discussions about the trial. There were feelings of injustice engendered by the ostracism of their neighbours, who were angered not by the cruelty that had been exposed, but by the thought that their source of cheap labour may be coming to an end. Anonymous pamphlets were published vilifying Mudie and Larnach, which Larnach ignored; but Mudie hounded anyone who spoke against him, and his efforts resulted in the probable suicide of one man[8] and were a contributing factor to the resignation of Governor Bourke.

It was Bourke, however, who had the final word. Before resigning, he removed Mudie from the list of magistrates. This loss of prestige was too much for Mudie. He sold his farm for £7,000 and, leaving behind his married daughters, he left for England in 1836 to write a book, *The Felonry of New South Wales*. The object of the book was "to arraign at the bar of public opinion the conduct of His Excellency General Sir Richard Bourke and his functionaries in the government of New South Wales, and particularly as regards his favouritism towards the convicts." The book received quite favourable notices in the English press; but in Australia its vindictive comments and unjust allegations lost him his old friends. Mudie was snubbed by his benefactor, Sir Charles Forbes, who was "not at home" when Mudie called and who vehemently refused to see him.

In 1840, having remarried at the age of fifty-seven, Mudie arrived back in Australia. The welcome from his friends was distinctly frigid, but his eight Larnach grandchildren greeted him with interest, the older children having only a faint memory of him. Even the welcome from his dutiful daughters was lukewarm as the book had stirred up all the controversy again. One day soon after his arrival in Sydney, Mudie was walking along George Street when a strapping young man accosted him. He was the son of the aged attorney-general, Mr Kinchella, whose deafness Mudie had ridiculed in his book. Taking Mudie by surprise, the young Kinchella seized him and gave him a horse-whipping, the severity equalling any flogging Mudie himself might have ordered. For the elderly Mudie the humiliation exceeded the pain, and he sued Kinchella for damages. Mudie won the case, and was awarded £50, but the spectators in the courtroom passed round the hat and paid the damages for Kinchella. Within a short time, to the relief of his family, Mudie returned to England, where his death in 1852 aroused no publicity. He was buried in Tottenham Cemetery, unmourned by his daughters in Australia, who had lost all contact with him.

Chapter III

YOUNG WILLIAM

By 1835 visitors to Australia could recognise Australian-born children by their colonial accents. The Larnach children were no exception; they no longer spoke with their parents' Scottish burr. By the time young William was ten years old, John and Emily Larnach had nine living children. Their strictly disciplined upbringing by Emily and the dour John was aggravated by John's growing melancholia, and not helped by a decline in the Larnach family fortune.

As a result of the findings of the Select Committee on Transportation in London[1] (formed after the Castle Forbes inquiry), the British Government in 1839 decided to discontinue convict transportation to New South Wales. In 1842 the lack of cheap labour coincided with falling stock and wool prices, and John Larnach in desperation joined an association to import Indian "coolies". This scheme never eventuated, and gradually, as the convicts finished serving their time, farm wages began to rise alarmingly, eating into what had hitherto been handsome profits.

Assigned convicts were still employed for a number of years at Rosemount, as on most large estates. Many worked as domestic servants, cooks, butlers and nursemaids, and their effect on the children of these households was brought to the notice of the Select Committee on Transportation in London: "Being very much in the hands of assigned servants, children are aware of the condition of these servants, they look down on them with contempt . . . It creates an insolence of feeling and of bearing towards their elders."[2] What precocious little monster would not revel in the ability to threaten his nurse or housemaid with the promise of a flogging should his whims be denied. Servants got their revenge by teaching children anything from swearing to behaviour of a most deviant nature.

While future generations would play cowboys and Indians, William and his elder brother George played at being bushrangers or constabulary, capturing younger meddlesome brothers and tying them to a triangle for a fake flogging game. Pesky sisters were leg-roped, and punishments were doled out in their make-believe court.

Not many miles from Rosemount, the small village of Singleton was beginning to form on either side of the Main North Road. There were no schools in the area in the early 1840s, but the Rev. Mr Hetherington, recently from Edinburgh, was appointed the Presbyterian minister for the parish of Singleton, an area of 2400 sq km, and he devoted what spare time he had to the education of his parishioners' children. Possessing great clarity of thought and expression, Hetherington assiduously prepared his long sermons, but delivered them in such a monotonous manner it is said his parishioners suffered agonies of boredom. A humourless, painstaking teacher, it was under Hetherington's dry-as-dust tuition that young William Larnach received his early education, giving him a lifelong interest in history. Later William progressed to Sydney College where, in addition to the usual academic studies, musical evenings were given by a Mr Nathan and his "Corps Harmonique" in the presence of the governor and his wife. These seem to have impressed William and later caused him to place great emphasis on his own children's musical education.

Just a year after the Castle Forbes trial, John Larnach's younger brother, Donald, who had regretfully farewelled John from Wick some twelve years earlier, arrived at Rosemount. At seventeen years of age, Donald was the golden boy. Enthusiastic, with a considerate and pleasant nature, he would prove to have the Midas touch, and while John grew more withdrawn and embittered, Donald brought an air of cheerfulness to the rest of the family. He was quick to take advantage of the opportunities available in the colony, and soon achieved success. Within ten years of his arrival in New South Wales he had bought the steam flour mill in which he had been employed as manager, speculated in town lots in Sydney and Bathhurst, and acquired a run on the Lachlan River. In 1845, at the age of twenty-eight, he married Jane Elizabeth Walker, the daughter of a wealthy

Donald Larnach, founding director of the Bank of New South Wales in London, and the uncle and mentor to William Larnach.

Sydney merchant, at Trinity Church Sydney. In a letter to his aunt, William recalls her wedding years later. "Well do I remember, although a very little boy, reading an account of your wedding in a letter from my brother George, who was present. It is impressed on my memory that there were four white horses and you were driven to Penrith. I think postilions were mentioned."

Not only was Donald's bride wealthy, but her father was one of the Bank of New South Wales's largest shareholders, and in the same year as his wedding Donald was appointed an auditor of the bank. In 1852, justifying his father-in-law's faith in him, he was appointed president of the re-formed Bank of New South Wales. On the discovery of gold in Australia in 1851, Donald claimed the credit for initiating the bank's purchasing of gold on the goldfields, thereby doubling the bank's capital out of profits in one year.

By the time William Larnach left college, his Uncle Donald's success had already influenced the direction he wanted to take in his career. William's only reference to his father, John Larnach, was that "I never received any help from my father." So it was through his uncle's influence that he joined the staff of the Bank of New South Wales in 1850, and left the depressing atmosphere of Rosemount, never to mention the place again.

As a young bank clerk commencing his first position in Melbourne, William's arrival coincided with the discovery of gold in Victoria. With the influx of people attracted to the goldfields, "The accommodation of Melbourne was tried to its utmost extent; every house was filled and overflowing, and many respectable families were under the necessity of living in tents or sleeping in the open air."[3] There was only one thing on everyone's mind, and that was gold. Every male in the colony was gripped with gold fever. Shops closed down, ships were deserted, even the police force took off for the fields, leaving only two out of forty constables in Melbourne. The women left behind had to group together for their own protection.

Many also departed from Sydney in search of gold.

> . . . the road over the Blue Mountains was choked with a footsore, sluggishly winding column of men: clerks and grooms, grocers' assistants and sailors, lawyers and army deserters, oyster sellers and magistrates, government officials and ex-convicts — all trudging beneath the weight of tents, blankets, crowbars, picks, shovels, pans and billy cans, hastily bought at gouger's prices, stumbling towards unheard-of wealth in mud-balled boots, under the driving rains of the Australian autumn.[4]

Melbourne suffered a much greater exodus than Sydney, and it was from Melbourne that William joined the melange of men from all over the world who were rushing to take part in this great gamble. He was just eighteen years old, and as business was at a standstill in Melbourne he headed for

Sofala, on the Turon River, near where an Aboriginal had found the largest gold nugget in history, equal in weight to a hundred-weight sack of potatoes. It was William's first experience of life on the diggings.

> I found two or three schoolfellows at Paterson's Point, on the Turon, who had a claim there; they invited me to join them, and I did so, following a digger's life for four months. We could always obtain about half an ounce a day (gold was reaching 60 shillings an ounce) simply digging a spade deep on the surface on the banks of the Turon, and this served to put us in funds to tackle our bed-claim. The bed-claim was capable of producing 50 ounces a day. An adjoining claim was worked by "old hands" (ex-convicts) as they were then called, who made from 50 to 52 ounces a day; but the quantity of water met with was so great that it was too much for us to continue at. However, after spending a very happy time for four months, the discovery of gold at Ballarat was announced, and I determined to go back to Victoria where I had a position kept open for me. [5]

Not only did William have a position kept for him at the bank, so too did his brother George. Both began as clerks. George stayed for only eighteen months, but was replaced by a younger brother, John, who later held managerial positions. Uncle Donald also placed his own brother, the light-fingered James Larnach, recently arrived from Wick, as an accountant at the Mount Alexander diggings near Castlemaine, an appointment that proved to be an embarrassment for Donald Larnach. Although on a salary of £600 per annum, £150 more than the accountant at Geelong to compensate for the discomfort and hand-to-mouth existence of life on the goldfields, greed got the better of James Larnach. He began fiddling the funds to his own advantage.

James's fraud was very ill-timed as far as the bank was concerned. Another charge of embezzlement had just received enormous publicity. The accused was George Dunmore Lang, manager of the Ballarat Bank of

New South Wales where William Larnach was a clerk. George Lang and his accountant received five years hard labour, working on the roads, for the theft of £900. The publicity focused on George Lang because he was the son of the Rev. John Dunmore Lang, the first Presbyterian minister in Sydney. The Rev. Lang was also a member of the New South Wales Legislative Council, an educationalist, an historian, and an aggressive Old Testament preacher.

The Rev. Lang refused to accept his son's guilt, and published a letter in the Melbourne *Argus* denying the fairness of the trial. He was then charged with contempt of court, but, after defending himself, was acquitted by the jury. With that small victory behind him, instead of leaving things well alone, he published a pamphlet entitled, "The Convict's Bank, or a Plain Statement of the Case of Alleged Embezzlement." The Bank of New South Wales retaliated by suing the Rev. Lang for libel, and won their case. Despite a petition of 10,000 signatures, the Rev. Lang was imprisoned for six months.

This highly publicised trial had just finished when it was discovered that James Larnach was dealing privately in discounts for his own profits, and had embezzled a much larger amount than George Lang, more than £5,000. Not only did the bank not want any more bad publicity about the dishonesty of its officers, but as James was the brother of Donald Larnach, one of the bank's most respected officers and now manager of the London branch, they went to great trouble to cover up the offence. After selling property owned by James Larnach, the bank claimed £3,690 from Donald Larnach to make up the shortfall. Donald Larnach paid the money and immediately offered to resign, but the directors, convinced that the matter had been hushed up, persuaded him to stay on, "as the affair has been resolved without the least public exposure, and as the institution will not lose by it." [6]

The matter had not escaped the notice of the Rev. John Lang, still languishing in jail, but after his libel case he was losing his venom, and wrote a letter to the press merely hinting at irregularities at Castlemaine, and pointing out the relationship of James Larnach to his brother Donald.

William was very aware of the rumours circulating, not only among the banking fraternity, but by the press also, who were not going to forget the bank's preferential treatment of the Larnachs. The effects of past scandals about his father and grandfather had not faded from William's memory, and under John Babcock, his superior banking officer and the man who had uncovered James Larnach's fraud, William hoped to restore some honour to the family name by his scrupulous accounting of the bank's funds.

Chapter IV

THE GOLDFIELDS OF VICTORIA

During his time as a bank officer opening up new branches as more gold-fields were discovered, William suffered the same hardships his uncle James had recorded in letters to his Melbourne manager. In April 1853 James Larnach wrote, "The winter is now settling in, and the tent is getting very cold and uncomfortable in the evenings. I will feel obliged if you will cause a small stove to be purchased and sent up before the roads are impassible [sic]. Let the pipe be sufficiently long to carry the smoke clear of the tent, say twelve feet."[1] A month later James wrote, "I am sorry to say that our good dog Brindle has fallen a victim to the epidemic now raging so furiously at the diggings. We are left unprotected at present, but I do hope to pick up a useful animal soon."[2] And in December of that year, after a customer complaint, he explained, "Mr Melville's complaint is correct, but had I waited to serve him and the many others who were around the tent, I would have had the disagreeable pleasure of sleeping with all the money and gold in the tent that evening, and this I did not choose to risk."[3]

There were no massive ledgers, impregnable strong-rooms or handsomely carved cedar counters on which to conduct transactions. William was required to provide "a tent or other building, gold safe, scales and other office equipment",[4] which was usually just an empty gin case to transact business on, and a carpet bag doubling as a safe. The carpet bag never left the bank officer's side, making him an easy target for robbery. He often travelled long distances on horseback, purchasing gold from the widely scattered storekeepers, and carrying the prized nuggets back many miles, his revolver at the ready, until he reached the dubious safety of a shanty dignified by the title, "Hotel". There, for want of a vault, the carpet bag was stowed each night under his stretcher-bed.

It was not a comfortable life, nor was it for the faint-hearted, but because of the ever present fear of bushrangers and Aborigines in the Hunter Valley, the young William Larnach had been brought up by his father to be alert to personal danger. It was second nature for him to watch over his shoulder, and his revolver was an accessory he was never without. At night, any suspicious movement caused the officers to follow a policy of shoot now, ask questions later. In the bank records there is an entry from William for "Subscription for defending Mr Taylor, who shot a burglar — £2. 2s."

William's trustworthiness and his ability to endure hardship did not go unnoticed by his superiors. In 1857, he was sent to open a branch of the bank at Ararat. According to the writer Lorna Birchfield, "Cloud capped mountains, ravines and slopes beautifully adorned with trees and shrubs, and wild red fuchsia everywhere in rich profusion"[5] adorned the hills into the township. But there the beauty stopped; Ararat was lined with grog shops and five or six public houses of distinctly shoddy character. One bright spot was Dobson's reading room and letter office, where many a homesick exile was able to read news of his distant homeland in the English, American, German and Italian papers there.

Once again, William set up his office in a tent, guarded by two dogs. He describes his role there with pride, saying that he was "a trusted officer of the Bank of New South Wales, who was frequently selected to open up branches on new rushes or goldfields. It came to my turn at one of the larger rushes at Ararat, where there were some 16,000 people, and a very rough time I had of it there for over four months."[6] Ararat was in every meaning of the word a lawless place; there was no police or magisterial control. "Scarcely a week passes but we have to record some fresh crime. Murders, holdups of individuals and stores would really seem the great feature of the day."[7] Ruffians plundered those who had laboured hard and honestly for their gold. Successful diggers became filled not only with euphoria at their new prosperity, but with large quantities of alcohol, while failures drank to excess from profound despair until compelled by hunger to leave the gold-fields in search of employment. Drunken orgies dominated the social life of the town.

Being among the diggers was a great leveller, and any pretensions to social superiority quickly disappeared. The educated, the uneducated, the rough, the refined, all needed to meet the same criteria of health and stamina. A little money helped, but initially picks, shovels and sluicing pans were sufficient to pursue their dreams of wealth. It was there that William met Richard Seddon and Julius Vogel, who would both make their mark in New Zealand; R.H.J. Reeves and Vincent Pyke, future New Zealand parliamentarians with William; and a young Dane, Niels Hjorring, escaping from the boredom of mercantile life in Copenhagen in the hope of making his fortune, and whose son would later marry William's granddaughter.

Observing the miners during these years was to benefit William in later life. "I used to take considerable interest in the work of the miners, and mixed with them a great deal whenever I had the opportunity on the goldfields. Therefore I had good facilities for laying in a store of information and practical knowledge that I felt sure was to be of use to me."[8]

After the miners' uprising at Eureka in 1854, he had seen the miners' hated licence fee of £8 per year replaced by the £1 miners' "rights," which also entitled the miner to vote for the Legislative Assembly in Victoria, a right they had not previously enjoyed. He was aware of their fear, shared by all in Victoria, that the Emperor of China would soon lay claim to the land, judging by the large numbers of Chinese descending on the goldfields; there were 24,000 by 1857, only six of whom were women. The Chinese, while content to work for a pittance on those claims given up as hopeless by others, were then accused of sending their money back to China.

Nor did it escape William's attention that it was the shopkeepers, quietly reaping in the gold for their over-priced goods, who were the most affluent men in town. Their tantalising array of a cosmopolitan selection of wares enticed the newly rich to spend on the variety of luxuries stored in their canvas emporiums. On 8 October 1857, the very day the *Mount Ararat Advertiser* proclaimed the opening of the Bank of New South Wales by W.J.M. Larnach, the "Old Established Manchester Drapery Store of Boag, Bergin and Company" advertised an "extensive consignment of spring goods." There were black and coloured silk and moire taffeta; wool,

Eliza Jane Larnach, née Guise, the first wife of William Larnach.

silk, velvet and French cashmere shawls; Coburg artificial flowers; kid gloves; bonnets; satin ribbons; kid boots; and fancy soaps and perfumes. For the men there were military trimmings, water-tight boots, enamelled Napoleon thigh boots, Bedford cord riding jackets, shooting coats and white and drab doe-skin gloves. These emporiums sold every accessory the well-dressed miner and his lady needed to promenade up and down the muddy main street of Ararat.

William remained in Ararat until February 1858, and spent an unforgettable Christmas surrounded by the bush fires that were raging on the surrounding hills. Despite the danger to the town, the Ararat Turf Club ignored the fire, and held its first ever race meeting. The principal steeplechase of 3 km, worth 150 sovereigns, was seen by hopeful punters through a pall of smoke. They watched with dismay as one horse after another fell at the jumps until only one was left, and it too unsportingly somersaulted at the last water jump.

William anticipated his return to Melbourne with pleasure at the prospect of re-acquainting himself with Eliza Jane Guise, the beautiful and apparently wealthy young daughter of the late Richard Guise jnr. Eliza was to become his future wife. No photos remain of the young beauty. In photos of Eliza taken with William and their children in 1878, it seems that years of child-bearing have taken their toll. She presents to the viewer a rather stolid appearance, and the happy nature revealed by her letters is also well concealed.

Eliza Jane lived in style with her sisters, mother and boastful stepfather in Barkly Street, Brighton, Melbourne. At the time of her marriage to William, Eliza was seventeen years old, and as a beneficiary of a large inherited family property, she was a ward of the Supreme Court of New South Wales. Articles of Agreement for the marriage were drawn up, whereby the court appointed John Babcock, William's superior and manager of the Melbourne branch of the Bank of New South Wales, and Laurence Cockburn, as trustees of Eliza's money until she came of age.

An announcement in the Melbourne *Argus* read: "On 15th June, 1859, at St. Andrew's Church, Brighton, Melbourne, by the Reverend Samuel Taylor, William James Mudie, second son of John Larnach, of Rosemount, Hunter's River, N.S.W. To Eliza Jane, only daughter of the late Richard Guise jnr."

From the very beginning, Eliza's marriage was marked by long periods of separation from William. While he remained on the goldfields for another two years, she stayed in Melbourne. Having lived much of her young life in the outbacks of the Murrumbidgee River, where even the most fundamental needs of life had to be hauled hundreds of miles by bullock wagons, loneliness was no stranger to her. No letters from Eliza to William during this period were kept by him, only details of her financial affairs, yet this should not imply that he married her for her money, as it proved to be a very happy marriage. Some pressed flowers and one small item among his papers give us an inkling as to her interests. The item is a small painting by Eliza of a dusty road winding through ghost gums and scrub, and is very well executed considering it has been painted on a gum leaf.

THE GUISE FAMILY

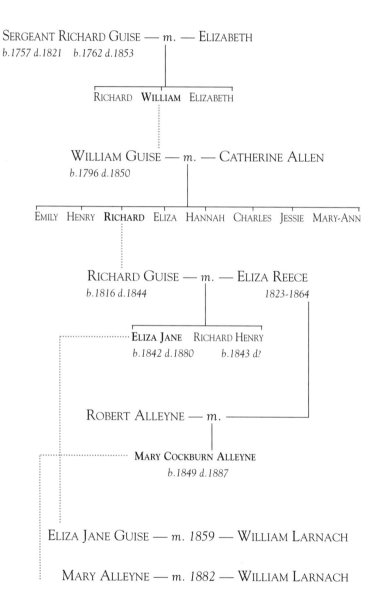

SERGEANT RICHARD GUISE — m. — ELIZABETH
b.1757 d.1821   b.1762 d.1853

RICHARD   **WILLIAM**   ELIZABETH

WILLIAM GUISE — m. — CATHERINE ALLEN
b.1796 d.1850

EMILY HENRY **RICHARD** ELIZA HANNAH CHARLES JESSIE MARY-ANN

RICHARD GUISE — m. — ELIZA REECE
b.1816 d.1844   1823-1864

ELIZA JANE   RICHARD HENRY
b.1842 d.1880   b.1843 d.?

ROBERT ALLEYNE — m.

MARY COCKBURN ALLEYNE
b.1849 d.1887

ELIZA JANE GUISE — m. 1859 — WILLIAM LARNACH

MARY ALLEYNE — m. 1882 — WILLIAM LARNACH

Chapter V

THE FRENCH CONNECTION

Imagine a noble young duke from the ancient family de Guise of France fleeing the French Revolution; consider also that he is the alleged illegitimate son of Louis XV, and you have a story that family histories thrive on. Richard Guise arrived in Australia in 1790 and began life anew in the half-starved colony of New South Wales, far from the cake-filled kitchens of the French court. And with each generation, the myths about his nobility multiplied.

Eliza Jane Guise, born in Australia in 1842, was the great-granddaughter of this romantic figure, and her ducal connections have often been referred to in articles about William Larnach and his wife Eliza Jane. Alas, Des Archives National de France can find no evidence of such an illustrious lineage to Louis XV, or any close relationship of Richard Guise to Les Ducs de Guise. The direct line of the ducal Guise family of Lorraine became extinct on the death in 1675 of the seventh duke, François Joseph, so any trace of nobility was well watered down by the time Richard Guise was born in 1757. The inheritance laws of France at the time of the Revolution divided a given piece of land among more and more inheritors, creating a growth of landless men. The lesser nobility — the poor relations — were fleeing the country not so much from fear, but from a very real need to find alternative means of support.

The first evidence of any true facts about Richard Guise is his enlistment in England with the New South Wales Corps, on 14 August 1789, exactly one month after the storming of the Bastille. This new unit was especially tailored for service in Australia, to guard convicts, and the drawcard was the offer of 10 ha of free land to any members of the corps on arrival in Australia. In fact the corps became notorious for the perks received by its members, particularly that allowing to pass through their hands all cargo and rum supplies, thus giving them an economic edge over the ordinary civilian. Two companies of the NSW Corps, one of which Richard Guise was a member, were brought out by the three ships of the Second Fleet, a voyage considered the most horrendous in the whole history of penal transportation. From a total of 1006 prisoners, carried in the three ships, 267 died at sea and at least 150 more on arrival at Sydney Cove. The ships had been contracted by the government from former African slave traders, and the prisoners were shackled by short rigid bolts about 22 cm long, fixed between the ankles, which incapacitated them to the degree of breaking their legs should they attempt to walk.

On their arrival at Sydney Cove, the vermin-infested and half-starved convicts disembarked. They were met by an even more traumatised group who had already spent two years in Australia and, being ignorant of agricultural knowledge, had proved incapable of cultivating any crops or raising livestock. Waiting on the shore were emaciated marines in tattered uniforms and cadaverous convicts dressed in rags. They were all so exhausted by starvation they could hardly comprehend that, after two years in which no ships had come from England, their desperately needed food supplies had at last arrived.

A few months after his arrival in Sydney, Richard Guise was promoted to sergeant. He married, and had three children. In Sydney he served under another Frenchman, Major Joseph Foveaux, who recommended that Guise receive several land grants of 12.3 ha each. Guise acquired a wine and spirit licence, and became the licensee of the White Hart pub in Sydney, living comfortably in his own house in Pitt's Row, with the help of fifteen convict servants. There was no denying the good fortune of the men serving in the NSW Corps.

After fourteen years in the corps, Richard Guise obtained a discharge and retired to yet another land grant, at Casula, which today is a suburb of Liverpool — a town on the outskirts of Sydney. There he enjoyed a profitable agricultural venture until his death in 1821 from liver failure. Guise had the doubtful distinction of being the first person to be buried in the old Liverpool cemetery, which has now been converted to a pioneer memorial park.

Ten years after Richard Guise's death land grants were abolished, and this persuaded men to push well beyond the fringes of settlement to land that had not yet been surveyed for sale or lease. Richard Guise's second son, William, with his wife and family, became part of this ever-growing exodus of hardy men, women and children who travelled over the Blue Mountains into the hinterland and on to the huge Riverina Plains, bounded by the Murrumbidgee and Murray Rivers. They arrived to settle on the plains only a year after Captain Sturt and his small party of explorers had returned to Sydney with news of the area. Because these settlers sought to occupy land without the consent of government and paid nothing for it, they became known as squatters.

The Guise family travelled for three months, with bullocks dragging the loaded drays. A horseman would ride ahead choosing the route according to the availability of water, essential for this lumbering migratory menagerie. The family, accompanied by shepherds, stockmen, teamsters, sheep, horned cattle, horses, a few pigs, working bullocks, caged poultry, and numerous varieties of dogs, ambled their way towards the southern banks of the Murrumbidgee close to the junction of the Lachlan River, where William Guise staked out his first run, Cunningdroo. It was the most westerly run in the district and therefore the most isolated. It was also the hunting and fishing ground of the Aboriginal Wiradjuri tribe, and the raiding parties of their chief tribesman, Windardyne, were greatly feared.

In 1836, the surveyor-general, Thomas Livingstone Mitchell, recording in his journal on his return from Australia Felix (Western Australia), wrote that the first sign of habitation he located and stayed at was the head station of William Guise at Cunningdroo. Mitchell carried out a prodigious survey in a desperate drive to gain control of the land from squatters such as Guise, who had claimed the land at least two years before this mighty mapping and gridding was completed. In 1836 Bourke's Squatting Act enabled men to legally occupy vacant land, without limit, for an annual licence fee of £10. Once again men rushed to acquire land, exercising feats of daring and courage and sometimes breaking the law in their lust for land.

William Guise, together with William Charles Wentworth,[1] were described by a contemporary squatter as "two of the eight dirty dogs of the area". It is not clear how they succeeded in getting possession of other squatters' runs. It may have been acquired by "dummying", where a squatter employed other people to select land, live on it for a year, then transfer it back to him; or perhaps by manipulating the government, or simply breaking the law. What ever they did they were successful, and, ignoring the bitterness of their neighbours, William Guise added 90,200 ha to his holdings and eventually extended the family holdings to thirteen runs in the Riverina district.

After years of extreme hardship and primitive living conditions, William Guise's move to the Murrumbidgee area was eventually of great financial gain to him, but his children paid a high price for living in such a remote and lonely place. His five daughters could barely read or write at the time of their marriages. Drinking, smoking and yarning were the main forms of entertainment, and his sons put as much effort into their drinking as they did to their heavy and often lonely work. The hip flask was their greatest companion and it contributed significantly to the tragedies that beset the Guise family.

* * *

In 1840 the eldest son of William Guise, Richard jnr, married Eliza Reece, a courageous and resourceful young woman of seventeen. She was to become the mother of two of William Larnach's future wives, Eliza Jane Guise and Mary Cockburn Alleyne. In the year of their marriage, Richard Guise jnr and his bride took over the 23,780 ha cattle run Uroly from an early settler, Charles Byrne. Extending 14 km along the southern banks of the Murrumbidgee River, the run was bordered on the west by waterless sandhills, and to the east sparsely wooded plains stretched as far as the Edward River. In May 1842, at the start of the winter fogs which shroud the area, the birth of Eliza Jane Guise took place, and was followed a year later by that of her brother Dick.

A slab hut was home to Richard and Eliza Guise and their children. It was built in the style typical of the Australian outback, with clay daubed between the timber to weatherproof the outer walls from wind and rain. Strips of bark from living trees were placed on the roof and held down by logs to prevent them from curling, as nails were scarce and expensive. The interior walls were pasted with newspaper or calico. Although these temporary huts were often extended and reclad, permanent houses were rarely built until after the 1860s, when it became possible to freehold the land.

The Guises' hut was situated among the wooded billabong area close to the river, on cracked sun-baked land. In summer, dust permeated everything, but it could be transformed into a sea of mud when the mighty Murrumbidgee breached its banks during its periodic flooding. The early childhood surroundings of Eliza Jane Guise were a far cry from those of William Larnach, spent in his parents' comfortable home with its polished floors and well-oiled furniture kept gleaming by an abundance of cheap convict labour. Convict labour had not been available so far inland, and by the time Eliza Jane was born the transportation of convicts to New South Wales had ceased. Apart from the help of a few stockmen, all the work was done by Richard and his wife. Raising cattle, sheep and horses was the main activity of Richard Guise, while Eliza tended the poultry and pigs, grew vegetables, ground flour from the wheat grown on the station for "breadstuff", mended clothes and cooked. Her cooking left much to be desired. A visitor, complaining about meals at the Guise station, wrote: "Although there were wild turkeys and ducks to be shot, we never had anything but tough beef and mutton chops swimming in fat to eat, for it never enters the minds of the squatters to care for such things at their stations." [2]

In October 1844, Richard Guise went to Melbourne to sell some horses. Eliza remained at Uroly with her two small children, the one-year-old baby Dick and two-year-old Eliza Jane. Uroly occupied 145 sq km, so when her husband was absent from the property, it was no exaggeration to say that Eliza Guise was isolated.

On Monday 13 October, heavy rain began to fall and the river rose alarmingly. When the flood waters first began to rise, Eliza Guise piled their belongings onto tables and chairs, their usual plan of action. Soon, however, the ever-rising water level left her no option but to climb onto the roof of her cottage, taking her two young children with her. From her precarious perch, she watched the efforts of their four years' work being undermined. Fences were flattened, the vegetable garden ruined, and drowned sheep and cattle floated past in the seething waters. For three sodden days and nights she remained on the roof, having enveloped her two children in her skirt and bound them to her, fearful lest she fell asleep and lost her grip on them. On the third day the unappetizing form of a drowned fowl floated past and was eagerly seized by Eliza, who made a raw meal for the hungry trio. They were finally rescued by some friendly Aborigines who, in frail bark canoes, delivered them to higher ground to await the subsiding waters.

Eliza's woes were far from over. Her husband failed to return from his horse trading venture in Melbourne, and on 17 December 1844 it was reported by the *Sydney Herald* that,

> Much excitement prevailed a few weeks back from the reported loss of Mr Richard Guise jnr. A rigid search having been instituted, his lifeless body was discovered in the neighbourhood of Little River, half way between Geelong and Melbourne. He had made himself a bed of grass and expired on it. So many statements are in circulation as to the manner in which he met his end that I deem it better to confine myself to the abstract fact of his loss and death than adopt any of the numerous rumours that are afloat. It is not apprehended, however, that any violence was offered to his person. Mrs Guise, who was lately subjected to such imminent peril during the flood, is now a widow. The event is a most melancholy one.

Although the *Sydney Herald* was loathe to report the real cause of death, it was not an unusual fate for those travelling in the bush. The experience is well described in David Denholm's book, *The Colonial Australians*.

> The solitude is awful. There is not a sound except the faint buzzing of the social flies, which stick to me by the hundreds. I wonder

what they live on, I wish I could see a snake. I begin to speculate what it is like to be lost in the bush — to wander round and round in a circle, helplessly trying to detect a landmark in the hideous gumtrees; to follow a trail leading to a rabbit hole; to lie down and die within a few yards of succour; or to go mad as so many have gone mad in this bush. [3]

What was known as the Bush Horrors (Delirium tremens), brought about by excessive use of alcohol, caused the death of Richard Guise.

Richard Guise died intestate in November 1844, and Eliza, a widow at twenty-one years of age, then became one of the first pioneer female squatters in the Riverina district. Richard was indebted to his father for the purchase of Uroly, and it was arranged between William Guise and his daughter-in-law that he should take Uroly in payment for his son's debt, and settle the property on his grandchildren, Eliza Jane and Dick. This was duly executed on 6 June 1845, and John Jobbins, George Watson and Henry Lintott were appointed as trustees. The sum of £100 per annum was to be taken from the profits of the run for the maintenance of the children, and the rest of the income was to go to his daughter-in-law, Eliza Guise. At the coming of age of the two children, the property was to be divided equally between the pair. This settlement was the source of Eliza Jane Larnach's wealth.

Within a short time, two more sons of William Guise died tragically, so he moved from the district, to take up more land at Gundaroo, but not before arranging with an impecunious Irishman from Limerick, Robert Joseph Alleyne, owner of the adjacent property to Uroly, to work under Eliza Guise's management. This arrangement ended in romance, and Eliza Guise and Robert Alleyne were married in February 1847. The newly weds and the two children moved to Robert Alleyne's much smaller run and Uroly was left to decline under the disinterested management of the trustees appointed by William Guise.

When Eliza Jane Guise was seven, Mary Cockburn Alleyne was born, and the two half-sisters formed a great bond that was to keep them together for most of their lives. Robert Alleyne outwardly displayed a kindly manner towards his step-children, while secretly filching their fortune. Their mother, now Eliza Alleyne, was at first an astute woman, investing her money from Uroly carefully, but gradually she became infected with her husband's extravagance and they both spent money too lavishly.

Even so, Eliza Alleyne acquired on her own behalf three adjoining stations: Groongal, Bringagee and Benerembah, totalling 48,380 ha. The parish of Alleyne is now named after her. Eliza's land was not freehold, but for £10 per annum, plus a tax of one halfpenny per head of cattle, a licence to occupy was granted. The value of the land lay in the amount of cattle the land could sustain. It was a time of great farming prosperity, and labour was becoming cheaper as so many disenchanted gold miners looked for farm work.

With the death of William Guise in 1850, the trustees lost all interest in Uroly. Because of their indifference, but without obtaining their permission, Robert Alleyne took over the management of Uroly, saving it, in his words, "from utter destruction". He began by selling cattle from his step-children's trust to reimburse himself for his trouble. He then instituted a suit in the Equity Court of New South Wales to remove the trustees from their duties, duties they were only too happy to relinquish. Alleyne maintained to the court that as stepfather to the Guise children, he was their guardian and trustee also. The court seemed to be mesmerised by this fast-talking Irishman and consented to his wishes.

Alleyne's next step was to obtain a decree from the Supreme Court in Sydney for the sale of Uroly, with the proceeds to go to the children's trust. He neglected to enlighten the court that he, as the children's trustee, would be the seller as well as the buyer of the property; that the auctioneer, Thomas Mort, would lend him the money to buy it, and that the conditions were so rigged that it precluded other purchasers from a fair chance of buying. The full price was to be paid in cash on the fall of the hammer.

In December 1853 the property was advertised as having 1800 cattle, and described as "one of the best runs on the Murrumbidgee, from which cattle never stray." Yet when the cattle were mustered from this flat country, though there was scarcely a place of concealment on the property only

1200 cattle were found to sell. Surprisingly, 600 cattle had "been stolen, strayed or died," according to Alleyne. The remaining 1200 were sold at £6 1s. per head. But some months after the sale was completed, Alleyne even more surprisingly found the 600 head of cattle, which he then sold for £12 each, pocketing the money for himself.

When Uroly was sold, Alleyne wrote to his wife who was in Melbourne, saying he had deposited £10,809 into the trust account. "Just think what Eliza Jane and Dick are worth, over £5,000 each," he wrote. In fact he had put in only £7,000, but it was to be some years before this was discovered. A year later, he on-sold Uroly, without stock, to a neighbouring squatter, John Peters, for £3,000.

By the time Eliza Jane was ten, barges laden with wool bales and paddle steamers carrying passengers began to appear on the Murray and Murrumbidgee Rivers. This transport was an enormous asset to the station owners, as well as freeing them from isolation. The Alleyne family were lured to travel, and frequently took the paddle steamer to Echuca, then a Cobb and Co. coach on the bone-shaking trip to Melbourne. The journey was not without its dangers, but brake failure on steep roads, holdups by bushrangers, or the thought of hurtling along behind a team of bolting horses did not deter them. They bought a house at Barkly Street, Brighton, and it was here, in 1853, that the twin daughters of Robert and Eliza Alleyne were born.

A family scandal made Eliza Alleyne anxious to distance the family, especially Eliza Jane and her brother Dick, from the Riverina area, so the Alleynes took up permanent residence in Melbourne. Eliza Jane's aunt, twenty-three-year-old Mary Ann Brownlow (née Guise), had been convicted for murdering her husband and sentenced to death by hanging. The sentence was the subject of enormous debate in the district, and a petition with numerous signatures was presented to the Governor General, asking him to commute her sentence to one of life imprisonment.

Once again alcohol had been involved in the tragedy. The couple had argued over the sale of a lease, and after the argument Mary Ann had asked her husband, George, to join her in a drink. When he refused, she accused him of "preferring to drink with his fancy woman" and as he left the house, she had rushed at him, "stabbing him in his side with a knife, whilst in a state of phrenzy [sic] caused by jealousy and stimulated by drink," the court was told.

The Chief Justice had spared her nothing when passing judgment. He remarked that "it was dreadful thing to have to pass sentence of death upon a woman, the mother of children . . . It appeared the cause was jealousy, and whether well or ill-founded, was no excuse for committing murder. Some allusions had been made to drink, but drunkenness was no excuse for a crime only worthy of a fiend." He trusted she would not delude herself with false hopes, "for her life was forfeited, and it was his imperative duty to pass upon her the extreme sentence of the law."

On the 10 October 1855 the scaffold was set up in the precincts of Goulburn Prison. Mary's quiet demeanour in prison had charmed not only her jailers, but the whole town.

> All who came in contact with her pitied her and were kind to her . . . indeed no case within the annals of the gallows can furnish a more conclusive argument against the iniquity, impolicy and sinfulness of capital punishment . . . so deep is the sympathy caused by her punishment, that it is feared in many minds that the sense of her crime is almost lost sight of in pity for her. She is so young, her previous character had been impeachable, except that it has been asserted that she was addicted to drink. By her death three infants, the baby only two months old, born in jail, are rendered orphans.[4]

Hopeful that clemency would be extended to Mary Ann Brownlow, the deputy sheriff delayed the hanging in the expectation of a reprieve from the Governor General, but to no avail. Shortly before four o'clock, the witnesses were stationed round the foot of the scaffold. Mary Ann had spent the afternoon in prayer with the Rev. Dr Waugh, who had persuaded her distraught sisters to leave her to concentrate her thoughts on eternity.

Her frame was greatly attenuated, and the languor mingled with resignation visibly depicted on her interesting countenance occasioned a hushed murmur of emotion amongst the beholders as she approached the scaffold. On reaching the platform, she thanked her minister, murmured a brief prayer, then resigned herself into the hands of the executioner. Even while the rope was being adjusted round her neck, her fortitude never forsook her; the hood was drawn over her features, the bolt withdrawn, and she fell through the aperture, dying instantly, without a struggle.[5]

Before and after the execution all shops and public houses in the town were closed. Her body was conveyed to the cemetery of the Church of England, and there laid to rest.

Mary Ann Brownlow had been illiterate, and did not learn to read until she was imprisoned. Education was still difficult for remote squatters, and Eliza Alleyne was eager to ensure her children had a better education than their ill-fated aunt. Robert Alleyne, never one to miss an opportunity of making some money on the side, applied to the Equity Court for £780 per year to educate his step-children. This was a large sum considering that in that year a young gentleman could board at Goulburn Grammar for £70 a year, where the syllabus included French, dancing and drawing. The courts were not so lavish in their thinking, deeming £280 a year as sufficient.

The doors to society had been opened to the Alleynes since Robert had been made a magistrate in 1855. The beach resort of Brighton was becoming a fashionable suburb of Melbourne. Squatters like the Alleynes now kept town houses in Sydney or Melbourne, their sons attending schools such as Geelong Grammar, and their daughters learning music, art and needlework at ladies colleges in the hope of preparing them to become accomplished wives for wealthy husbands.

Girls were encouraged to marry at an early age. Soon to come into Eliza Jane's life was the young banker from the Hunter Valley, William James Mudie Larnach. Described as a jaunty dresser with a penchant for velvet jackets, his neck encircled by a "masher collar" — a high stiff cravat of starched linen — and swinging a silver topped cane, William, in 1857, was the very model of a young banker about Melbourne. When the half-sisters first met the man they were both destined to marry, Eliza Jane, at fifteen years of age, was blossoming into a beauty, while Mary Alleyne was just eight years old.

Chapter VI

GEELONG

When the marriage of Eliza Jane Guise and William James Mudie Larnach took place in 1859, the young couple could be said to be truly Australian. It had been sixty-nine years since Sergeant Richard Guise first set foot on Australian soil, followed by John Larnach thirty-two years later.

In the first six years of William and Eliza Jane's marriage, four of their six children were born in Victoria — Donald Guise Larnach on 1 March 1860, followed two years later by Kate Emily, then Douglas John in 1863 and Colleen Shawn in 1865. Alice Jane was born in Dunedin in 1868, and ten years later their youngest, Gladys Beryl, was born in London.

For two years after their marriage, Eliza stayed in Melbourne while William continued his banking career on the goldfields, until he was promoted as manager of the Bank of New South Wales in Geelong. The salary for branch managers ranged from £400 to £800, in addition to housing allowances. Geelong was a substantial looking town, it had been a rival of Melbourne before the railway was completed between Ballarat and Melbourne, but now it was losing trade to the other centres. When Larnach was appointed to the struggling Geelong branch, the branch was not covering expenses; but he later recorded that "when I left the business, I had made shrewd profits, equal to £10,000 per annum."[1] His term of office there coincided with the end of a small recession, and this may have accounted for his success.

A year after Larnach's appointment, the bank moved from the temporary accommodation it had occupied since first opening in 1852, to a stately two-storied stone building on the corner of Malop and Kardinia Streets. The new building was officially opened on 17 March 1862, and the Larnach family took up residence on the second floor. It was here that Douglas and Colleen Larnach were born. From the six large double-hung windows of the upper floor, the view across the dusty wind-swept road was of other banking and trading establishments. Not far away, what is now a beautiful park was then the eyesore known as La Trobe's Cesspool, a dam harbouring many dead animals, with offal from butchers' shops floating on its surface. It was not a town in which William intended to make his permanent home.

For William, life in Geelong was not entirely centered around banking. He became involved in several court cases, and one in particular related to Eliza Jane's inheritance. There has been much speculation about Eliza's wealth and the financial backing she gave William to embark on his many business ventures; £80,000 has been the figure most often quoted, a figure that has never been supported by evidence. The actual amount from the sale of Uroly station, placed in the Supreme Court in Sydney in February 1854, was £6,140 18s 10d, and that sum was to be divided between Eliza Jane and her brother Dick.

After discovering a large discrepancy in Eliza Jane's inheritance, William took his stepfather-in-law, Robert Alleyne, to court. The loquacious Alleyne was an easy-going rough diamond, always on the make and eager and successful in impressing people, but never able to hold onto his money or his tongue for long. It was Alleyne himself who first planted the seeds of suspicion in William's mind regarding the stewardship of Eliza Jane's inheritance. Alleyne couldn't resist boasting to William of the great price he had received for the 600 head of cattle found on Uroly after the sale in 1853, exactly twice the price that had been realised by the children's trust, and remarked to William, "Who had a better right to the money than me?" He doubled up with laughter recalling the muster he had organised and the stampede he had contrived of the 600 frightened cattle, which had conveniently disappeared until well after the sale. The more he talked to William the more he incriminated himself. He lacked the brains to recognise the banker's psyche in Larnach, who believed every penny should be accounted for. In William's eyes, Alleyne's conduct amounted to nothing more than cattle stealing.

When William conveyed this information to his mother-in-law, she realised that Robert Alleyne had not only bought Uroly at a greatly under-valued price, but had deposited in the children's trust account nearly £4,000 less than he had told her. Although she had always condoned the fact that he had made some money out of the trust for himself, this great deception turned the indulgent feelings of a wife into those of a fiercely protective mother, and in her fury she not only banished him from their Brighton home, but gave William all the letters Alleyne had written to her concerning Uroly, to be used in evidence against her husband.

The Larnach versus Alleyne case was commenced in the Equity Court in Melbourne in 1861. Robert Alleyne hired the most expensive and fash-ionable lawyer in Melbourne, Archibald Michie, later knighted. The case lasted nineteen days. There was much mud slinging and it was recorded in great detail by the press, giving the public copious reading matter and fill-ing the lawyers' wallets with exorbitant fees.

At the end of the case, Mr Justice Chapman declared the sale of Uroly Station and stock to be fraudulent and void, and decreed that Alleyne should account for all the monies which he had received, or which, "with-out his wilful default" might have been received for the station and cattle since the sale eight years previously. However, the judge decreed that each party had to bear the massive court costs.

Judge Chapman died soon after the case, and Robert Alleyne appealed to the Supreme Court. It was not until 1865 that the appeal was heard before three judges. Their Honours took two years to make up their minds, overruling a portion of Judge Chapman's decision. It says much for the excellent work of Mr Michie, aided by Alleyne's gift of the blarney, that Alleyne was discharged of fraud, but liable for costs.

At the time of the Supreme Court's decision, Robert Alleyne was liv-ing on the Camaroo station in a remote area of Queensland and was prac-tically penniless, his money having gone on his lawyer's fees. His solicitor applied for leave to appeal to the Privy Council against this judgment, and Justice Molesworth gave this permission, but directed that the costs for which Alleyne was liable be paid into court. Mr J.W. Stephens, the solici-tor for the prosecution, believed it was immaterial whether costs were awarded, as it was not likely any money would be got from the now poverty stricken Alleyne.

The appeal did not go to the Privy Council, nor did Alleyne repay one penny to Eliza Jane Larnach and her brother Dick Guise. The matter always rankled with William, and thirty years later he was still trying to recover the money. In a letter dated 3 November 1897, to F.N. Dougal and Company at 62 The Strand, London, he wrote: "Dear Sirs, in looking through your Unclaimed Money Registry Pamphlet, I have come across the name Alleyne, in whom I am interested in learning more about, and I see for a fee of £2. 2s., you supply full copies with names and dates of papers in which the name appeared. . . . I am prepared to remit you the price if it is forwarded to my address."[2]

The whole unhappy episode of the Larnach versus Alleyne case was compounded by the failing health of Eliza Alleyne. After long suffering, she died at the age of forty-one years in 1864 without ever knowing the outcome of the court case, which had not only ruined her marriage, but further depleted her children's inheritance by the hefty legal costs. Eliza was buried with her first husband, Richard Guise, at Towang on the Hume River.

The three stations in Eliza Alleyne's name were only leasehold, but on her death the sale of cattle realised close to £40,000. In the unlikely belief that there were no debts and her husband had no claim on the money from her estate, her five children — Eliza Jane and Dick Guise, Mary, and the twins Edith and Emily Alleyne — would each receive about £8,000. (There is no evidence that Mary Alleyne ever had any money.) Looking at the best prospect and adding the £8,000 to the £3,000 from Uroly, Eliza Jane's inheritance still falls far short of the often quoted £80,000. William Larnach's financial start in life could not be entirely attributed to his wife's money.

Eliza Jane and William Larnach were now well established in Geelong, but on the death of Eliza Alleyne, Mary Alleyne and her twin sisters went to Queensland to live a transient life with their father. It was to be the longest time that Eliza Jane and Mary would be separated. Dick Guise married and went to Sydney, where his daughter was born the following year.

If William thought life would now settle into an uncomplicated pattern and the Larnach name would cease to feature in the press, he was mistaken. On the 4 March 1864, William discovered that his trusted accountant, Alfred Etheridge, had embezzled £200, fled the country and left his wife and child to fend for themselves. William had the unpleasant duty of laying charges of embezzlement against his employee. When the name of Alfred Etheridge appeared in the *Police Gazette*, *The Geelong Advertiser* wasted no time in bringing to the public's attention the name of James Larnach, and the suppression by the same bank of any searching inquiry into his £5,000 swindle. "When the defalcation of Etheridge was made the subject of rumour, we determined to wait and see what action the Bank would take. . . . It is satisfactory to find that on this occasion there is no room for fault finding."[3] The press, however, did question how Etheridge's new found affluence had gone unnoticed by his manager, William Larnach. However, William's mind was on other things. The first of his many ventures in land speculation was about to take place, in partnership with his brother George and others.

On 26 March 1864, the leading article in the *Adelaide Telegraph* described a proposal put forward by George Larnach, together with six unnamed men from Victoria and New South Wales, for an extensive land grant of two million acres (820,000 ha) of unexplored land in Western Australia. This proposal was presented to Dr J.S. Hampton, governor of Western Australia, with instructions that all correspondence be addressed to William Larnach in Geelong.

The enormity of the proposal emerges in reading the despatches sent from Governor Hampton to the Secretary of State, the Duke of Newcastle. George Larnach had "applied for himself and six un-named persons of great wealth resident in Victoria and New South Wales, for a grant of extensive, pre-emptive and exclusive rights over large tracts of unsettled parts of this Colony." George Larnach wanted the exclusive privilege of exploring the land within a radius of 480 km north and east of Cape Pasley, consisting of no less than one million acres (410,000 ha) to be held by the consortium for twelve years, with unrestricted rights for eight years to purchase any portions they chose at 10/- an acre, in quantities of not less than 1000 acres. They would stock the land with sheep, cattle and horses. They requested certain concessions, and if these were agreed to the partners had a second proposal: to drive overland from Cape Pasley to the Exmouth Gulf on the north-west coast a flock of not less than 2000 sheep. In return, George Larnach wanted another one million acres in the Exmouth Gulf area, with the same pre-emptive rights to purchase, commencing with the arrival of the sheep at the Exmouth Gulf.

One look at the map of Australia, taking a rough estimate of the distance George Larnach promised to take the sheep, gives an indication of the audacious nature of this scheme. The distance from Cape Pasley in the south east, overlooking the Great Australian Bight, to the Exmouth Gulf on the Indian Ocean, above the Tropic of Capricorn, is about 1600 km as the crow flies, and the last 480 km were at that time unexplored. [4]

The people of Perth were gripped by George Larnach's proposal. It was the first offer of capital of any substance to come to Western Australia and gave the colonists hope of opening up the huge areas of land that had remained unexplored for want of money. Governor Hampton thought George Larnach "an energetic, pushing man", well qualified to carry out the proposed enterprise to 'Terra Incognito' as he called the northern parts of Western Australia. Yet while the governor yearned for the input of capital coming into the colony, he could not agree to the proposal as it departed so radically from the Regulations of 1862, which only permitted land grants of 100,000 acres (41,000 ha).

Everyone had an opinion on the matter. The colonial secretary thought no such offer was likely to occur again, "so I commend the proposal." The attorney general, the colonial treasurer, the butcher, the baker, the candlestick maker, the bankers and businessmen of Perth were all in favour of the prospect of capital into the struggling colony, and all signed a petition which they sent to the Duke of Newcastle, asking him to accede to George Larnach's plan. With it went another petition from George Larnach and the people of Perth for the abandonment of convict transportation to

Western Australia. George Larnach and the colonists knew free immigration was needed for his scheme to be a success. Convict labour was quite unsuited for the purpose of settlement, and fraught with labour problems, as George and William Larnach well knew from their father's experience.

On 4 June 1866, a letter from Downing Street came with a resounding "No" to the land deals, but recommended that each man took up 100,000 acres allowed under the existing regulations. Apart from 4000 acres already held by George Larnach, there is no evidence that the other six men took up any land. It would seem that the most important outcome of the whole exercise was the success of the petition for the abandonment of convict transportation. It, along with other petitions, achieved their aim. The last shipment of convicts to Australia arrived at Fremantle on 10 January 1868, eighty years to the month since the first fleet anchored in Sydney Cove. In a generation of one family, from father to son, the change of attitude is apparent. John Larnach, having inadvertently and unwillingly helped precipitate the beginning of the end of convict transportation, a scheme he favoured for its cheap labour, lived to see his sons George and William recognise the damage transportation had caused Australia and petition for its ending.

Whether George and William Larnach were involved in other land deals during these years is not known, but it is highly likely. William was amassing money over and above a bank manager's salary. He owned land near Frankston, in the shire of Mornington, Victoria — a popular beach resort in the mid 1800s, where paddle steamers used to bring picnickers from the city — but there is no other evidence of land held by William in Australia.

By 1866, living in Geelong had begun to pall. At the invitation of his uncle, Donald Larnach, William, Eliza Jane and their four children left for London. Their departure was marked by a complimentary dinner held at Mack's Hotel, and they were presented with a framed "beautifully inscribed expression of esteem" from the bank's staff, which still hangs in the castle rooms today. "We hope that you and Mrs Larnach and Family may derive every benefit from your trip to England, and that you will return among us. William Larnach's name will long live among us for his past Charity and Gentlemanly Kindness to all men."

Chapter VII

DUNEDIN

The attraction of mid-Victorian London for William and Eliza Jane was immediate. They were welcomed to the town house at 21 Kensington Palace Gardens by William's aunt and uncle, Jane and Donald Larnach. Their arrival coincided with the start of the London season, with its round of lunches, dinners and balls, held at houses whose elegance far surpassed anything the young Larnachs had seen in Australia.

Donald Larnach did not enjoy the social whirl, but he used the occasions to advance his nephew's career. He introduced William to many influential banking associates, such as Lord Rothschild, through whom Donald Larnach had just negotiated a loan of £300 million for the Bank of New South Wales. William was also introduced to Sir Francis Baring and his brother Thomas. The Barings looked down on Rothschild as a parvenue in the world of banking, as he was only a third generation member of the German banking family. But it was the men from the London financial community who in 1863 had formed the Bank of Otago to exploit the profits from gold in that province whom Donald Larnach hoped William would impress with his experience of banking in the goldfields.

Donald Larnach had an "incurable optimism" about New Zealand, and his influence on William was profound. It went far beyond an uncle helping his nephew in his career. William set out to emulate his uncle in every way, not only in business, but in his personal lifestyle as well. While William and Eliza were in London, Donald Larnach bought Brambletye, a country estate in Sussex, the house an ivy-mantled ruin built in 1631. He discussed his plans with William, describing the commodious ornamental stone house he would build and the extensive gardens that he hoped to create. This fired William's imagination and filled him with a burning ambition for a similar estate of his own. In later years the huge conservatory at

Brambletye would house New Zealand plants sent by William to add to his uncle's noted plant collection from around the world. Likewise, the Black Hamburg grapes still flourishing on the Otago Peninsula were cuttings from the vines at Brambletye.

Under the wings of Aunt Jane Larnach, who was born in Australia but had come to London fourteen years previously, Eliza delighted in the sight-seeing, the social life of London, the shopping and the theatres, which were only just becoming acceptable places for respectable women to attend. Although she had four children under six years of age, Eliza was only twenty-four, and life in Geelong had been remote even from the excite-ment of Melbourne. She was captivated by London, and for her the visit came to an end all too quickly.

On 6 October 1866, the passenger ship *Superb*, 1451 tonnes, sailed from the East India Dock in the Port of London for Melbourne. Included in the first class passenger list were the names of Mr and Mrs William Larnach and their four children. For the sum of £187 10s for the entire fam-ily, they were allowed 40 cubic feet (1.2 cubic metres) of luggage each, and were to be "victualled during the voyage and at ports of call, but no wine, beer or spirits were permitted in the cabins, and servants must mess with the crew."

Almost a year after the family returned to Melbourne, the position of chief colonial manager of the Bank of Otago was offered to William by the London directors. He was to replace Thomas Bathgate, a manager they had found unsatisfactory. Once again leaving Eliza and the children in Melbourne, William made the first of many crossings of the Tasman Sea. The Larnach family would make so many trips across that rough stretch of water that the master of the *Tararua*, Captain McLean, and his wife and daughters became great friends of the Larnachs and frequently stayed with them.

When he caught his first glimpse of New Zealand from the decks of the *Tararua*, William was not impressed. It was a dismal September day in 1867. The first port of call was Bluff, seen from the ship through heavy rain. They were detained there for two days before reaching Dunedin. "What

with the work I had to do, which was not of a very happy kind and therefore had something to do with my determination, had I not engaged to stay
for five years I would have turned back and been away again within a
month," recollected Larnach twenty years later.

Dunedin was evolving from an insanitary little town — its filthy streets
were compared to seventeenth-century Edinburgh — to one of substance.
Most buildings were being replaced by brick or stone after fire had swept
the town a few years earlier.[1] Many of the businesses in operation then are
still known today: F.G. Dalgetys, Wholesale and Importing Co; William
Gregg, coffee, spices, cordials and aerated waters; Duncan and Wilson, malt
importers and whisky makers; Moses Joel, brewer; Charles Begg, musical
instruments and sheet music; Speight's beer; Cadbury's chocolate; Richard
Hudson's Excelsior Biscuit Factory; Sargood & Co., warehousemen; A. and
T. Burt's engineering firm; and Ross and Glendining, about to form their
partnership.

The Dunedin Club was the meeting place for a clique of merchants,
pastoralists, professionals and financiers, who were unconsciously forming
a strata of society they had hoped to leave behind when they emigrated,
and from which many of them would have been excluded in Britain. It was
here that William Larnach made friends and met business acquaintances.
James Macandrew, for a decade the enterprising and popular superintendent of the Otago Provincial Council, who on being jailed for the debt of
£40,000 declared his house a jail; Robert Stout, a puritanical man with
a zeal for education and reform; and Henry Driver, an American card-
playing land speculator, were a few of the diverse friends Larnach made at
the club.

With seventeen years of banking behind him, William Larnach was
thirty-four years of age when he became colonial manager of the bank.
Banks from Australia and Britain were well represented in the town, but
the Bank of Otago, in Princes Street, was the most impressive banking
establishment. The bank's business was derived mainly from dealings with
gold prospectors and importers, and possibly a few transactions with pastoralists, but there is no evidence of other activities.[2] The bank had suffered

The Bank of Otago about the time Larnach was manager. It is the tall building with the four ornamental urns on the skyline. The lower building with the clock tower later became the Colonial Bank of which Larnach was a director.

two setbacks which seem to have been responsible for the resignation of John Bathgate. The first serious loss was the result of the crash of the London financial house Overend and Gurney in 1866, and further losses were incurred from holding part of the overdrawn Southland Provincial Government account, as Larnach soon discovered. "On arrival in New Zealand, I found that my predecessor had locked up almost the whole of the Bank's capital by a fixed loan made for several years to the Southland Provincial Government. The Bank's shares, with £10 paid, were selling at £4. 2s. 6d., and there were many doubtful advances to deal with."

William's arrival in New Zealand coincided with a time of general prosperity, and Otago in particular was progressing. The Cook Strait cable had been laid, giving Dunedin telegraphic communication with the North Island. The Otago Provincial Government could now afford to deepen the notoriously shallow harbour. The construction of the railway which would eventually link Christchurch to Invercargill had commenced. Of particular interest to bankers were the executions of three notorious bushrangers — Burgers, Levy and Kelly — who were responsible for many murders in Otago, Westland and Nelson, and had especially targeted the gold escorts. In that year Dunedin opened its first public school and its first steam-powered flour mill. Wool prices were buoyant, and the *Southland News* excitedly announced the successful acclimatisation of rabbits.

Once William was established in Dunedin, Eliza and the children followed, and again they took up residence above the bank. The living quarters were somewhat cramped with the four children, and made more so by the arrival of the rather forlorn figure of Mary Alleyne. Torn between choosing to live with her father, who detested William Larnach, or taking up residence with Eliza, she had chosen the Larnachs. That same year Robert Alleyne had remarried, and Mary Alleyne left her father, stepmother and twin sister in Queensland to live in Dunedin. Mary Alleyne was eighteen years of age at the time, and it says much for her feelings towards Eliza and William that although their efforts to recoup Eliza's money had resulted in the collapse of her parents' marriage and the ruination of her father, Mary still preferred to live with them. Eliza, a motherly woman, welcomed her younger sister's company. Mary became part of the Larnach household, and was included in every facet of their life.

Another arrival from Australia that year who left his mark on William's life was the formidable W.J.T. Clarke, one of the largest landholders in Australia and generally known as "Monied Clarke". He was widely feared for his ruthless land hunger, but respected for his consummate ability in pursuit of fortune.[3] Years later, the *Tuapeka Times* in acknowledging his death paid him this tribute: "W.J.T. Clarke has died, the richest, meanest man in Victoria." Clarke had had dealings with William Larnach in Victoria, and was possibly one of those involved in the Western Australian land claim initiated by George and William Larnach, as it had all the hallmarks of the way Clarke worked — anonymously, pushing into previously unexplored land and laying claim to it.

Clarke had visited New Zealand ten years previously, and now was returning with the purpose of expanding his pastoral empire, but not by buying land outright, he was too shrewd for that. His ploy was to lend run-holders large sums of money, bide his time, and when times became tough, step in and buy the run-holder out.

In the musty old leather-bound Larnach scrap book is a Bill of Exchange for £41,000 on account of George M. Bell to the Hon. W.J.T. Clarke, dated 1 October 1869 and signed by W.J.M. Larnach, reassigning land in the Awamoko and Maerewhenua survey districts of North Otago.[4] This document is the first indication of Larnach's association with Clarke as Clarke's agent in New Zealand, and also with George Meredith Bell, a successful Southland wheat grower. Bell also was to become involved in later land deals with Larnach.

W.J.T. Clarke gained notoriety in New Zealand with his negotiations over the Otago run named Moa Flat, a property that had impressed Clarke when he first saw its rich river flats and well grassed slopes on the banks of the Clutha River, some 80 km west of Dunedin. The Crown lease of Moa Flat was held by the Chalmers brothers, originally bankers from Melbourne, who should have stayed with banking, being quite unsuited to farming. When speculation in sheep ended disastrously, they found the crippling interest rates of twenty per cent on their £20,000 loan from Clarke impossible to pay. Clarke was quick to take advantage of their misfortune by insisting that the brothers mortgage their Crown lease of Moa Flat to him as additional security. His uncanny sense of anticipating others' misfortune was soon realised. In 1868 a sudden recession hit Otago, affecting sheep farmers badly. Clarke foreclosed on the Crown lease mortgage, assigning William Larnach as his agent. The press condemned Clarke, accusing him "of foreclosing on the Chalmers without going about the business in a proper legal manner."[5]

The Chalmers were bitter, in their eyes the 70,000 acres (28,700 ha) and stock were worth more than £20,000. They felt they had suffered the privations of pioneering the land for seventeen years for no reward. Their threats to sue Clarke came to nothing, and they left New Zealand. As soon as the foreclosure proceedings were resolved, Clarke sent for his most competent Tasmanian station manager, John Fry Kitchings, to restore the run-down property, and at Clarke's request the Provincial Government issued a fresh lease in the name of W.J.T. Clarke's son, William John Clarke jnr.

Clarke's low level of popularity was counterbalanced by his continued good luck. In May 1871, the Otago Provincial Government found to its embarrassment that its account with the Bank of New Zealand was over-drawn by £88,000, and the bank made it very clear they would not honour any cheques after 1 October. The Provincial Government treasurer, J.B. Bradshaw, was convinced that the only way to raise the money was to sell 50,000 acres (20,500 ha) of Crown land as quickly as possible, at the price fixed by law of £1 per acre. The most obvious person likely to produce that amount of cash at short notice was "Monied Clarke", and Bradshaw wrote to Larnach, as Clarke's agent, to make an offer to Clarke.

Clarke was delighted with the proposal. He knew the exact 50,000 acres he wanted, but he was a wily negotiator. He wrote two letters, one to Bradshaw saying that he would be an unwilling buyer — the price was too high. The other letter was to Larnach: "Come to Melbourne immediately. You are to bring full information regarding a possible freehold purchase of Moa Flat, and you will regard this business as confidential."[6]

Larnach responded to the summons, arriving in Melbourne within two weeks. He told Clarke of the Provincial Government's panic and their hopes of solvency by selling to Clarke. "The two men drafted an offer. The terms were tough. Clarke would be prepared to buy 50,000 acres of Moa Flat Station only, and no other. He would pay £1 per acre, to be reduced by 2/6 an acre for the cancellation of the Crown Lease he already owned, and a further reduction of 2/- an acre to survey the land by his own surveyor. The Otago Government was to pay a 1 per cent commission to Larnach, amounting to £500." The proposed terms effectively reduced the offer to Clarke to 14s. 8d. an acre. [7]

Clarke instructed Larnach to return to Dunedin and deliver the terms in person. On 16 September, Larnach presented the terms to the executive committee of the Otago Provincial Government and gave them exactly two days to accept the offer. The executive committee was depleted by the absence of Superintendent James Macandrew; the Provincial Government treasurer, J.B. Bradshaw; Donald Reid and two other members, who were all in Wellington attending Parliamentary sittings. It was left to the acting treasurer, W.H. Cutten, to receive the ultimatum, knowing that the Bank of New Zealand had reaffirmed its refusal to extend the overdraft, which placed in jeopardy money many private individuals were owed by the Provincial Government.

Cutten wasted the first day by sending a despatch to Larnach querying his status as Clarke's agent. Larnach replied by messenger: "If you are doubtful about my authority to speak for Mr Clarke, there is no necessity to communicate with me. If your Government is not going to come to terms with my client, then there is no further need for him to keep £40,000 to £50,000 uninvested in order to pay for land." This reply alarmed Cutten and he was reduced from "bureaucratic high-handedness to nervous prostration." [8] Urgent telegrams flew between Dunedin and Wellington, with procrastinating replies. "We will write," replied the executives attending Parliamentary sittings, who were happily isolated by the slowness of communications from making a decision they knew would sacrifice political principles; yet where else could they raise the money?

In desperation Acting Treasurer Cutten telegraphed Bradshaw: "Cannot wait for your letter, Clarke's agent limits time offer. I will resign tomorrow." But despite his threats, Cutten continued discussions not only with Larnach, but with the station manager John Kitchings and Clarke's son William, who had arrived in Dunedin with his father's power of attorney. The ultimatum expired at noon on 19 September. Cutten, with still no word from Wellington, decided to sell not only Moa Flat, at 15 shillings an acre, but was persuaded to sell 11,000 extra acres (4450 ha) that had been reserved for small farmers. The chairman of the Waste Land Board signed on behalf of the Provincial Government. William Clarke jnr. signed, papers were exchanged and the sale of Moa Flat was completed. An hour after the expiration of the ultimatum, Bradshaw telegraphed from Wellington: "I hope you will close with Clarke, and thus enable us to open the remainder of Moa Flat for agricultural purposes." Cutten replied, "Clarke insisted on his own terms, which I have accepted. There was no help for it, or Treasury must have closed on 2 October."

When Bradshaw received the terms of the sale in Wellington friends "feared for his sanity". The 61,000 acres (25,000 ha) had realised only £45,750. Bradshaw was aghast and fearful for the safety of his seat in Parliament, as were all the Otago members. They persuaded the Legislative Council to form a select committee to look into the matter, but Clarke and Larnach had done their homework, the contract was legally watertight, and the Government could take no action. Even so, the whole province called on the Government to "repent of their bargain", and engaged lawyers to have the sale declared invalid.

Again Larnach sailed for Melbourne to warn Clarke of the impending legal battle. Clarke advised Larnach to engage lawyers to represent his youngest son, Joseph, to whom he had by then transferred the property, and to grant some concessions to appease public opinion. Larnach left Melbourne with Clarke's power of attorney personally made out to him. This was a sign of the faith this miserly millionaire, a man who rarely trusted anyone, had in Larnach.

At the legal proceedings in Dunedin instigated by the Provincial Government, Larnach proposed as a concession that ten acres be reserved for a school site, which met with approval. The Waste Land Board would agree to the sale if Clarke would return 1950 acres (800 ha) of the 11,000 acres that had originally been set aside for small farmers. Larnach reminded them that Clarke would not accept one acre less than the area surveyed, but if they would agree to exchange 1950 acres of river frontage next to Moa Flat for the land they wanted returned, then Larnach would be satisfied. The possession of this desirable river frontage was Larnach's aim. This was granted, the legal battle was over, and the title confirmed to the absentee owner, W.J.T. Clarke's lucky son, Joseph Clarke.

The Provincial Treasury had only repaid half their overdraft, and the bank was still demanding full payment. For the third time Larnach went to Melbourne, this time with a personal interest in adding to Moa Flat. He convinced Clarke to offer the Provincial Treasury £16,000 for 20,000 acres (8200 ha) of leased land across the river from Moa Flat, at Teviot. This provided seven and a half miles (12 km) of river frontage, with command of 500,000 acres (205,000 ha) of hill country that would otherwise lack summer water for stock. The Provincial Government made no opposition to this sale; they were happy to be financial again. In fact all those involved with the sale were happy. The Bank of New Zealand, W.J.T. Clarke, William Larnach, not to mention the Waste Land Board, who were so delighted with Larnach that they commissioned him to negotiate further purchases for them. Only the scapegoat, the Acting Treasurer Cutten, lampooned daily by the press for several weeks, was not so thrilled, and the general public were still infuriated at the sale to the wealthy Australian squatter at the expense of men of little capital.

During all these negotiations, Larnach had thoroughly acquainted himself with Moa Flat, and was as impressed with the property as W.J.T. Clarke had been on first viewing it. Joseph Clarke, now the owner of Moa Flat, was living a gentleman's life on a property in Tasmania given to him by his father, and he was not really interested in Moa Flat. But Larnach, together with W.J.T. Clarke's Tasmanian station manager John Kitchings, could see its possibilities. One month after the sale of Moa Flat was completed, Larnach lodged with Joseph Clarke title deeds of land he owned on the Otago Peninsula, North East Harbour, the town of Palmerston, and properties in McLaggan St, Cumberland St, and buildings in Dunedin and Winton, as security to lease Moa Flat from Joseph Clarke.

Larnach formed a partnership with John Kitchings and the recently bankrupted Henry Driver, who was a land and stock agent. The three men set about with enthusiasm to create a model station, combining their knowledge of livestock, and importing top quality stock of all kinds. "The mighty Lord Salisbury was brought out from Scotland at a cost of 1,500 guineas, the highest price up to that time for a Clydesdale horse in North Britain."[9] This horse, with quality mares from Tasmania, established great progeny, which were featured in the New Zealand Stud Book for many years. Thoroughbred horses were imported and a racing stud with training stables was formed. Shorthorn cattle, Lincoln sheep, Berkshire pigs, prize poultry, greyhounds and collie dogs were all imported. Large areas of land were cultivated to provide winter feed for the stock. The station promised to become the showcase of Otago livestock.

The syndicate not only acquired livestock. Every bit of freehold land they could get was bought, until the property comprised half a million acres (205,000 ha). Its boundaries ran 96 km north along the Clutha River from Beaumont to the ranges facing Clyde, the gullies covered in matagouri scrub and clumps of manuka, the higher land treeless, with rocky outcrops, and it was a long day's ride for a hardened horseman to reach the Old Man Range, the western boundary.

It was a place Eliza, Mary and the children loved to visit. Mr Kitchings, who managed the property, kept ponies for the children to ride, and Eliza noted that he provided her "with huge turkeys and turkey eggs" which she loved. "Dear Mr Kitchings," wrote Eliza, "I think his hands are now too fat to hold his pen and he will soon not be able to see out of his eyes with all the hair on his face. Baby loves him, as long as he doesn't kiss her."[10] It was a popular holiday spot for the Driver and Larnach families, and many of their Dunedin friends were entertained there.

Chapter VIII

THE BANK OF OTAGO

William Larnach had been managing the Bank of Otago for four years when the sale of Moa Flat to Joseph Clarke took place in 1871. That same year, he commenced the building of his house on the Peninsula. With a view to future subdivision he laid out the town of Portobello, reserving land for a cemetery and Anglican and Presbyterian churches. He also established the "Big Mill", in the Catlins district, half way between Dunedin and Invercargill, which made Owaka into a thriving little timber town with its own school and store.

No wonder it was a common criticism from London directors that colonial bank managers often made private investments at odds with their position, for Larnach was not unique in this matter. But this was a criticism made by men far removed from the excitement of participating in colonial opportunities. Where Larnach saw an opportunity, he took it. During the six years of his management of the bank, thirteen branches were opened throughout the goldfields of Southland and Otago, and as a profitable sideline for himself, he began arranging for basic foodstuffs to be sent into the mining towns, where food was sold at a premium.

While the directors in London were unable to fault his management, they were not particularly pleased with the bank's results, which by 1871, were being affected by the decline in gold returns. This decline, suffered by all banks in New Zealand, made it necessary for them to call for more capital from England — not a popular move with the English directors and shareholders, who wished only to take money out of New Zealand. Because the Bank of Otago's London directors' policy had been to confine the activities of the bank to the Otago goldfields, the Bank of Otago suffered more heavily from the decline than their competitors, such as the Bank of New Zealand, the Union Bank, the Bank of New South Wales, and the Bank of Australasia, all of which had branches throughout the country. The time had come for the London directors to take stock of the bank's position; either it had to expand throughout the colony or be left behind by more progressive institutions.[1]

Very little is known of the Bank of Otago. The minutes of meetings of directors and shareholders or letters between New Zealand and London would no doubt have provided interesting reading, but no records have survived.[2] In fact Larnach's own account gives as much detail as any that remains.

> I stuck to the office I had undertaken for nearly seven years, and had built up a good safe business for the Bank of Otago, when the Directors in London agreed to transfer the business to the National Bank of New Zealand, rather than increase its capital . . . Notwithstanding that the Bank of Otago received nothing for the goodwill of its business, which was only taken over at a capital valuation; the Premises, representing fourteen branches were accepted for £1,200 more than they stood in the books of the Bank, and only £13,000 in advances, out of nearly £300,000 were declined as not worth 20/- in the pound.
>
> Although more than £100,000 of the Bank's capital before I had assumed the general management, and a hurried liquidation in the end, was made of the Bank's affairs, shareholders received a return of £8 15s. per share for £10 originally paid.[3]

The shares had been worth £4 2s. 6d. when Larnach took over in 1867.

Local opinions differed about Larnach's management of the Bank of Otago. The *Tapanui Courier* of 19 October 1898, (always an opponent of Larnach's views) asserted that Larnach was the means of the downfall of the Bank of Otago. "He was storekeeping in a large way at Lawrence and other goldfield centres, and at the decline of the Otago fields, when the rush took place to the West Coast, his liability to the Bank was exceedingly large, and hence the downfall of that institution and its absorption by the National Bank."

Another opinion came from a cautious man with frugal habits, John Bathgate, whom Larnach had replaced as manager of the Otago Bank. Bathgate says in his autobiography that "Larnach was an able man, and well received." Ross Gore in his history of the National Bank describes Larnach as a man who had riches thrust upon him, was open-handed, extravagant, ambitious and adventurous in business, a man of whom it has been written "that it is only necessary to inform him that a thing is impossible in order to ensure his attempting it forthwith."[4] Other contemporaries had faith in him, shown in this letter dated 5 September 1872, written to Charles Magniac Esq., Chairman of the National Bank of New Zealand, 34 Clements Lane, EC, London. The sender's name is indecipherable, but could possibly be a shareholder. It reads:

We ourselves suffered as much anxiety and pecuniary loss in the first appointment we made of our Bank, that we venture to suggest that a responsible position in the National Bank in New Zealand should be offered to Mr Larnach. This gentleman has been our chief Colonial Manager for the last five years, and by his energy, zeal and thorough knowledge of banking has restored in great part, if not altogether, our lost capital, weeded our books from bad accounts, increased the number of good ones, and won generally the confidence of the Settlers in Otago and Southland.

The takeover of the Bank of Otago by the National Bank occurred on 1 July 1873. The agreement was that management and staff would be kept on for one year. Immediately there was antipathy between Larnach and the London directors of the National Bank. Writing to Adam Burnes, the National Bank general manager in New Zealand, Larnach asserts that he should be left to get on with the business of managing, and that interference from London should stop. By November the directors had resolved that Larnach should not be kept on any longer than the agreed twelve months, but Larnach immediately offered his resignation rather than suffer the ignominy of being sacked, pleading his own business interests would now prevent him from having the time to fulfil responsibilities to the bank. Whether this was the real reason for his resignation is hard to tell. One area of the directors' displeasure with Larnach concerned the newly formed National Insurance Company, of which Larnach was one of the founders. Larnach had attempted to place the company's account with the National Bank on favourable terms to the insurance company, to give it time to estab-lish itself, before getting the best terms for the bank. This coloured the directors' thinking that "Larnach was too responsive to local pressure."

Negotiations for the takeover by the National Bank were, however, speedy and outwardly amicable. It was later that relations with Larnach would publicly deteriorate. After Larnach's resignation from the bank, in a friendly arrangement with the new manager, Mr Bartleman, the Larnachs, now with five children, stayed on in the bank's accommodation for a year, as their house on the Peninsula was unfinished. Larnach felt entitled to do so, as the takeover agreement had given staff a year's grace. The London directors felt otherwise, but not wishing to offend Larnach, now a valued client, they took their venom out on Mr Bartleman, cancelling his £100 a year housing allowance, an amount in those days which would have seri-ously embarrassed a branch manager.

Poor Mr Bartleman thought he had acted in the best interests of the bank. William Larnach had recently formed a partnership with a promi-nent manufacturer in Otago, Walter Guthrie, and the business was escalat-ing. The new firm of Guthrie and Larnach was now a major client of the bank, and Larnach's personal account alone made him a customer not to be slighted. While the London directors had been delighted at Larnach's res-ignation, he now became another source of irritation to them. Not only was he still living in their premises, but he was actively promoting the opening of the Colonial Bank, in opposition to the National. Equally annoying was the popularity of Larnach with the local people, which was making it difficult to establish the National Bank in the province. The Otago people found the new English bank too restrictive, and not as responsive to their needs as its predecessor, who understood the speculative nature of most colonial borrowers.

This feeling among the local people was influential in the founding of the new local bank, the Colonial Bank. William Larnach was its first chairman, and would remain faithful to it until its demise in 1895. Many of the staff and customers of the National Bank transferred to the Colonial Bank, and for twenty years the National Bank experienced keen competition from the Colonial.[5] However, back in 1874, the National Bank still held the overdraft of Guthrie and Larnach, and its size was already causing the bank concern.

The partnership of Guthrie and Larnach resulted in the largest trading company in Australasia during the 1870s. It employed a thousand men, and owned fourteen vessels.[6] The partners originally set up a chain of hardware and timber stores, and in 1873 became "Guthrie and Larnach's New Zealand Timber and Woodware Factories Company Limited. Ironmongers, Hardware Merchants and Sawmillers." The leading industrial and financial city in New Zealand, Dunedin was also the most populated. There was a demand for kauri houses, and Guthrie and Larnach's catalogue presented a cornucopia of choice for the home builder. There was a huge selection of mouldings, architraves, skirting boards and fretwork, carved with every conceivable combination of curlicues and flourishes. Double hung windows, arched windows, rose windows, casement windows, and columns, Corinthian, Ionic or Doric, were offered. There were handsomely turned spindles, balusters and newel posts for stairways. Also illustrated were doors and gates for every type of entrance, however grand or humble. The choice of panelling, palings, pickets, even pulpits and pews must have confused the buyer.

Country dwellers were not forgotten. Prefabricated two-storied houses and cottages, complete with finials, could be transported by drays and reassembled. Guthrie and Larnach's ironworks in Cumberland Street and their other covered premises in Princes and Bond Street were big enough to keep all their stock and timber dry, an advantage in the days of horse and wagon transport, as this considerably lightened the load for the purchaser.

The firm imported directly from Great Britain, America and Europe.

They claimed they had coastal vessels especially employed to guarantee prompt despatch of important orders. Timber from their mill at Owaka was shipped from the hazardous Catlins harbour, and in 1878 an even larger milling venture was entered into, in the Waitakere Ranges west of Auckland, where Guthrie and Larnach purchased Nicholas Gibbon's mill at Whatipu and William Foote's mill at Pararaha, together with forests esti-mated to contain 70 million feet of kauri. [7]

No wonder undertakings on such a grand scale made the National Bank nervous. The London directors wrote to Adam Burnes in 1874, about "some of these permanent and objectionable overdrafts . . . these accounts must be reduced by half . . . You will of course advise the manager to pro-ceed with great caution . . . it is plain therefore, if anything happened to Guthrie and Larnach the result might be disastrous for the Bank." Later in the year came another warning from London: "With regard to Guthrie and Larnach's account, I am to say that the reduction thereof is not a matter of option with the local board, but that the London Board's positive order is that it must be reduced." [8] To this was added the cautionary adjunct not to offend Larnach — "of course with all due care and judgment."

In 1875 John Bridges, the National Bank's inspector, arrived in Dunedin from London with full powers to act for the bank. He was not a tactful man. He has been described as "a man of violent temper and antipathies", with a vitriolic tongue to match. In the convivial atmosphere of Dunedin's Fernhill Club, housed in the elegant Oamaru stone mansion of Fernhill, John Bridges, before members of the club committee, charged Larnach with "dishonourable conduct". No official records remain as to the nature of the accusations, as the Club records were destroyed by fire. The episode caused a stir, and rumours abounded. Larnach was not without his enemies, one in particular being John Macfarlane Ritchie, a prominent Dunedin merchant and a fellow director of many companies with Larnach. In a letter to his business partner in London, John Ritchie describes Larnach as "bad" and "dishonest." He reports John Bridges as saying "Larnach gutted the Bank when he left and took many things belonging to it away. Bridges rendered an account of £300 which Larnach indignantly refused to pay, but eventually sent a cheque for the amount."[9] As evidence given by John Bridges on another occasion was discredited, these remarks may not be true.

There were other versions. "The event of the month has been the strong public feeling against the National Bank and Bridges their manager in particular," wrote Robert Gillies to William H. Cutten in England. He went on to explain:

> It seems that some of his dispatches to his directors have found their way out here, or rather copies of them; and as they reflect severely on the whole place they have been very generally resented. I believe Larnach went about with a horsewhip for a day or two to punish him, but thought better of it. Bridges has been turned out of the Club and was refused admittance into one or two hotels in town. It seems he told Bird, the manager of the Club, some tittle tattle story about Larnach ruining Hanky and Bird. Larnach told it before the Committee of the Club and Bridges was summoned before them. Cargill and a number of others wishing to shield Bridges and the matter would have ended on his denying Bird's statement, but he, Bridges, was so elated at his success that as the Committee was rising he volunteered the statement that he, Bridges, knew however that Larnach was so and so and had done so and so. Cargill then got angry and told him he must remember he was there in the Club by courtesy as a stranger and such conduct could not be tolerated, and as he had now given proof of what he was accused of, the Committee proceeded to inform him that he had been guilty of conduct unworthy of a gentleman and so must find lodgings elsewhere. They then handed to Larnach the words in writing which Bridges had used (I don't care to repeat them) and I believe an action for defamation will be the result.[10]

Enraged by the indictments made at the club, Larnach retaliated by writing a sub-leader in the *Otago Daily Times*, of which he was a director. On 27 July 1875 he wrote:

It must suffice to put on record the fact that with ominous speed the business of one of our banking corporations (National) is going to the wall, and that is chiefly due to the freaks of an eccentric individual who seems at least as ignorant of his proper business as he is of the routine of banking in a colony, or the customs of honest men. . . . To damage the reputation of businessmen by a series of malicious falsehoods, and underhand and cruel statements seem to be his delight. . . . We desire indignantly to repudiate the vile and untrue statements that have been freely circulated from the centre to which we refer, concerning the commercial soundness of Dunedin.

Two days later the *Bruce Herald* (30 July 1875) reported that an article in the *Otago Daily Times* had given scandal lovers a rare treat. It was about a certain bank inspector, who they thought deserved "a good horsewhipping", but they questioned if the author of the article, without mentioning Larnach's name, should have used the editorial columns and the editorial "we" to settle personal grievances.

Whatever Larnach said to Bridges privately on the matter might have had some bearing on the actions taken by Bridges a few months later. The Public Accounts Committee in Wellington was taking evidence from John Bridges about his allegations concerning the Bank of New Zealand loans to Julius Vogel, when Bridges, usually so outspoken, refused to speak until a special amendment was passed on the Parliamentary Privileges Act of 1865 giving Bridges complete immunity from libel. Eventually Bridge's evidence was totally discredited.[11]

Overall, despite a few detractors, William Larnach retained his popularity. If the citizens of Dunedin thought he was a rogue, then they considered him a likeable one. He was providing employment to a large number of people and was considered a fair employer. He was riding on the crest of the wave of financial success, oblivious of the undercurrents of economic recession slowly forming which would eventually dump him on the relent-less rocks of failure. Life would never be as kind to William Larnach as it was in the 1870s.

Chapter IX

THE CASTLE

Restricted during the week to "living over the shop", William and his two sons, nine-year-old Donald and six-year-old Douglas, spent the weekends riding or walking in the country on the outskirts of Dunedin. Never let it be said that William walked only for sheer pleasure, anything so fruitless was not in his nature. His walks were carefully monitored by the pedometer he wore on his watch chain, which counted the number of steps he took and the miles he covered.

It was on such a walk with his father on the Otago Peninsula that nine-year-old Donald Larnach ran up a bush-covered hill and drew his father's attention to the panorama extending from the wild rugged beauty of the Peninsula that faces the Pacific to the warm, sheltered, lake-like harbour that encompassed Dunedin, and stretched to Port Chalmers. At that time the Peninsula was mostly covered in bush and sparsely occupied. Under armed guard, Maori prisoners of war from the North Island were forming a road round the harbour, and a few scattered little farms, their paddocks divided by dry stone walls, could be seen.

Captivated by the area, William lost no time in acquiring the land. On 19 January 1870, a deed was duly signed by "our trusty and well beloved Sir George Ferguson Bowen . . . Governor and Commander-in-Chief over the Colony of New Zealand," and William Larnach became the owner of 40 ha of Block 11 Otago Peninsula, 14 ha of which he would devote to garden. After purchasing more land, the rest would form a 410 ha stud for a superior herd of Alderney cattle.

The founding of Otago had taken place only twenty years previously, and the Peninsula was still an inaccessible place, covered in bush and stone, and subject to gales and fog. Many obstacles had to be faced before building commenced. Initially a temporary cottage was built where the family could escape the confines of the bank premises at the weekends, and enjoy country life. The cottage became known as "The Camp", a name which eventually was transferred to what is now known as Larnach Castle, while the original cottage was then referred to as "The Old Homestead". William Larnach never referred to his home as a castle, rather it was a name given by the local people. Quite substantial farm buildings were then erected. William enjoyed labouring on the property and even built dry stone walls by lantern-light at the end of a hard day's work.

The plans for the main house originated in England, and with modifications stipulated by Larnach were drawn up by R.A. Lawson, the renowned architect of First Church, Dunedin. Speculations as to the origin of the design have implied that it was copied from an ancestral castle in Scotland, or was a replica of William's birthplace, Castle Forbes in New South Wales. It is neither; he was simply a follower of fashion, and the Gothic style was the fashion of the time. The Victorian age had abandoned Georgian simplicity and preferred a riot of decoration. In 1874, Mark Twain moved into his newly completed home in Connecticut, described as a picturesque palace, with its turrets and gables. Closer to home, Henry Dangar's son, who bought John Larnach's estate, Rosemount, built a town house in Sydney, and his brother, describing the crenellated castle in a letter, added, "All we need is a dozen cannon!" While in England, John Ruskin, author of *The Seven Lamps of Architecture*, despaired at the insensitive and inappropriate applications of Gothic ideas, but that criticism fell on deaf ears in New Zealand in the early 1870s.

Larnach had a significant imput into the design; the whole process was looked on as an absorbing hobby by him, which would culminate in a grand residence for Eliza and his children. Everything was to be of the highest quality; money, in this era of great borrowing, was not to be spared. By English standards the house is not remarkable for its size; there are twenty-five rooms, including the 27 m by 9 m ballroom. Its uniqueness lies in the many inventive and varied features, displaying both the talents of the designers and the skills of the craftsmen employed on the building. Larnach's own innovations are still apparent, and are technically advanced even today. The huge double hung windows, double-glazed and hung not on cords, but on brass chains, still function effortlessly and have an ingenious method of ventilation which regulates the air in all weathers.

The magnificent chandeliers throughout the house were lit using methane gas, collected from a crenellated outhouse built in the shape of a Maltese Cross and euphemistically called "The Gas Generator". The outhouse was a commodious version in every sense of the word of that necessary structure, the "privy". Inside this inconspicuously sited outhouse for the servants' use were two rooms, each containing two large-holed and two small-holed "long drops", complete with handsome brass ashtrays to hand. The accumulated gases were pumped up to the various light fittings throughout the house. A two-tonne trapdoor trip-tipped the contents of the cans from each lavatory into a large cesspool under the floor on which the generator stood, and the contents eventually emptied down a tunnel to a sump 180 m away, to be used in the making of compost. Whether Larnach was ecologically minded or just canny, his ideas were years ahead of his time.

A man-made waterfall fed by two artificial reservoirs still falls onto an old water wheel, and beside it, remains can be seen of a bed for an engine, suggesting that Larnach had also considered a hydroelectric scheme. His attention to the tiniest detail covered every aspect of the building, from specifying different coloured bell pulls in each room, to exacting instructions on the way he wished the scaffolding to be stacked on completion of the contract.

The foreman of works for the building of the castle was a joiner, Walter Riddell, who arrived in New Zealand in 1865. He kept a diary which documents the hard work of clearing the property that took place during the early 1870s: "Started to saw for Larnach's house this week, awful hard and ugly timber, have had two pairs sawing for two months," wrote Riddell on 14 January 1871. Riddell received £50 for this labour. Growing among the bush were large broadleaf, kowai, black and red pine, and totara. A month later, Riddell records: "stopped sawing, started grubbing at £20 per acre for Larnach, an awful bad job, will make about three shillings a day." Access had to be cut along the contour of the hill from Pukehiki, approximately on the line of the present road to the top of the hill where the house was to be built. To enable a level site, the top of the hill was blasted until a rock base was reached, and the topsoil was removed and reserved for the gardens.

The extensive resources of the newly formed business, Guthrie and Larnach, were utilised during the years of building. Their shipping interests enabled Larnach to bring out as ballast such materials as fire bricks from Glasgow, Italian marble mantelpieces, black and white Belgium marble tiles, mosaics, and multi-coloured Roman tiles. Thousands of cobblestones from Marseilles, at sixpence each, were landed for the stable floors. Flagstones came from Scotland and glass from Venice, engraved with the family crest, mottoes and leaf motifs of England, Ireland, Scotland, Canada and New Zealand. These can still be seen in the foyer of the castle today. All the materials, whether imported or local, had to be punted across the harbour from Port Chalmers, then ox-drawn up the steep Camp road, with its gradient of one in seven. When one considers the transporting of 20 tonnes of $1^1/_2$ cm plate glass on drays, Larnach's motto, *Sans peur* (without fear), takes on a new meaning. Two heavy marble baths, reproductions of an ancient one buried at Herculaneum by the eruption of Vesuvius in AD 79 (the original is now at the Vatican), were brought out from Italy. One of these baths is still on the nursery floor, the other graces a paddock on the Peninsula as a horse trough. [1]

Heart kauri came from the north for the magnificent entrance gates, long since demolished, and was used for the 3 cm thick kauri floors, which today are shown to advantage in the Ladies Drawing Room. Guthrie and Larnach's saw-mill at Owaka provided much of the timber for the building, and their factory in Dunedin, equipped with the latest machinery, turned the wood into mouldings, architraves and skirtings. In hindsight, it would almost seem that Larnach's motive in forming Guthrie and Larnach was to facilitate the building of his house. The specifications stipulated that much of the building material — in particular, stone, wood and iron — would be supplied by Larnach, but the contractors — masons Dick, Page and Co.,

and Roger, Riddell and Co., the carpenters — had the most difficult assignment; they were to undertake the cartage to the site.

As much as possible of the browny-grey stone for the exterior of the
building was quarried from the property and the rest was carted from nearby Harbour Cone. Where work of an ornamental nature was required,
Oamaru stone, being softer, was used. Four brothers from the Dick family
were the stone masons employed on the job, and according to an article in
a 1925 newspaper by "Old Timer", recounting a stone mason's memories,
Larnach was very well liked by the workmen. Larnach shouted them a
whisky every morning, and on completion of the job each workman
received a patent lever watch with chain and seal, engraved by jeweller
John Hislop with the words "A souvenir for good and faithful work at The
Camp for W.J.M. Larnach 1876."

Larnach engaged Louis John Godfrey, a skilled and respected architec-
tural sculptor, to work on the house. Godfrey had arrived in Dunedin several years before Larnach, and was in demand for the many stone commercial buildings being erected at that time. He rarely did domestic work.
Godfrey, and later his sons, worked intermittently at The Camp for many
years. Other craftsmen came to New Zealand at Larnach's invitation, a
Frenchman called François, and an Italian artist, of unknown name.

The French and Italian men were responsible for the delicately
coloured and wonderfully moulded plasterwork throughout the building.
They treated the ceilings as a canvas to embellish. These two men, and Louis
Godfrey worked periodically for twelve years on the liberally decorated
wood carvings and plaster work, six years alone being spent on the magnificent ceiling of the foyer. On the light English oak panels of the dining
room ceiling, Louis Godfrey carved flowers, birds and butterflies in full
relief in mahogany. He was also responsible for the carving of the imperious lions that with bared teeth guard each side of the entrance steps. As
visitors ascend, eagles with prey in their talons eye them arrogantly, while
griffins on the top level support the standard lamps which illuminate the
steps. Overlooking all, that symbol of death and disaster the owl, with rap-
torial beak, directs its large eyes at the family escutcheon below. This was

Top: Mosaic paving on the entrance floor of the castle.
Above: The cat surrounded by Larnach's punning motto, Sans Peur,
set in a window on the staircase.

jokingly devised by Larnach, and consists of a shield decorated with a glum-
looking European wildcat and the punning motto, *Sans peur*.

Through the entrance doors to the tessellated foyer, Larnach's tongue-
in-cheek humour is again displayed. His personal name for the castle, "The
Camp", is set in mosaic on the floor, but any pretence to life under canvas
is immediately dispelled. The foyer must be one of the finest examples in
New Zealand of wood carving and panelling. The panelled walls are of
Spanish mahogany, kauri, mottled kauri and Burmese teak. The dadoes are
of ebony and New Zealand honeysuckle, and the doors, with their Gothic
panels, are of English oak, kauri and mahogany.

Unique in the Southern Hemisphere, a hanging spiral staircase of late Georgian design leads to the upper floors. With no supporting centre post from which a spiral staircase generally radiates, its complex curves derive their strength from the precise and careful workmanship of Walter Riddell. The bannisters are of mahogany, the steps of oak, and the handrail is not steam bent as would be expected, but carved from solid kauri. All the woodwork was dowelled, not nailed.

Opposite the first floor landing is the master bedroom, directly above the main entrance. On either side of Larnach's room are two bedrooms; one was occupied by Eliza and the other by Mary Alleyne, giving rise to some gossip among the household staff as to the relationship of the trio. The nursery floor is on the top level, and the main room on that floor, which is directly above Larnach's bedroom, commands wonderful views and all day sun. It has had various uses, first as a nursery, and later as a painting and embroidery room for Eliza and Mary. In the 1880s it became a smoking room furnished with leather settee and chairs, and as it provided a great view of the shipping lanes, a cupboard containing code flags was close at hand.

On the same floor, after passing through the children's shelved library, a steep stone spiral staircase is reached. This would make a convincing backdrop for any swashbuckling swordsman. It leads up to the roof and the battlements, 320 m above sea level. One of the few happy memories of her two years spent at the castle in 1891-92, recalled by Larnach's grand-daughter, Gretchen Guise Hjorring, was of New Year's Eve. It was cele-brated with great Scottish fervour. The family gathered on the roof of the turret, each carrying a lantern, and her grandfather excitedly waited for the stroke of midnight, when his carefully coordinated display of fireworks and rockets would erupt, to be seen for miles around.

The only features reminiscent of Larnach's father's house were the open verandahs. But this was not the warm Hunter Valley, and as early in the year as March, Eliza had occasion to write: "We have had dreadful weather and fogs. This is such a cold day I can hardly hold my pen."[2] The following year the delicate iron castings and columns that went round the four sides of the house were backed with plate glass, "so that we do not feel the Wind or the Rain."

It was some time before the softening effect of trees and shrubs grew to fulfil the landscape designs Larnach had in mind. He began by planting a shelter belt 40 m wide round the property, which consisted of native and exotic trees and shrubs. Glasshouses for stone fruit were built, and rolled plate glass covered the curved vinery to protect the Black Hamburg grape vines that had been sent out from Brambletye. The abundance of fruit was well known. The Fernhill Club was anxious to buy the produce, but Larnach, with no wish to upset the small fruiterers of Dunedin, replied, "I ought not to agree to your wishes even to oblige you . . . at the same time, whenever you are unable to purchase fruit and vegetables, butters, etc. in Dunedin, I shall have pleasure in making you a present of all things grown by me on the property." Hot houses and ferneries were equally successful, and Larnach sent over fifty varieties of native trees and shrubs to his uncle in London, with precise instructions as to their care. Extensive pergolas were built, entwined with roses and creepers, and underplanted with Larnach's favourite flower, the foxglove. There was a raised Italian garden, a fish pond, and a wishing well in the centre of a lawn, which was edged with box hedging. Peacocks and guinea fowls roamed the gardens. Monkeys and llamas were imported for the children's entertainment, as were many dogs — the Newfoundland being the favourite breed. A cock fighting pit was another source of entertainment.

Of all the animals on the estate, horses were Larnach's greatest love. In the 1880s, there were fifty-eight horses and four foals on the property, and the children kept tiny ponies when they were young. For heavy dray work there were Clydesdales, but on steep unmetalled surfaces mules and oxen were used. Many tales are told of the speed with which Larnach liked to ride to Dunedin, often challenging other riders from the district to a race into town. It has been said he could spend twelve hours in the saddle and not tire, and he would not own a horse that could not trot from town to The Camp. The best of his bloodstock horses he kept in the Stars and Stripes field — a field planted with trees into patterns resembling the

American flag. This field, which was entered through an archway of whale bones, still stands today, and was often used for picnics and church bazaars. There were twelve carriage horses; six light grey and six black, and all bloodstock. His carriage and team of four spanking greys dashing through the rough streets of Dunedin always aroused attention. In 1882, there were eight buggy horses — Kelpie, Stockings, Baldy, Blackboy, Knottingly, Moa, Nelson and Traveller. Traveller would later be the one to pull the hearse with Larnach's coffin to the Northern Cemetery in 1898.

The spacious stables, paved with Marseilles cobbles, contained grooms' quarters, coach houses and harness rooms, and were adjacent to the cow byre, forge house, poultry, piggery and goat houses. Close by were liquid manure pits and huge stone compost bins. Everything was at hand to ensure good animal husbandry. Farm workers' cottages, a coachman's house and a four-roomed residential laundry completed the buildings on the property.

The farm was of tremendous satisfaction to Larnach. It is remarkable that with all his involvements in the 1870s, and his entry into Parliament in 1876, he found the time to make such a success of farming. He was the first dairy farmer on the Peninsula, and through careful cross-breeding he reared cattle that gave high quality dairy produce. His Alderney bulls were sought after and commanded high prices. Throughout his life, he was in demand as a cattle judge at Agricultural Shows in the South Island. On 13 April 1876, a meeting was held at the Criterion Hotel in Dunedin to promote a Christmas fat stock exhibition, and the newly formed Agricultural and Pastoral Society was constituted. William Larnach, being the pioneer of the dairying industry in Otago, was elected the first president. [3]

His cultivation of the soil showed his proficiency as a farmer. After burning the land, it was planted in turnips, potatoes and oats for three years before it was laid down in permanent pasture. The farm was divided by dry stone walls and post and rail fences. Larnach was one of the first to use wire fences, and his detailed letters placing orders for the posts and wire meticulously stipulate the number of wires and the measurements between them.

The castle in 1874, about the time the family moved in.
Photographed by American photographers Phillippi and Pearson
who were in New Zealand to photograph the Transit of Venus.

On 3 February 1875, the *Otago Daily Times* accords the estate high praise.

Everything and everybody connected to the estate looks well-to-do and happy; the cattle grazing on the rich pasture, or the sheep browsing on the hillsides, are alike well-conditioned and well cared for . . . even the sleek and shiny coated horses frisk about the paddocks as if they would seem to say, this is the right sort of place to live. When a gentleman by his business tact and ability has achieved an honourable and independent position in a newly settled country, how much more satisfactory it is to see him founding for himself and his family a home in that land where the sun of prosperity has shone on him, than to find him husbanding his gains to be expended in some favourite part of Europe . . . Mr Larnach is a colonist in the true sense of the word, and his efforts in founding such a home in his adopted country are well worthy of emulation.

*   *   *

When the family moved into the house in 1874, it was far from finished. Workmens' tools lay on the mud that was to become the front lawn, and there were still another eight years of work before the interior would be completed. Nevertheless, a large party was held to celebrate their move. Friends from Dunedin, neighbours and all those who had worked on the building were invited. The Peninsula was considered remote, and rather than let his Dunedin guests be deterred by the 19 km road which was often shrouded in fog, Larnach, in anticipation of the entertaining he hoped to enjoy, had a red brick hotel built across the road from Mathieson's Springfield farm and Cheese Factory. There his visitors could either stay the night or rest before completing the journey.

At the time of the move, there were then five Larnach children. Alice the youngest of the five, born in Dunedin in 1868, was six. A governess, Miss Campbell, was employed, and Donald, the eldest son, was sent to Christ's College in Canterbury. In spite of the grand exterior of the house, it was very much a family home. Tennis racquets were in the library; boxes of games, card games, and shell collections were in the drawing room; croquet sets and targets for archery were in the back hall; and a small piano in the breakfast room was piled with music books. In spite of a large number of servants, all the family clutter still managed to make the place looked lived in. It would seem that Eliza had very little say in the design and furnishing of the house, nor did she seem very interested. While furnishing a town house in 1880, Eliza wrote to her daughters: "We are having all the old carpets made to fit the rooms of the Town House, but I am sure Papa will not have curtains. Some of the furniture has been sent from The Camp, I expect Papa will be getting some new things as well." Eliza's time was devoted to the children and organising the running of the household while playing hostess to their numerous visitors, again mostly of William's choosing. Eliza complained in a letter to her daughter Kate, "I can hardly write as Mrs Boyce and Aunt are talking. Papa asked Mrs Boyce to come up and have dinner with him this evening, so Aunt and I have all the trouble of entertaining her."

Many notable people passed through the entrance foyer as guests of the Larnachs. At least four future prime ministers — Julius Vogel, Robert Stout, Richard Seddon and Joseph Ward — were to enjoy their hospitality. Among their great friends was the erudite medical practitioner, Dr Hocken — whose huge collection of books was to form the nucleus of the Hocken Library — and his wife Julia, a particularly close friend of Eliza Larnach. Other guests were Dr and Mrs Millen Caughtrey, the professor of anatomy and physiology at Otago University, and a keen rugby advocate; the geologist Dr Black; the poet Thomas Bracken, responsible for the words of "God Defend New Zealand" and who is said to have written the poem "Not Understood" at The Camp. Also there was Dunedin's superintendent, the colourful and popular James Macandrew, a warm-hearted and impulsive man with a mind full of schemes to advance the commercial interests of Otago. Another great friend was Edward Wakefield, a parliamentarian and journalist, and nephew of Edward Gibbon Wakefield. Eliza writes to her daughter Kate, who was staying with her uncle George Larnach in Sydney: "Mrs Edward Wakefield and her three children have been staying here for the last fortnight. Mr Wakefield came down last Friday and stayed till Monday. Chunkie has grown a tall thin boy, very much spoilt. Papa gets so cross with him and feels he would like to exercise his five fingers upon him. Oliver is a great fat fellow, too lazy to speak. As long as he has enough to eat and drink and plenty of sleep, he is all right." Edward Wakefield was a fluent speaker and gifted lecturer, and had considerable influence in Parliament. Larnach wrote to Julius Vogel: "Wakefield and his wife stayed here for a month. He has been a total abstainer for two years." This was a step Larnach was later to take himself.

From Australia came a steady stream of guests also. The sons of "Monied Clarke", William and Joseph Clarke called, and William Larnach's sisters, brothers, uncles, aunts and cousins frequently crossed the Tasman to visit. Eliza was not enamoured of her sister-in-law, Louisa Larnach, and accused her of filching her finery. She writes: "Mrs Fanny Jones asked for the loan of Colleen's riding suit, but I could not find it, so I suppose your Aunt Louisa has given it away with a lot of my clothes I miss since she was staying here."[4]

Larnach's favourite room in the house was the library, which contained his large collection of specially leather-bound books. After his death, the sale of his books was described by the auctioneers as "probably the largest of its kind ever held in the Colony." Early Australian, American and Scottish history, as well as natural history, were the topics that interested him. Ordering a copy of W.L. Buller's history of The Birds of New Zealand, from the Sydney booksellers Angus and Robertson in 1888, he comments: "[this book] is now looked upon by many in this Colony, capable of judging, as a fraud perpetrated on the public," and follows this statement with a request for a discount. In true Victorian style, any spare wall space in the library was crammed with oil paintings, water-colours, oleographs and engravings. Guns in leather cases, field glasses, microscopes and sundry other objects fought for room in this masculine domain.

It was in the library of The Camp that the radical Robert Stout and the liberal Richard Seddon were reputed to have first argued the pros and cons of giving women the vote, with Larnach acting as umpire between the opposing opinions. Richard Seddon, with his interests in the hotel trade, was nervous of the influence of women voters, who might push for Prohibition, but Robert Stout eventually won the argument, and the vote was passed as law in 1893.

Many dinner parties were held under the magnificently carved ceiling in the dining room, with its furniture carved to match the elaborate panelling. The ladies retired after dinner to the drawing room, with its crimson leather walnut chaise and matching chairs, and heavy crimson curtains looped up with gold tassels, the rich colours muted under the flickering mellow light of the gas powered chandeliers. A grand piano stood in the corner of the room, and women at that time were expected to sing or play an instrument with a tolerable degree of ability. Larnach placed great emphasis on these talents, spending thousands of pounds on his children's musical education, with minimal success.

Upstairs the rooms were plainly furnished. Larnach's bedroom consisted of a double iron bedstead, supporting a combination of straw palliasse topped with two horsehair mattresses, bolster and pillows, a chest of drawers, two wardrobes, a marble-topped washstand with blue and white china bowl and jug, and, completing the furnishings, a bedside table on which sat three pistols in cases, a habit which had remained from William's early banking days on the goldfields. The only floor coverings were two white skin rugs, one beside the bed and the other by the worktable.

The bedrooms of Eliza and Mary Alleyne had a more feminine atmosphere. Carved wooden double beds dominated each room. There were writing desks, camphor wood chests, and marble-topped washstands with pink and white china. Small tables held Dresden tête-a-tête sets in readiness for morning tea, and to step onto on a frosty morning, there were sealskin rugs, possibly from the seal colony on the Otago Peninsula.[5]

The number of domestic staff needed to run the establishment has been estimated at about twenty. There were five women employed just to run the laundry, which was a building fairly remote from the main house. It contained a large fireplace where the irons were heated and in front of which the linen was aired. Water came from a spring over a mile away, where a large reservoir had been excavated and the water was carried by 44 cm pipes to the house and grounds. Two maids did nothing else but attend to the numerous kerosene light fittings throughout the house, cleaning them, and replenishing and replacing them, as well as keeping the chandeliers free of dust. Nearly every room had a fireplace, and a fire was lit every day, which meant wood and coal had to be carried and grates had to be cleaned every morning. Each piece of coal that went into the private family rooms had to be individually wrapped to prevent the ladies soiling their fingers. A dungeon under the rear of the house was the storage place for all the wood and coal.

There were two enormous kitchens, one above the other, both equipped with a long row of black coal ranges. The lower kitchen, known as the pastry kitchen, had a 5-cm-thick white marble bench round three walls, and also a butchery nearby. There were two cooks and two under-cooks. On Fridays, a side of beef was delivered to the kitchen, along with dozens of eggs, vegetables from the kitchen garden, milk and butter from the dairy, and buckets of raspberries and strawberries in season. The place was completely self-sufficient.

Many of the staff came from the Peninsula. Larnach gave preference to the locals, and their descendants today often enquire as to the positions their ancestors held. Unfortunately the surnames of the domestic staff are not recorded, but Christian names are mentioned in Eliza's letters. In 1880 the cook was Elizabeth; Rose was in charge of the laundry; the baby Gladys's nurse before Emma Karetai took the position was called Eliza. One of the men who looked after the horses was referred to as Old Steve, and D. Hughes was the head gardener. Another gardener was William Morris, a man who lived and died on the Peninsula, and whose permission had to be obtained before a single flower could be picked. A German gardener's sole job was to look after the vinery. A married couple, Kenneth and Jeanie, were also mentioned, as were Pat, Mrs Salter, Mrs Kerwin and Jane. Each member of the family had a personal maid, and there was also a but-ler. Later, with the family's frequent absences, it must have seemed to Larnach that he kept the place solely for the staff's enjoyment.

The expense of maintaining the house, staff and property must have been enormous, not to mention the actual building costs. There have been many guesses made as to the amount, but as no financial records remain, it is all speculation. The early years spent in the new house were carefree times, money was plentiful, and before parliamentary obligations kept him in Wellington, there was time for Larnach to indulge in some of his favourite pastimes, such as race meetings out on the Taieri. These were day-long affairs, where at lunch-time damask cloths were laid on the ground and spread with exquisite crockery, shining silver, and the sumptuous contents of the picnic hampers. It was an event where people were to be seen as much as to see. Larnach

> dressed after the manner of an old English gentleman of the time, wore a velvet coat, loose pants and gaiters, and he carried a hunting crop. There was a row among the roughs and light-fingered gentry, the honourable gentleman was looking on, and was gradually drawn closer and closer, until he was surrounded, but did any of those gentry interfere with him or any of his valuables? No, they knew their man. . . . Next day, dressed as a city magnate, he was in town attending to his duties as a businessman. He evidently likes to observe all phases of life. So it is in the House [of Representatives]; none of the members attack or find fault with him. They, like the aforesaid roughs, know when they are well off. They do not care to start a row and so he gets through the session without any rumpus. All round he is admitted to be 18 carat. Long may he wave. [6]

Chapter X

IN A STEW OVER RABBITS

If the author Beatrix Potter had felt a need for inspiration for further *Tales of Peter Rabbit*, the annals of the Waimea Plains would have provided her with plenty of material. There, Peter Rabbit's colonial relations were involved in exploits unheard of in the rustic kitchen gardens of England. What English rabbits could lay claim to upsetting the balance of power in Parliament because of their fertility? Yet this is exactly what happened.

Encouraged by the success of Moa Flat, now well established and prospering, William Larnach and Henry Driver, again with the financial backing of Joseph Clarke, acquired the large Southland run, Middle Dome, the first of many runs on the Waimea Plains. The name "Waimea Plains" would become etched on Larnach's mind. This land would one day be considered the best wheat-growing area in New Zealand, and would have prospered even as early as 1875, but for one thing — a plague of rabbits. Between 1875 and 1877, falling wool prices created a great demand for agricultural land fit for "bonanza" wheat-farming. [1] But while the boom continued in other parts of the country, rabbits were rapidly over-running the Waimea Plains. They nibbled their way through lush pastures, not only reducing stock-carrying capacities and causing heavy declines in stock yields, but gnawing away at healthy black bank balances until they became blood red. The never ending cost of rabbit extermination forced many runs to be abandoned. As he watched his profits disappear, Larnach was convinced that with government help the catastrophe could be alleviated, and the best person for securing that help would be himself, as a member of the government.

To say that Larnach entered politics in 1875 with the sole intention of saving his investment in the Waimea Plains would not be far from the truth. He often spoke openly of his private interests as the most significant reason for his entry into politics. He made no secret of the fact that to him, good government went hand in hand with a flourishing business sector.[2] If as a prominent businessman, Larnach felt a duty to the country to enter politics, he never mentioned it.

Larnach's first foray into politics was unsuccessful. In August 1875, he stood for the Caversham seat (Dunedin), where his opponent was Robert Stout. Stout was the antithesis of the gregarious Larnach. He was a zealous reformer, stern and doctrinaire. Born in the Shetland Islands, he came to New Zealand during the gold rushes. Unable to find work as a surveyor, he became a teacher, then trained as a lawyer, and in 1872 became a member of the Otago Provincial Council. He also was standing for Parliament for the first time.[3]

The by-election was fought on the big question of the day, whether or not to abolish the provincial governments and amalgamate into one central government. Larnach favoured abolition, Stout was opposed to abolition. Because of Stout's rigid views, the *Otago Daily Times* favoured the more popular Larnach, while admitting they knew little of his policy. The outcome of the election was very close, only a matter of twelve votes in Stout's favour. Larnach, always gracious in defeat when he felt it had been fairly won, declared the narrow margin made it "a glorious defeat". The *Otago Daily Times* reported that "three cheers were given for Mr Larnach, and the crowd seized him and carried him away shoulder high."

Larnach's evident popularity made it no surprise that he was successful in the general elections a few months later. He stood for one of the three Dunedin City seats, and this time he stood with, rather than against, Stout. The other candidate forming this odd trio was James Macandrew. Where Stout was straight-laced, Macandrew, although an elder of the First Church, was like Larnach — a gambler and a speculator. Macandrew's enthusiasm for speculation had lost him £40,000, and earned him a prison sentence for defrauding the council funds of the same amount while he was the superintendent of the Provincial Council. Fearing Her Majesty's prison might be a little overcrowded for his comfort, he declared his home, Carisbrook House, a jail. This innovative idea was unfavourably received and, stripped of his authority, he was forced to endure his punishment in the local prison. These events had taken place a decade before, but such was his charisma that all had been forgiven and he was now back in favour.

In the build up to the general election, Larnach assumed the political ploy of vagueness when he spoke in favour of free trade, waffling that he would "support any fair and reasonable tax, either on property or on any product of the colony that would bear it."[4] But on the subject of land he had definite views. He thought people should be financed onto the land with a deferred payment scheme. He was against large landholdings, believing that when leases fell due, large runs should be cut up and leased by auction. This was consistent with his later views on cutting up the Waimea Plains, but how he rationalised his huge holdings at Moa Flat with this theory remains a puzzle. At that time Moa Flat was a highly successful farming project and he had no desire to release it for small farms. However, on his property on the Peninsula, a large number of farmers leased land from him, and by means of extra work provided by Larnach in the upkeep of his castle and grounds, these struggling local men could subsidise their earnings from their farms.

Having made the statement that "he believed in a man if he forms an opinion and thinks it is proper, that he should consistently adhere to it",[5] Larnach, to the surprise of many, did exactly the opposite and joined Stout and Macandrew as a strong anti-abolitionists of provincial government, suffering no loss of popularity in the process. The three men had little trouble convincing the voters that the wealth of Otago and Canterbury was being plundered by central government to finance the Maori Wars in the North Island. The Otago Daily Times explains Larnach's success: "The truth is that the personal popularity of Mr Larnach rendered him an exceptionally good third to put on the ticket with the two tried politicians. Along with this, the electors were well aware that their interests required a businessman to look after them."[6] The electors also recognised in him a good employer, and they liked his flamboyance, his slightly outrageous dressing, his love of fast horses and his ability to mix with all social strata, although the upper crust of Dunedin society viewed him with some reserve.

Leaving his beloved Camp in the hands of Eliza and Mary, who would cope with the many workmen still there, he arrived by boat on the first of many trips to Wellington, a place he never liked, and moved into lodgings in Pipitea Street. His magnificent white horse, Reindeer, came with him. "I went for a ride by myself last afternoon on Reindeer, and he was somewhat fresh. I need not say that the people of Wellington were considerably interested with the gallant white steed and his interesting rider. I made three attempts to get out of town but each one failed being stopped by a gate or a hill. I begin to think that there is really only one road out of this blessed hole and that one does not lead to heaven but to the lower hut [sic] another name I fancy for that other place," he wrote to Kate. He missed his family and told them so repeatedly. In July Donald spent his school holidays in Wellington. "Donald seems quite contented here, having a horse to ride, no lessons to learn and plenty of books to read; as he is great company for me I am not sorry to have him with me."

Larnach's first session in the House was uneventful. He was no orator, there was no fine rhetoric. His speeches showed deep thought and were plainly delivered. He held decidedly democratic, even extreme views, and had an open mind willing to consider a variety of issues. He was a man of independent spirit, and something of a showman. Found tucked away in a wallet owned by his son Donald was this undated newspaper cutting describing his father:

As a member, the Hon. W.J.M. Larnach is liked and respected. Is always well 'groomed' and jaunty looking. His clothes are always well made, and fit him to a T. It is true he affects at times checks of large patterns and pronounced hues; sometimes wears a vest of saddlecloth pattern, and at other times one of brilliant colours, but that's his trouble. He has a paucity of jewelry, but then it is of the best. His hat is often pulled over his forehead or gently placed on his ear, whilst his face radiates with smiles; judging from the numerous winks and nods he indulges in, he seems to get a lot of fun out of life, and to enjoy the peculiarities of his fellow members.

Despite having come to Wellington to support the Atkinson Government,

Larnach quickly found himself in another about turn, voting against them. He stated he would support any government "so long as they are acting in fairness to the Country."[7] When Sir George Grey initiated the debate that there should be two local governments, one in each island, instead of the thirty-nine counties promoted by Atkinson, Larnach agreed with Grey, airing his views that the country was over-governed and extravagantly so. He was critical of the huge sums Public Works had spent financing immigrants, while producing only poorly built railways, especially in Otago. He was quite open that his support for Sir George Grey was not party motivated, but that his political views were coloured by his personal interests, which he was not prepared to neglect, and would therefore vote for the most efficient system of government that would promote his interests. It was no secret that men like Larnach had their own financial interest in public policy. This combination of political and financial interest was a feature of nineteenth century politics, and on many occasions private enterprise, with political help, carried out many useful developments that would otherwise have been postponed for years.[8]

Despite emphasis on promoting his business pursuits in Parliament, Larnach was not completely self-centred. He was always willing to discuss issues completely divorced from business, and had a great empathy for the average man. He was aware that many able men, lacking money, were prevented from entering politics. In the days before payment to members of Parliament, political talent was restricted to those wealthy enough to support themselves and their families during their years in Parliament. Larnach raised the question in the House of honorariums for members. At that time (1876) he was at the peak of his prosperity and was earning £10,000 annually from land investments alone, so the money would have held little interest for him. He felt it would ensure a better representation of members if the less affluent man in the street was given a chance to have his say in the running of the country. This idea met with some opposition, a few members fearing men "of an inferior class"[9] would enter politics. An allowance was granted in 1884, but it was not until 1892 that the Payment of Members Act provided an annual sum for members of Parliament.

The social life of Wellington did not appeal to Larnach. While he loved to entertain in his own home, he didn't enjoy being a guest. "I am asked to dine at the Hon. John Johnson's tonight and at Sir Julius Vogel's on Saturday next, you know how I hate these sort of things." On another occasion he was invited to an "At Home" at Lady Vogel's but "I preferred coming home to my lodgings to write letters." He wrote to each member of the family in turn, but only the letters to his "dearest Kate" have survived. The family and The Camp were always on his mind. "My dearest Kate I have only time to thank you for your kind note and to say that I love you very much. . . . Tell Mother that she must not encourage Harry Smith to be coming out to The Camp too often as the youngster is not too well known to me and he may be getting spoilt. I would not be too thick with him." Even from Wellington he ruled the household. "Do you and Miss Campbell [the governess] sleep as long in the mornings as ever because it is a very bad habit and one that you must both get out of now the warmer weather is coming, and you are unusually afraid to get into the cold bath water." Eliza also received detailed instructions to direct the carpenters about making shelves and wardrobes: "and if the doors of the wardrobe do not open clear of the bookcases and the skirting boards, say to your Mother she had better have them removed into the room opposite your auntie's, but say to your Mother that no plugs or nails are to be driven into the wood. The shelving can be simply fixed on stands made purposely which will screw to the floor. These are merely suggestions that your Mother can have carried out if she likes."

While keeping tabs on what was happening at The Camp, the Waimea Plains were not forgotten. Having already stated his intention of protecting his business interests, and with the Waimea Plains in mind, Larnach wasted no time in getting elected to the Rabbit Nuisance Committee. Here the pros and cons of importing ferrets, stoats, weasels, and even poachers to control the menace were discussed. Some deplored the importation of any predators that might kill the quail and pheasant they so dearly loved to shoot. Rabbits were not the only pest that worried Larnach. He was one of the few people at that time interested in native flora and fauna. He wished to see the game laws changed to remove hares from the protected animal list, as he felt they also would become a pest, and he was against the importation of weasels to control rabbits. He proposed that a gun tax should be levied, as he was concerned that "young lads were constantly seen carrying guns on the highways on holidays and Sundays, and had become a great nuisance, for they went shooting along the roads, destroying native birds merely for the pleasure of killing them. It is very important that this sort of thing be stopped, so that the few native birds that remain in the Colony might be preserved." Surprise was expressed by Mr Holmes, a member of the committee, that there were any native birds worth saving in New Zealand. Holmes believed "There were only a few parrots and the kiwi, a bird they only saw in the live state about once in seven years."[10] Mr Holmes then personally imported one hundred weasels, which embarrassed him by ignoring the rabbits and eating the birds.

Despite all the legislation, the rabbit situation continued to deteriorate. Larnach's entry into Parliament had done nothing to eliminate the pests. The seed of what has been described by some historians as a highly questionable scheme began to take root in his head. He planned to float a company in London and sell the Waimea Plains to it. In New Zealand, no one in their right mind would contemplate buying into the area, but Larnach had a theory that by subdividing the large runs into much smaller holdings, the closer settlement of land would check the rabbits' progress. He felt that sprawling sheep runs with their small bands of shepherds could not cope with the onslaught of the rabbit hoards. Like Edward Gibbon Wakefield, he envisaged turning the large runs into towns, villages and small farms, all serviced by railways, preferably of course, provided by the government.

His theory involved plenty of preparation. He began by building a coterie of political supporters interested in the idea of his company. Shortly before the beginning of the 1877 Session, Robert Stout, who had decided to resign from Parliament, was persuaded by Larnach to withdraw his resignation and remain in the House a short time longer. Stout was already Larnach's legal adviser and would remain as his solicitor when the new company was formed. John Ballance, a great friend of Stout's, became interested in the company also, and later Sir Julius Vogel joined them. Vogel had been premier from 1873 to 1876, and both Stout and Ballance would become future premiers.

The four men looked on the profits they hoped to get from the land from very different angles. Ballance and Stout saw the breaking up of large estates held by individuals or companies into small holdings as a highly desirable public service. Larnach, while happy to be looked on as public benefactor, really just wanted to recoup his losses. Vogel, whose appointment in London as Agent General was soon to be terminated, needed an alternative source of income to fund his extravagant lifestyle. Not only were they all intelligent men, who must have been aware of the pitfalls of the land they were foisting on the unsuspecting British public, but they were an unusual alliance, and their different aspirations for the company they would float would cause the making and unmaking of government ministries. Larnach, usually dismissed as an unimportant parliamentarian and hardly mentioned in history books, played a significant role when his interests were at stake. Looking back on the Session of 1876, there was nothing of great moment that would mark Larnach as the man who would end, for some years, what was referred to as the "Continuous Ministry" — a group of men that included Fox, Vogel, McLean, Hall, Whitaker and Atkinson, who in varying combinations had governed New Zealand for the previous thirteen years.

* * *

With his parliamentary associates all ready to spring into action on the part of the company, Larnach, accompanied by Eliza and Mary Alleyne, left for Melbourne in June 1877 to persuade the wealthy Joseph Clarke of the benefits of becoming a shareholder. On the death of his father in 1874, Joseph Clarke had inherited all the Tasmanian, South Australian and New Zealand pastoral lands owned by his father, "Monied Clarke". He also inherited £1,350,000, slightly less than his elder brother, William, who received £1,500,000. Immediately his father died, in almost indecent haste, Joseph Clarke left Tasmania and bought a large Melbourne house, renamed it Manderville Hall, and with his wife and two sons lived in a style that would have outraged his frugal father. Likewise, his elder brother added enormous extensions to his home, Rupertswood at Sunbury, near Melbourne, and he and his wife entertained in the grand manner, bringing their guests by private train to their own railway station at Rupertswood. [11] It was understandable that the Larnachs and Mary Alleyne looked forward to visiting Melbourne and being entertained by the Clarkes.

Their crossing of the Tasman was far from smooth. "Oh mercy, it was rough," wrote Eliza to the children left at The Camp. "We had a fearful sea in our cabin one night. I had nothing spoilt or wet as I was very sharp in lifting our things off the floor . . . I was seasick only once or twice on the voyage. I feel quite proud of myself being such a good sailor."

Cold weather greeted them on arrival, "colder than I have ever felt in Dunedin." They stayed at the Felix Hotel, Spencer Street.

I do not remember of ever enjoying myself so much in Melbourne before. We are either going to dinners or theatres every night, and have the use of two carriages, Mrs Joe Clarke's and Mr Goldburg's [sic] every day. We have a great deal of driving about. We went out and called at Government House last Thursday, there were over a hundred people in the drawing room when I went in, I knew such a number. To my surprise who should be there but old Judge Chapman, he was walking about and talking to the ladies like a young man. He leaves tomorrow by the "Arawata", I should like to be going at the same time, I am sure we would have some fun with him.

Your papa went to a large coursing party [chasing hares on foot with hounds] at Rupertswood, there were over 400 gentlemen there, he was so tired when he came home in the evening, with all the walking, he only went out for a short time after dinner. . . . We are going out to lunch at Mr Were's today. I suppose it will be another "big stuff" — people in Melbourne only seem to live for eating.

While William Larnach was busy discussing with Clarke the nature of the new company, Eliza and Mary were enjoying that perennial favourite of most women, shopping. Writing to her fifteen-year-old daughter, Eliza shows herself in her letters to be a canny person.

My dear old Kate, I bought you a new dress and hat the other day which I hope you will like, besides four nightdresses and two petticoats, they are very pretty, and I also got collars and cuffs. I would have got you more only you are growing so much. I did not think Coll [Colleen] and Chook [Alice] cared for your "farmed off clothes" as they called them.

Your Papa has given me a new sealskin jacket, and my other I intend having the fur collar taken off and made down for you. All the sealskin jackets are trimmed with furs of different kinds, but I much prefer them quite plain. . . . I want you to get on and get as much as you can with getting the children's clothes ready for Wellington, and the mending of Donnie's socks, all his old ones will do to wear on the Steamer to England, and then he can throw them away when they are dirty.

Two of William's sisters visited them at the Felix Hotel.

Your Aunt Amelia, left for Belfast a few hours after we arrived last Monday. Morven has grown such an ugly girl, her teeth are all black and all that pretty hair she had is short and thin. Willie is a splendid little fellow, and so is the wee girl, she is the brightest of the lot. Fancy your Aunt Emily Gill coming to see us, Papa told her she ought to be ashamed of herself for painting her cheeks. Of course she flew up in a temper at the very idea of such a thing!

Eliza always remembered her staff at The Camp in her letters, and Kate was to tell them so.

Remember me to Pat, Jennie, Mrs Salter and Jane. Tell Elizabeth and the girls we are all well. I will write to the old black-headed cook soon. How does Mrs Kerwin and Elizabeth get on? Many a stand up fight they will have I think . . . Make those boys take you for a ride every day the weather is fine. Now my dear old daughter Kate, I must say goodbye, take care of yourself dear Kate, with love to Miss Campbell, Your affectionate Mother. E.J.L.

Eliza refers to letters she wrote to the other children, but the letters to Kate are the only ones to have survived the years. When these letters were written, Donald was seventeen, and about to leave Christ's College for England to read law at Oxford. Douglas was fourteen, Colleen twelve and Alice nine; these three remained at The Camp in the charge of their governess Miss Campbell.

The hectic round of entertainments were taking their toll on Eliza and Mary. It was time for Eliza to put her delicately etched silver visiting card case in her reticule and start packing. Now the weather was too warm.

Colleen Shawn Larnach aged thirteen.

Your Aunt and I are dreadfully tired. I have not had a good night's sleep since I left home, the bedrooms are much warmer here than they are at home. It seems such a long time since I saw you all, we shall be leaving Melbourne this day week by the "Arawata". Your Papa told Captain McLean to put our names down as passengers, so we will be going for certain. I would like to stay another week but for Donnie going Home, and having to go up to Wellington." [12]

The Melbourne visit had been successful. Joseph Clarke was convinced of the soundness of the scheme. For Eliza and Mary it had been an exciting change from The Camp. Not only were they returning home with evidence of their shopping in their bulging portmanteaux and hat boxes, but with cages of birds for the aviary — rosellas, parakeets, and cockatoos, reminders to both women of the bird calls of their childhood. The proprietors of the hotel, Mr and Mrs Felix, had given them a little dog for the children, which also accompanied them on the journey home. Then it was off to Wellington to farewell Donald on his voyage to England, and while William returned to Parliament to put his plans for the Waimea Plains into action, Eliza, Mary and the children returned to the isolated life at The Camp.

For William, The Camp was like a splendid holiday retreat, where he could relax, entertain his friends, enjoy the farm life and leave the place always feeling he wanted to spend more time there. But his wife and family, who were so often left there without William, felt that their "holiday" lasted too long. The Camp was too far from Dunedin for a frequent exchange of visiting cards inviting lady friends to call for an exchange of gossip, fashion and world affairs over cucumber sandwiches and afternoon tea, in the accepted manner of well-to-do matrons of that time. The lives of Eliza and Mary revolved around the children — their education, their ponies and their clothes — and the lives of the servants, and the local Portobello Presbyterian church, the building costs of which Eliza had donated. Although she was mistress of a beautiful home, Eliza would have preferred to be closer to Dunedin.

Chapter XI

THE GODFATHER OF THE GREY GOVERNMENT

The lack-lustre Atkinson Government was still in power, in August 1877 when Larnach returned from Melbourne to Wellington. Atkinson, alarmed by the size of the country's debt, announced a policy of "political rest", just as Prime Minister David Lange, a century later, suggested the country "stop for a cup of tea", but the members made it clear this was not to their liking; they were used to a rich diet of heavy borrowing and lavish spending. The official leader of the Opposition was that grizzled old veteran Sir George Grey. But other opposing factions were appearing, the most prominent being "The Middle Party", led by William Montgomery, William Gisborne, William Larnach and Henry Tancred, men who were all driven by their own financial interests, and who wanted a continuation of borrowing and expenditure on Public Works.

The Abolition of the Provinces Act had been finally passed on 1 November 1876, and now the Government was having to face embarrassing questions on the sale of the Piako Swamp.[1] This swamp, comprising 32,800 ha in the Waikato, had been sold illegally by the Government at a bargain price to a strong Government supporter, the ruthless and plausible Auckland solicitor and Bank of New Zealand director, Thomas Russell. Another controversial issue was the printing of the *Waka Maori* newspaper at public expense, a newspaper which published libellous material in its columns in defiance of the vote of the House.

Cashing in on the Government's discomfort, on 27 September 1877 Larnach brought forward a motion of censure against the Government concerning the *Waka Maori* newspaper. The debate was heated, much scandalous information surfaced, and despite Robert Stout's strong condemnation the Government won the debate, but were shortly afterwards defeated on another no-confidence vote, also moved by Larnach. The subject of this debate was, "that the Government does not possess the confidence of this House."

Before the debate began, Mr C. Woodcock (Gray Valley) asked the House who would form the new ministry if the motion succeeded. He found it a difficult question as there were "contradictory and unsavoury" elements among the Opposition, but despite this he had confidence in Larnach.

> With regard to the Honourable Gentleman who has brought for-ward this motion, I do not agree with what has been said with reference to him, that he would not be able to form a Ministry. I differ from those who made that statement. I would rather trust that Honourable Gentleman to select gentlemen to assist him in the formation of a government than anyone I know of among the so-called leaders of the Opposition, because I believe that if he carries this vote he will snap his fingers at the aspirants for this office, and he will take in to assist him those he believes will be the most efficient members of the Government, and who will best be able to carry on the administration of the affairs of this country."[2]

The Government, unalarmed by this speech, sat back relaxed and confi-dent in their claim that there was no group in the House capable of form-ing a ministry, and certainly not Larnach. But their confidence was short-lived, and the result of the debate "that the Government does not possess the confidence of this House", was carried by a majority of four votes; forty-two against the Government and thirty-eight for. The House was adjourned, and the following day, the Governor, Lord Normanby, acting on the advice of Major Atkinson, sent for Larnach.[3]

Larnach called on the Governor, then reported back to the House that the Governor had given him twenty-four hours to consult his political friends, with a view to forming a ministry. "I now feel the deep responsibil-ity which is put upon me," he said.[4] Larnach knew the Middle Party was quite unequal to the task of forming a government; its members had no true unity or any policy beyond their interest in Public Works, and, in spite of previous promises, not one member was willing to come forth and lead the ministry. Larnach felt betrayed.

It will be in the recollection of some of those Honourable Gentlemen who were associated with me in the want of confidence motion which I brought forward a few days ago, that before doing so I stipulated that, in the event of its being successful, I should not be asked to take office. I did this, not because I had any objection to associate myself with an Administration formed from my own party, but because my business ramifications in this Colony were so extensive and my position such that to be compelled to take office would mean I should submit myself to a very considerable monetary sacrifice. On that account I desired to be free from office in any Ministry formed. But immediately I began an attempt to form an Administration, I found difficulties surrounding me on every side — difficulties that I did not contemplate nor had any right to anticipate would arise — because during my lifetime I have been accustomed to regard pledges and words of men with much respect. But in this instance I was disappointed. [5]

There was no surprise when it was announced that Sir George Grey and not Larnach was to be the head of the new Government. The choice of Sir George Grey was a last resort, not only for Larnach, but for many in the House. "My difficulties did not lessen or disappear after associating myself with the Honourable member for Thames [Sir George Grey] but why they did not I have yet failed to learn any good reason." [6]

Thus the Middle Party passed from the stage of history; it had lasted just long enough to facilitate the coming to power for two memorable years of the "Knight of Kawau". On 12 October 1877, a letter with the gold-embossed crest of Government House was delivered to Larnach. It read:

Dear Mr Larnach, His Excellency has ventured the enquiry as to the usual Custom in this Colony on a new Government being sworn in, and he finds that it has not been customary to issue any summons. If you will therefore come over to Government House accompanied by Sir George Grey, Mr Macandrew and Mr Sheehan at 12 o'clock tomorrow, His Excellency will be pleased to administer the Oaths of Office. [7]

Sir George Grey has variously been described as headstrong, difficult, opinionated, intolerant, autocratic, yet with a strong sympathy for the labouring classes and the oppressed of this world. It is not surprising that this complex man with his inability to get on with people was not a success as a political leader. He was in Parliament to attack corruption, and he saw corruption most clearly in the dealings of land speculators. He believed they were keeping the small man off the land, and using their financial and political power to advance their own fortunes. [8]

It has been implied by some historians with the benefit of hindsight that Grey, unaware of the so-called machinations of his political and speculating allies, had been swept, ageing and unsuspecting, into power, with the sole purpose of promoting the new agricultural company Larnach was about to set in motion. Yet questions have to be asked. If Larnach had arranged the vote of no confidence with the sole purpose of setting up a company, and forming a new ministry for this end, why would he have chosen Grey, such a despiser of speculators? Why, when he had the brief opportunity, did Larnach not take up the leadership himself, when he could have appointed ministers of his own choosing to aid the company? Whatever the answer, it is still open to question if Larnach planned the demise of the Atkinson ministry solely to further his own ends, or perhaps he was an opportunist, quickly able to assess a situation and benefit from it. Larnach became known as the "godfather" of the Grey ministry — a title of benign meaning in 1877, but where dealings with the New Zealand Agricultural Company are concerned, some might think closer to the Mafia connotations of today.

It was Sir George Grey who addressed the House after the Governor had sworn in the new ministry. He explained that

> Within the last few days what is called "a Ministerial Crisis" occurred; my honourable friend, the member for Dunedin City, having proposed a want of confidence in the Administration, carried the vote, and it thereupon became incumbent upon him to assume the responsibility of forming a Ministry. He having requested my assistance, I felt it my duty to attempt to give effect to what was the manifest will of this House, namely, that a change of Administration should take place. I had very great difficulty in bringing that object about, for, as Honourable gentlemen know, the House was divided into three parties, and it became exceedingly difficult to reconcile the differences which had arisen.[9]

When Grey announced his ministry, it comprised of only four men, Larnach, Macandrew, J. Sheehan, James Fisher, and later Colonel Whitmore. "Five colleagues who had never willingly committed an act of self-denial in their whole lives, and who had each in his own way, proved himself to be so remarkably untrustworthy."[10] Such was the jaundiced view of Mr Alfred Saunders, a contemporary of these men.

Another view of these men, which was equally unflattering, was that of the Governor, the snobbish Lord Normanby, who detested Grey and thought him "a dangerous and unscrupulous man who would shirk at nothing, provided he could do it with safety to himself." Normanby also wrote, "Mr Larnach is a sick man, but a wild speculator, and a getter up of companies; Mr Shean [sic] is a pettifogging lawyer, the son of a *Public House-keeper* in Auckland. Mr Macandrew's character has been found not to bear very strict interrogation, and Mr Fisher two or three years ago was a common labourer."[11]

On 15 October, Grey assumed office as Premier, Secretary and Commissioner of Customs; Larnach as Colonial Treasurer, Minister of Public Works and Commissioner of Stamp Duties; Macandrew as Secretary for Crown Lands and Minister of Immigration; Sheehan as Native Minister and Minister of Justice, and Mr Fisher as Postmaster General and Commissioner of Telegraphs.

Three days later the leader in the *Saturday Advertiser* promoted Larnach the premier in all but name with the heading "The Coming Man", and prefaced the article with a quote from *Julius Caesar*:

> I am no orator as Brutus is. But as you all know me, a plain blunt man. Mr Larnach is now the leader pro tem. There is little doubt that he will be able to form a government, however short a time it may last. Some may question his qualifications for so important a task. We do not. He has no pretensions as an orator, but it is not orators we want at the present crisis. . . . At this juncture, the country wants the services of a good businessman, who can grasp the whole of its financial details and submit a clear and distinct balance sheet which any ordinary person can comprehend. . . . His experience as a bank manager, and his power of organisation, mark him as the right man in the right place, as our Chancellor of the Exchequer. He has a good sagacious and sensible head for business, and we shall be content to leave the oratorial display to others. [12]

Almost immediately trouble arose. Atkinson, unresigned to his defeat, tried to unseat the Grey ministry, but without success. At last the House settled to the long neglected business of the Session, which was the financial reorganisation made necessary by the Abolition of the Provinces Act, a job that fell to Larnach as Colonial Treasurer. He found that the Atkinson Government had been appropriating the Land Revenue in an underhand way, and in presenting his budget Larnach told an amazed House that he proposed to treat the Land Fund as part of the General Colonial Revenue, and that only twenty per cent of the land funds from each county would now go back to the county in which it had accrued. In colonialising the Land Fund, he would tie it into development — developing railway branch lines for instance, in order to increase land values — and this would prevent the government from using the Land Fund for other purposes. [13]

The effect of this statement was instantaneous. "The Colonialisation of the Land Fund . . . has been like the wave of a fairy's wand in a transformation scene . . . and the Grey Ministry are found with a following at their back which must be a surprise to their most sanguine supporters." [14] Other items in the Larnach budget were for a fairer distribution of taxes; earlier meetings of Parliament, and abolishing the use of Treasury Bills as a stop-gap measure for balancing the books. Larnach concluded his speech by telling the House of the urgent need of the Government to raise a loan of £4 million on the London money market. The measure of success of Larnach's budget could be gauged by the vote counts: 40 for, 14 against.

By December 1877, at a cabinet meeting at which Grey was conveniently absent, Larnach warned his colleagues that if authority for further borrowing was not sent to London immediately, he would not take responsibility for the outcome. In a flurry of activity it was decided to raise the £2.5 million just authorised by Parliament, and a further £1 million authorised in 1876 and as yet un-negotiated. [15]

Larnach's rapid rise to ministerial ranks was short-lived. He had spent only two months in Parliament as Colonial Treasurer before hurrying home to arrange his trip to London to personally raise the loan there, and at the same time use the opportunity to promote his agricultural company in Britain.

A letter from his uncle, Donald Larnach, awaited William at The Camp, reassuring him that William's son, Donald Guise Larnach, was settling in well at Oxford, and he was sure young Donald would live within his income of £600 a year, a surmise that would prove to be quite wrong. As an afterthought Uncle Donald added, "Things are very dull in England, and as land and sheep are becoming cheaper in New Zealand, I may as well buy a station for Herbert [his son]." The news of falling land prices in New Zealand having reached English ears was not what William really wanted to hear as he prepared to launch his land on the English market.

"Stick to one thing," Uncle Donald had advised William at one time, but this was not in William's nature. Even on the eve of his departure for England, another project was taking place. It was the acquisition by Guthrie and Larnach of the large timber mills and kauri forests on

Auckland's west coast. This move was taken by Larnach and his partner Walter Guthrie to cash in on the prosperous times that were continuing in Auckland and to help prop up the flagging Otago trade, where the first signs of economic depression were being felt. They purchased Nicholas Gibbon's mill at Whatipu and William Foote's mill at Pararaha, together with forests estimated to contain 70 million feet of timber.

The mills were soon cutting up to 100,000 feet of timber a week under the supervision of Charles Primrose Murdoch, who had worked for Guthrie and Larnach in Dunedin and who became a well-known identity on the Auckland west coast. No obstacle was too great for the firm to tackle. To move the timber to the company ships, a tram line was hacked and blasted at the foot of the wild cliffs south of Karekare and a locomotive, the first to be built in New Zealand, was brought up from Thames to service the line. To enable it to pass under overhanging rock ledges, its funnel was made retractable. Despite this forbidding terrain, with surf constantly battering the cliff, the timber went through, and encouraged by generous bank over-drafts, Guthrie and Larnach's insatiable hunger for kauri ensured the pre-carious platform carved into rock forming the wharf at Whatipu was a remarkably busy place.[16]

Guthrie and Larnach had the funnel on this locomotive made retractable so it could pass under the overhanging cliffs near Whatipu.

Chapter XII

LONDON, A LOAN AND A LAND COMPANY

After hurried arrangements, the new colonial treasurer and his family left for London on 2 February 1878 on the ship *Wakatipu*. It was quite an entourage, consisting of William, Eliza and the children, plus Mary Alleyne, a governess and a ladies' maid. When they arrived in San Francisco, a group photograph was taken as a memento of their visit. Although Sir George Grey, in a letter to Sir Julius Vogel,[1] remarked that "Larnach had left in a great hurry", this haste was not apparent in their leisurely tour across America. Affairs of State were stalled by Eliza; an event had taken place of which the Colonial Treasurer had failed to consider the consequences. On reaching San Francisco, Eliza's sea sickness had metamorphosed into morning sickness, and this required the trip across America to proceed at a more sedate pace.

The Larnach Family in San Francisco, 1878. From left seated: unidentified woman, possibly one of Mary Alleyne's sisters (Edith or Emily), Colleen, Eliza, Alice and Mary Alleyne. Standing: William Larnach, possibly Edith or Emily, Douglas and Kate.

William Larnach in San Francisco, 1878, on the way to London as Colonial Treasurer to raise the Government Loan.

While Eliza rested, William took the opportunity to explore an area that had always fascinated him, the scenes of the great Californian goldrush of 1849 from which so many miners had come to try their luck in Australia. As a young man on the goldfields, he had listened to the tales of these fortune hunting optimists, many of whom had experienced disappointment in California yet had continued full of hope in their quest for gold. This was an optimism he found it easy to identify with.

Travelling across America by train, the interiors of which were richly velveted and thickly tasselled, with ornate mirrors and brass cuspidors, was a novel experience for the family. As Minister of Railways, Larnach was eager to see how the development of railways in America had opened up land for farming and forestry, and he had a particular interest in the size of railway gauges. New Zealand railways covered only a small mileage then, yet had three different gauge sizes. He was not impressed with America, and wrote to Sir George Grey that he "thought more of Australia and New Zealand after having travelled through America."

Arriving in the throes of an English heat wave, the family were welcomed by son Donald, and Uncle Donald and Aunt Jane. London had changed in the twelve years since William and Eliza had first visited there. Many large and lavish department stores were opening in the city, with Harrods leading the way. Gilbert and Sullivan had been collaborating since 1871, and their show *H.M.S. Pinafore* was delighting London audiences. The year before, the All England Croquet and Lawn Tennis Club had held its first lawn tennis tournament at Wimbledon. But the threat of war with Russia hung over the city, and London was in a state of apprehension when the Larnach family arrived in May 1878.

It was to be another month before the Congress of Berlin was convened, giving Britain Cyprus as compensation for Russia's gains in Caucasia. Yet even this did not inspire much confidence; the financial situation in the city remained extremely cautious. There had been too many ruined men, ashen-faced and suicidal, lamenting fortunes lost on loans to exotic governments like Turkey, Mexico and Peru for much optimism to be felt in financing small governments on the other side of the world.

Two days after his arrival in London, Larnach wrote pessimistically to Sir George Grey:

The still unsettled state of feeling existing regarding Russia makes it imprudent, if not impossible to attain any hope of success to float our new loan. My uncle, Donald Larnach, strongly advises if possible to wait until July before communicating with the public on the subject, and from a long conversation I had with Sir Penrose Julyan last afternoon, I feel convinced that undue haste must not be exercised in the negotiation of the three and a half million loan. It is therefore my intention to arrange through the Crown Agents for any temporary borrowing necessary for protecting the Credit and wants of the Colony meanwhile, until the time has arrived for operating promptly in connection with the loans. I have not seen Sir Julius Vogel yet, as he had occasion to go to the country the morning after my arrival, . . . I can say plainly that financial men here think we have already borrowed more money than the population of New Zealand warrants us in doing.[2]

Sir Julius Vogel had taken to the country soon after Larnach's arrival in a fit of pique that Larnach was negotiating with the Crown Agents instead of himself. He had had a disagreement with the Crown Agents in 1875, and they considered his requests extravagant. In fact, they begged never to be associated with him again.[3] It was usual for New Zealand loans to be issued through the office of the Crown Agents, a quasi-government bureau established in the 1830s to carry out financial and commercial operations in London for the colonies, and Sir Penrose Julyan, as senior Crown Agent of the Crown Colonies, was an influential figure in organising New Zealand finance.

It was to him that Larnach first mooted the idea of raising a loan from the Bank of England instead of loans from the private banking houses such as Baring brothers or Rothschilds. Uncle Donald Larnach was sceptical of William's idea that the Bank of England would even consider such a loan, even offering a bet of £500 that the Bank would not be interested, unusual from a man so frugal he wrote letters to his nephew on the back of already used paper. Donald Larnach thought the House of Rothschilds was the place William should approach.

In spite of his uncle's doubts, what William would term "the loan of '78", was successfully raised from the Bank of England. It was an important one for New Zealand, being the first of many times an Australasian colony would arrange such a loan. The loan was over-subscribed, but this probably reflected confidence in the Bank of England rather than the fiscal policy of New Zealand.[4]

Sir Julius Vogel was later to take all the credit for the idea of this loan, and it would not be the last time that successful and important ideas promoted by Larnach would be claimed by others as their brainchild. This particular instance rankled with Larnach for many years, and twenty years later he wrote to Sir Penrose Julyan asking him for his recollections as to the originator of the idea of the loan of '78.

My reason for asking you is that I have been informed Sir Julius Vogel takes credit for having been the author of the idea of proposals first made by me to you, that we should ask the Bank of England directors to act for New Zealand in respect of the 1878 loan, and future loans. I was in your office in Downing Street alone with you when I ventured to first make the suggestion — Sir Julius Vogel being at home in bed with a severe attack of Gout, which lasted several weeks on and off. You did not pooh-pooh my suggestion as my late Uncle Donald afterwards did, when I told him my plans, but you kindly took up the suggestion made by me and said you saw no reason why the Bank of England should decline to act, and that knowing the Governor and Deputy-Governor, you would see them and arrange a meeting if they were agreeable. The result being that the Bank of England, for the first time became the agents of one of the Australasian group of Colonies. [5]

Sir Penrose Julyan replied that it had indeed happened a long time ago, but that he had sent Sir Julius Vogel a copy of the correspondence "to correct a wrong impression, which for a long time was contained in his mind."

*   *   *

With the successful completion of the loan negotiations, Larnach resigned from his portfolio as Colonial Treasurer, and was replaced in New Zealand by John Ballance. Family affairs now occupied Larnach. With his expanding family, William and Eliza could no longer expect to enjoy the hospitality of Uncle Donald, so a house was bought in London at Courtfield Place, Kensington. Douglas was enrolled as a boarder at St Leonard's on Sea, the girls were placed under the tutorial eye of Miss Visick, and Donald Guise, at Pembroke College Oxford, was already showing signs of the extravagant lifestyle which would exasperate his father in the years to come. Brought up at the peak of his father's prosperity, and surrounded in England by the affluent ambience of his great-uncle, young Donald Guise Larnach could

Donald Guise Larnach in the Pembroke College Oxford Boat Club dress of straw boater, white flannel coat trimmed with cerise, and heraldic rose on the pocket, 1879.

see no virtue in frugality. Yet great-uncle was certainly not a spendthrift; he led a singularly quiet and unpretentious life, devoting himself to his bank and ignoring social and political life. Donald Larnach's success as a banker came at a time when the landed aristocracy found it respectable to marry into city money, and his sons, who lived only for their horses and were relieved of the necessity of earning a living, found wives among the aristocracy.

For the next five years, Donald Guise Larnach and Douglas Larnach would spend much time at their great-uncle's estate, Brambletye. On the crown of a hill overlooking the lovely valley that separated the town of East Grinstead from the village of Forest Row, the successful banker had built, in 1868, his country house on 820 ha, which commanded some of the most attractive views of Sussex. The 12,192 sq m house was renowned for its superbly frescoed ceilings, magnificent furniture and huge conservatory containing a valuable collection of rare plants from throughout the world, including some from the Otago Peninsula. The door to the conservatory consisted of one large pane of glass on which was scratched with a diamond the signatures not only of every member of the family, but every visitor who had stayed at the house. It was a huge contrast to the ten-roomed two-storied house, considered large by colonial standards, that had been home to Jane and Donald Larnach in 1848, at Rose Bank in Darlinghurst, Sydney.

William's sons, the colonial Larnach boys, spent much of their time riding to the hounds with their cousin James Walker Larnach, a dedicated horseman.[6] Hunting was considered an accomplishment on a par with the mastery of science or art in a certain strata of society then, but despite William Larnach's great love of horses, this was not the main achievement he had in mind for his sons. Indeed the times spent at Brambletye gave his sons a taste of life that was never to be theirs, and eventually only made them dissatisfied with their lot.

William attended the Paris Exhibition as one of two commissioners from New Zealand, a service which later in the year was rewarded with the Companion of the Order of St. Michael and St. George (C.M.G.), an honour Larnach did not want. Writing to Richard Seddon in 1897, he says, "Now I never asked for the C.M.G. ship but saw my name in print one morning in the London "Times" and I was going to decline acceptance, but Sir Robert Herbert and Vogel told me it would be discourteous to Her Majesty to do so."[7] It had not been modesty that had prompted his rejection of the honour, but a wish for greater prestige — a knighthood no less.

Towards the end of the year, on 2 November 1878, Eliza, at thirty-eight years of age, gave birth to her sixth and last child, Gladys Beryl Larnach, at Courtfield Place. Also about to be born was the prospectus for the Agricultural Company. In New Zealand, the wheels within wheels were turning in the gearing up of the company. In Parliament, Robert Stout and John Ballance were favourably placed to oil the wheels — Stout as Attorney-General and Minister of Lands and Immigration, and John

Ballance as Colonial Treasurer and Minister of Railways. Stout had persuaded Sir George Grey to give Ballance these portfolios. All was in readiness to expedite the floating of the New Zealand Agricutural Company on
the British public and to extol the virtues of the Waimea Plains.

*   *   *

The progress of the Agricultural Company was like a long drawn out pup-
pet show, with very little candy floss at the end of the performance. The
puppets themselves were pulling the strings, and they became entangled in
a mess of distorted allegiances both to themselves and to the governments
they were elected to serve.

The stars of the show were well known politicians of the day — Sir
Julius Vogel, Robert Stout (later knighted), John Ballance, Sir George
Grey, and less well known figures such as James Macandrew, William
Larnach, Henry Driver, Richard Oliver, Horace Bastings and P.K.
McCaughan. All were in Parliament at the same time and, with the excep-
tion of Sir George Grey, all were connected with the Agricultural
Company. They were supported by a cast of thousands — the rabbits.

The prelude to the performance of the Agricultural Company was
played on 15 October 1877, exactly two days after the Grey ministry had
come into power, when Robert Stout urged the ministry to take up the
Lands Administration Bill, which had been before the House during the
Atkinson ministry. After a difficult passage the bill was finally passed, setting up administrative machinery which provided for auction sales of pastoral leases and a deferred system of payment for the purchase of waste
lands. It also gave the Government control over the sale and settlement of
Crown Lands, [8] and simplified the selling of land.

On 7 June 1878, while Larnach was in London engaged in his duties as
Colonial Treasurer, a meeting was held in Dunedin to form a company for
the purpose of constructing a railway across the Waimea Plains. With one
exception, all who were to sell their land to Larnach's Agricutural
Company were enrolled as provisional directors of the Waimea Plains

Railway Company. Sievwright and Stout were named as the company's solicitors with Henry Driver as chairman and Larnach as director.

Four months later a second company was floated, both in New Zealand and England. This was to be known as "The New Zealand Land and Loan Company", with the object of providing loans to small farmers to buy land on reasonably moderate terms, with large profits accruing for the shareholders. It was hoped that these small farmers would buy land on the Waimea Plains. The names of John Ballance and Robert Stout again featured prominently amongst the directors of this second company, both men advertising their ministerial positions to add credence to the new company. Again the company solicitors were Sievwright and Stout, and when the company was advertised in the New Zealand papers, any mention of the Waimea Plains was carefully avoided.

When Larnach arrived in London it was at a low point in Sir Julius Vogel's career. The two men had known one another since their days on the Victorian goldfields, but with the antagonism on Vogel's part to Larnach's involvement with the loan for the New Zealand Government, their meeting in London was frosty. However, when Larnach waved the plans for the Agricultural Company before the eyes of Sir Julius Vogel, and invited him to join the company, all rancour was quickly forgotten. Vogel had always believed in the benefit of bringing more settlers to New Zealand, and in subdividing large estates, but it was the size of the commission that dazzled him. He desperately needed another source of income; he was receiving £1,500 per annum, but this was not sufficient for his extravagant lifestyle. According to the company prospectus, the total value of the land was £1,070,000, and the two men would receive a handsome commission of £40,000, each, which in 1995 would be the equivalent to £1,600,000 each.[9] Vogel and Larnach would have the responsibility of selling the land on the London market and inducing settlers to emigrate to New Zealand.

Launching the company could not have come at a worse time for Larnach and Vogel. Not only had they to contend with the failure of the City of Glasgow Bank, which had invested heavily in New Zealand, but three other banks as well, plus increasing depression in New Zealand, brought about by falling wool prices and poor wheat harvests. Vogel wrote to Henry Driver on 16 January 1879, "No businessman or company felt himself or itself safe. Men were actually frightened to assist us from fear it should be supposed they were contracting fresh liabilities."[10] It was a battle to recruit reputable London directors for the company, but eventually Vogel managed to secure Major-General Patrick Maxwell, Captain (later Admiral) R.C. Mayne, W. Clark (London) and T. Selby Tancred (a New Zealand sheep farmer) to join Larnach and himself on the board.

In composing the prospectus, the two men used every advertising trick available, stressing their rank in the New Zealand Government. Larnach appeared as "Late Colonial Treasurer and Minister of Railways" and Vogel as "Late Premier of New Zealand." The valuers were W.H. Pearson, Commissioner of Crown Lands for Southland, and Horace Bastings, a Member of the House of Representatives. These two men promised that the land was of first class quality, easily cultivated, with a high stock capacity. They wrote: "The line of railway running through the heart of the property will create a demand . . . for sites for towns and villages — lands which may be expected to realise very handsome prices."
In another letter to Henry Driver, Vogel writes,

> No description I could give would do justice to the work and anxiety Larnach and I have had. Picture to yourself someone coming to you, to ask you to buy a large estate 1200 miles distant of which you know nothing, bringing you no valuation and insisting on his own terms. Practically, this is what Larnach and I had to do. But that Larnach knew the property thoroughly and that we both have good positions and stand well in the estimation of people, the thing would have been impossible.

At the end of December 1878, the New Zealand Agricultural Company came into possession of eight stations, covering 126,690 ha, extending from the Hokonui Hills as far north as Athol and Eyre Peak, and including almost all the land between the Mataura and Oreti Rivers in Southland.

The company's prospectus was published at the end January 1879, with the Bank of England as bankers for the company. They offered shares of £20 each in the company for allegedly prime Southland land, and promised a dividend of seven per cent per annum as well as profits from future development. "The whole of the capital for the railway has been provided," stated the prospectus, yet a few months after the issuing of the prospectus, Henry Driver and George Bell were making urgent requests from Dunedin for funds for the railway without success. "This is a ticklish matter," wrote Vogel to Driver, "it would be most embarrassing to have to reveal that the statement in the prospectus was incorrect." [11]

All might have proceeded satisfactorily had that watch dog of the public, the London *Times*, not picked up the scent of rabbits and gone in for the kill. On 31 January 1878, *The Times* alleged to have received so many letters on the question of land value in New Zealand that it could not possibly print them all. They exposed the rabbit situation by printing an extract from the *Otago Daily Times* of 30 June 1876 compiled from a report on "the rabbit nuisance" by Richardson and W.H. Pearson, commissioner of Crown Lands in Southland, the very man who had carried out the valuation of the land for the company. The report stressed the seriousness of the problem, describing the affected lands from river bed to mountain top as perforated with rabbit warrens, making riding after stock a danger and railway embankments as unstable as honeycomb.

A week later *The Times* again questioned if it was not too much for the public to ask, before being invited to give over one million pounds to a company for rabbit infested land, that "testimony of a different character from that which the vendors now furnished should be forthcoming." They quoted from *New Zealand Hansard* of 17 August 1877 a statement made in the House of Representatives by William Larnach. "From my own experience I can speak of the evil from that part of the country from which I come. Whole tracts of country have been rendered almost valueless by the rabbit nuisance. A measure had been passed last year but it had not proved effective . . . on twenty-four holdings in the South last year, 1,059,000 rabbits were destroyed." (This had cost the farmer 3d. per rabbit.)

As soon as that piece of damaging evidence was published, Larnach, who was visiting his father's birth place in Scotland, quickly returned to London to compose a letter to *The Times*. He wrote explaining how in the two years since his statement in *Hansard* he had applied for stronger measures to be taken and had succeeded in getting an amendment to the Act. It enabled trustees to enter onto land where no preventative measures had been taken by the landholders. The trustees were empowered to take such action as was necessary to prevent the spread of destruction. That and a bonus offered for rabbit skins had checked the nuisance considerably, and Larnach was now satisfied that with further settlement the rabbits would disappear, and investors need have no apprehension on this account. He was able to conclude his letter with the words from a well-timed telegram which had just come to hand from the Colonial Treasurer, John Ballance: "Turned first sod of Waimea Plains Railway 27 January. Line through magnificent country. Success must contribute prosperity colony and remunerate proprietors."

Larnach's explanation and the apparent backing by the New Zealand Government seemed to have the desired effect. Within a few days investors rushed to subscribe, and Larnach and Vogel cabled the good news to the Dunedin board. In the first week £20,000 was realised, with quarter-acre sections selling for £45 and agricultural land for £15 per acre. By May 1879 half the shares were taken up, although this was not as profitable as it seemed, as 17,500 of these shares were given to the original owners of the land in part payment for selling to the company. An additional 4,442 shares were taken up by the vendors and the directors, leaving only 5,712 distributed among a large number of small and medium investors. Vogel and Larnach both took substantial share allotments, planning to finance these out of their commissions, which unhappily took years to materialise.[12]

Troubles now loomed on every front. Sir Julius Vogel suffered long and painful periods of gout, and was confined to his bed, worrying that because of his directorship of the Agricultural Company, the Government would terminate his lucrative position as Agent General. His concerns were justified. By April, the Cabinet had forced Vogel to resign as Agent General, but as a consolation prize he was appointed as agent for Inscribed Stock, with the proviso he was to resign from the Agricultural Company, something he managed to procrastinate about for a long time.

In New Zealand Robert Stout had presented Sir George Grey with the prospectus of the company and enthusiastically indicated to Grey that this great effort at patriotic colonisation deserved every assistance from him and his colleagues, by considering it a duty to join as a provisional director. When Grey discovered the large commission to be paid to Larnach and Vogel, he decided patriotism had little to do with the company. He refused to take any part in the proceeding, and insisted that Stout and Ballance refrain from involvement also, so he was far from pleased by the printing in the London *Times* of the telegram to Larnach from John Ballance in his capacity as Colonial Treasurer on the turning of the first sod of the Waimea Plains Railway, which predicted success for the venture.

As the full ramifications of the scheme dawned on Grey, he told Stout and Ballance they must resign either from the Agricultural Company or from Cabinet. The Government's financial position was deteriorating, and other policies were going badly. Grey was constantly clashing with Stout and Ballance on other issues, but on the issue of the Agricultural Company Stout and Ballance refused to bend to Grey's wishes. Stout resigned both from the Cabinet and the House, and Ballance from Cabinet.

Without his two most capable ministers, Grey's Government was defeated on 8 October 1879, exactly a year after coming into power through Larnach's initiative. Grey attributed his defeat by two votes to his refusal to sanction the government purchase of the Waimea Plains Railway Company, and other financially embarrassed rail companies, which were urging the Government to take over their debts. As three of those voting against Grey were shareholders in the Waimea Plains Railway, this was quite likely the case. For many years to come, Sir George Grey would fight against what he considered corrupt speculating companies having government backing.

When the Waimea Plains Railway Company was formed, it was proposed that the company should finance itself under the legislation of the

District Railway Act of 1877, by which the Government paid two per cent interest on the capital cost of construction, and the property owners, whose land the railway would cross, would contribute five per cent of the cost in the form of a special rate. Unfortunately that vital little piece of information was not in the prospectus of the Agricultural Company and, when it became known, was not well received by the landholders on the Waimea Plains. Most of the land on the Waimea Plains remained unsold, and the few landholders had discovered a legal loophole in the poorly constructed Act which prevented the company from forcing them to pay their unpopular rates. This meant that the company, with practically no money coming in, was unable to sell its debentures.

This problem was soon to be righted. On Grey's defeat, Richard Oliver, a shareholder in the Waimea Plains Railway, became Minister of Public Works in the incoming Hall Government. Despite steadfastly refusing to aid the Rotorua, Thames, Canterbury or Westland railway companies, Oliver, in the face of strong protest from Grey, succeeded in authorising the Government to advance £40,000 to the Waimea Plains Railway Company. This was a considerable help, but it was another four years before legislation was passed to enable the company to at last collect its rates. [13]

The structure Larnach and Vogel had worked so hard to erect to ensure the profitable disposal of the Waimea properties was showing signs of strain. The vendors and board in London were frequently at odds with Henry Driver (the manager) and the local directors in New Zealand. The New Zealand faction resented the control of the London directors, and began refusing them information on what was happening on the estates in Waimea. Because the company did not provide proper balance sheets, those in London were unable to declare a dividend.

Larnach was becoming despondent. News of his affairs in New Zealand was not good. At Moa Flat, what was to have been the showcase of Otago livestock had suffered severely in the snow of a harsh winter which had halved the 120,000 flock, burying them in frost-hardened snow drifts which stayed on the ground for six months. Even the huge woolshed had collapsed under the weight of snow. As if this was not enough, when the thaw set in, millions of rabbits took over the land, and even the bird life disappeared, poisoned by grain laid by gangs of Chinese employed to kill the rabbits.

Matters concerning Guthrie and Larnach were also disturbing. Larnach could see his £60,000 investment in the firm being eroded. Their huge milling venture on the west coast of Auckland was suffering from a drought, and the lack of water, an essential element for the efficient running of a saw-milling process, meant some mills had to be closed down. Then came the embarrassing news that Guthrie and Larnach had joined the queue with others who were dipping into the well of taxpayer's money. The scam, revealed by a Civil Service commission, found the commissioner of South Island Railways, Mr Conyers, had substantial capital invested in a firm contracted to the Railways to build twenty-six railway wagons, using "stringy bark" timber sold by Guthrie and Larnach at hard-wood prices. The appallingly bad workmanship, combined with poor quality timber, had caused these wagons, on their first trip from Dunedin, to literally rattle to bits by the time they reached Christchurch.

It was easy for those involved in this glaring robbery of taxpayer funds to deny the existence of the wagons, there was so little left of them. However one brave man, Christchurch locomotive superintendent Mr Allison D. Smith, in the face of strong denial from his superiors, sent several cases of samples to the House of Representatives. These samples showed "the whole jingling machinery — the pieces of wood hanging together, mortises without tenons, tenons without mortises, stringy bark used for iron bark, all the parts rattling together like a child's rattle." [14] The commissioners came to the conclusion that a more trustworthy head of railways was needed, and recommended that many of the appointments of highly paid, useless men, including some fifty engineers, clogging the service and neglecting their duties, should be cancelled.

As this all happened while Larnach was in London, he could hardly be held responsible, but he felt it was time to return home. On 23 October 1879, replying to a letter from Mr Robertson, manager of the Bank of New Zealand, Larnach wrote rather testily, "I have no control or say in the workings of Guthrie and Larnach. . . . It is hardly worth answering your letter as I hope to see you soon. I have taken my passage on the new steamship "Orient" and will leave here in ten days. With luck and no accidents, we should sail to Melbourne in about forty days."

With the exception of the baby Gladys, the children were to remain in England to further their education — Kate, Colleen and Alice with Miss Visick, Douglas at boarding school, and Donald at Oxford. The plan was that Eliza and William would return to England in a short time. Meanwhile Larnach would attend to his business matters in New Zealand, and try to solve some of the differences between the London and New Zealand directors of the Agricultural Company.

Leaving Vogel as chairman of directors of the Agricultural Company's London board, and appointing Benjamin Petersen as his agent for his personal affairs, the Larnachs and Mary Alleyne left for Melbourne, where a meeting was planned with Joseph Clarke to discuss matters relating to the company. Eliza left belongings in the London house in anticipation of her return, and farewelled her children for what she thought would just be a few months' separation.

Chapter XIII

ELIZA

The homecoming of William, Eliza and Mary Alleyne was accompanied by a feeling of gloom falling like the mantle of fog which so often shrouded The Camp. The splendid family home no longer resounded with the rough and tumble of childish fun. News from England that Douglas had suffered serious injuries in a riding accident intensified the feelings of loneliness and remoteness from the children, but William and Eliza considered their loneliness a small price to pay for the educational advantages the children would receive in England. While William loved the exhilaration of racing into Dunedin each day in his brougham to his office at Guthrie and Larnach's, Eliza and Mary found The Camp cold, dull and lonely. "There is so little going on out here," Eliza wrote to the children in England. "Don't you think that old Kate expects too much when she expects me to write her three sheets of foreign paper every mail? I would like to know where I am to find the news at The Camp, I have not been to town but once since we came home."

Yet Eliza enjoyed the country. After the autumn rains fell, she and Mary would be seen carrying large baskets.

Your aunt and I go out every morning mushrooming, we have found a great many in the paddock next to the vegetable garden, so we have kept Elizabeth pretty busy making catsup and pickles. Elizabeth is not married yet, nor do I fancy she will when the time comes. I find she certainly is the best cook in Dunedin — her temper is getting bad and I am sure I don't know why as she is humoured in every way. I will not be able to get another cook to suit Papa like her . . . Kenneth and Jeannie have left. Jeannie marched into town without asking either Papa or me, so Papa told

Kenneth they must both leave. I was not sorry as the children were always crying about the house. One of the men from the cottage looks after the horses and drays. Old Steve wishes me to give his best respects to you all, he always asks particularly after Miss Alice. Eliza [the baby's nurse] and Elizabeth [the cook] will answer Coll's letter by the next mail.

Last Sunday we went for a long walk in the quarry paddock to see all the ponies — there are two dear little foals, the smallest is the size of that black dog Mr Barth gave Papa, the other a little smaller.

Eliza repeatedly told the children how "desperately they missed them" and her loneliness for her children finally motivated William into renting a townhouse in Dunedin. In April 1880, the Larnachs and Mary Alleyne moved into Manor Place. Once again The Camp became a weekend retreat.

The move to Dunedin cheered Eliza.

We have at last come to Town, this is a comfortable little house and very warm, we do not require to keep great fires on as we did in the country. Dunedin has been quite lively with all the weddings. Ruth Edwards married a Mr Hall, I am informed they are both smaller than Dr and Mrs Hocken! Charles Tressle is married at last to a Miss Forbury, I am told she is a very pretty girl. The young lady that he was engaged to before has come into a lot of money. I expect he wishes now that he had married her instead of this one.

I suppose you have seen Mr Joseph Clarke before this, he promised to go and see you directly he arrived. I am sure Miss Visick will like him, perhaps he will take you to the theatre. I hope you did not make yourselves ill with the cake Aunt Jane took you, it was very kind of her to think of you.

Your old father and mother dined at Mr and Mrs Turnbull's

last night. The dinner was good but plain. We had two kinds of soups, fish, three entrees, Turkey, Saddle of Mutton, Ducks, Hams. Two puddings and creams, jellies, cheese and dessert. The wines were champagne, sherry, and for dessert, sherry, port and claret. We managed to get away at half-past eleven, and thinking the mail would be delivered, I asked Papa and Mr Ferrier to go off to the office to collect it, but my darlings, my heart was almost broken, there was not a word from any of you. That Donnie I must say is awfully careless, do some of you write regularly as we feel so miserable without a word from you twice a month. [1]

Eliza recounts each milestone in the baby Gladys's life with great affection, every tooth and gurgle of "your darling wee pet of a spoilt sister, you would love her so much if you could only see her. I expect Papa's letters are full of the wonderful doings she does in the twelve hours she is awake. It is most amusing to see Papa running up the stairs whenever he hears her cry. I don't think he could live without her now. Your aunt has made her two beautiful little crochet petticoats for the winter. I wish she would make haste and walk, I want to get her a red velvet cloak, I think it would suit her."

In July, they went back to The Camp. "I never felt anything like the cold. I used to have three and four hot bottles at night as well as a great fire. The wind used to blow me almost out of bed, for days it was impossible to go outside the door. The high winds and severe frosts have cut up many of the creepers along the trellis." In September 1880, Eliza employed a new nurse for the baby. "I have now Emma, a girl of sixteen, she is a good girl and keeps "Bow-Wow" [the baby] out the greater part of the day."

Emma was the granddaughter of Hone Karetai, a signatory to the Treaty of Waitangi, and one of the Maori chiefs who sailed to Sydney to negotiate with W.C. Wentworth on the sale of land in the South Island. Emma stayed with the Larnachs for several years, travelling to Wellington with them when Larnach was in Parliament, and after the return of Douglas and his three sisters from England, she endeavoured to teach them Maori, but with little success. Emma later married Louis Wallscott, and became an influential figure in the organisation of Maori land claim activity throughout her life, being a source of traditional knowledge for the Otakou people. It is recounted that her brother Timoti Karetai idolized William Larnach and followed him round like a shadow at The Camp.[2]

Before their trip to England, to make the journey to The Camp even easier for his guests, Larnach had built another hotel, this time on the beachfront at Waverley, to be called The Dandy Dimont. After the steep descent from The Camp, coach and horses could be left there and the journey continued by boat to Dunedin. But it was not just any boat. While in England, Larnach visited Denny's shipyard at Dunbarton, and ordered a steel double-ended 24 m-long ferry. His requirements were ambitious. He wanted a small ferry with a maximum draught of 71 cm, yet she was to have two decks, the upper deck for first class passengers and the lower deck for steerage passengers, for a journey that would take less than an hour. She was to be capable of carrying 100 people standing, should withstand the occasional run in rough weather, and was to steam at eight knots, with a maximum coal consumption of one hundredweight per hour. A special request was that the settees and couches in the cabins should be covered in red velvet. The price for the vessel was £1,750, and the machinery £750.[3]

The vessel, to be called the *Colleen*, was brought out to Port Chalmers on the *Canterbury*, arriving on 9 January 1880, and was assembled by Robert Spiers of Sparrow and Company, Dunedin, for William Larnach and James Smith, a solicitor. The *Colleen* was not entirely for pleasure. Larnach and James Smith were sub-dividing sections at Waverley, and in advertising the sections they promised a ferry service from Port Chalmers to Dunedin, calling at Portobello, Broad Bay, Waverley and Macandrew's Bay; the Waverley residents were to have free travel as an inducement to buy land there.

The *Otago Daily Times* had published an article declaring the land, "sub tropical, bathed in sunlight and far from the unhealthiness of a large

The Colleen, *commissioned by Larnach, proved unsuitable as a passenger ferry, having a tendency to capsize.*

city." The auction, conducted by Montegue Pym, was a great success. Many prominent names in Dunedin bought land there: Evan Prosser, chemist and druggist; Professor Black, of Otago University; Thomas Burt, of A. & T. Burt; Henry Lethaby, umbrella maker; Ralph Ewing, of Brown Ewing & Co.; Gustav Hirsch of the Dunedin Atheneum; and John Alexander Mackenzie, sharebroker. The roads round the Peninsula were narrow and winding, so the prospect of water transport was a great selling point.

Perhaps Larnach had had too much say in the design, for the boat was not a success; it was top heavy. Larnach wrote a restrained letter to the boat builder at Dunbarton on 8 November 1881: "I regret to say that the *Colleen* has not by a long way been up to expectations. . . . The boat carries plenty of steam, and will steer with regularity, but I may address you that with a number of passengers on board, with the slightest breeze blowing, it becomes dangerous." In fact on the Free Thought Association's picnic excursion to Quarantine Island one Sunday, the ferry had almost capsized.

Because of its unseaworthiness, the *Colleen* was taken off the ferry service at the beginning of 1882, and was eventually sold. It passed through many owners until, with the removal of its superstructure, it was used to barge coal on the Wanganui River.[4] The end of the ferry service meant the depreciation of the Waverley land by twenty-five per cent, and the angry landowners took the subdividers to court, which resulted in the subdividers having to refund the difference in the price of the sections.

Larnach's life was about to change irrevocably. He began to lose all interest in the Dandy Dimont hotel, and let it to a tenant. It would soon fall into a neglected state. Today the building, now known as the White House, still stands close to the waterfront road.

*   *   *

Since his return from England, Larnach's business associates in the Agricultural Company seemed to have conspired against him. Larnach had called into Melbourne on his way home and arranged with Joseph Clarke for a commission of £3,000 each to be paid to Julius Vogel and himself. Vogel received his £3,000 from the London branch of the company, but when Larnach arrived in New Zealand, the company coffers were empty. Contrary to their original agreement, Vogel, who had been so eager to join Larnach's venture, exhibited a "greedy and sanguine nature"[5] and refused to share his commission with him.

Larnach also found that Henry Driver "was going in for the management of the company's affairs, and on my arrival I found all cut and dried in that direction, so for the sake of harmony I offered no objection, but fell in with the views of the majority." Larnach found land prices had fallen dramatically and stock numbers were down, information he felt Henry Driver should have sent to London. When the situation was revealed by Larnach to the London directors, they did not want to hear the truth. Joseph Clarke and George Bell, the largest landholders, had just arrived in London to further promote the company, and writing to Vogel, Larnach complains

Clarke and Bell seem annoyed that I should have communicated to any of my Co-Directors in London the opinion I had formed after arrival here, of depreciation through sudden fall in the value of land and deficiency of stock, but considering that I was still a Member of the Head Office Directors, and that I found I, myself, had been deceived, through not having been made aware long before I had to leave London, I felt bound as an honourable man to make the facts known . . . and whether pleasing or not, I would do the same tomorrow. . . . I consider I was "sold" coming out here without powers of any kind to control the Management, and when you suggested that I should come empty-handed, I believe that you were playing into Driver's hands, knowing a good deal more of his views and wishes than I did at the time. . . . Do not be surprised to receive my resignation as a Director of the Company, I don't consider I have been fairly treated.[6]

His complaints were justified. Before the floating of the Agricultural Company, Larnach and Vogel had entered into a partnership to buy Lora Station, a run south of the Hokonui Hills and bordering the Waimea estates in Southland. It was purchased from W.H. Calder and J.P. Taylor, both members of the Southland Provincial Council, and the transaction took place while Calder was in London. It was intended that Larnach and Vogel would on-sell the property to the company, once it was launched. The agreement was that £3,000 be paid to Calder on the signing of the contract, and the rest of the money at a later date. Larnach deposited his share of £1,500 in January 1879, but by March 1880 Vogel still owed his share, despite frantic letters and cablegrams from the worried Larnach, who wrote

I have no letters from you to reply to. Your treatment of me in connection with the purchase of Lora Station is simply cruel and disgraceful. You are jointly interested with me and the purchase cannot be got rid of, yet I induced Clarke to agree in Melbourne to your drawing £3,000, but I cannot get sixpence of what is owing to me here, and you seem determined that I shall get no relief as no funds, either through the Company or otherwise, have yet to be called to settle with Calder. You don't even put me in the way of getting your share, and I am left to fight Calder and Taylor at Law to carry out the contract made by you and me. There is no defence, whether the Company take over the property, or it remains with us. Had my monies not all been locked up with the Guthrie and Larnach Company, I would have been able to settle with Calder meanwhile, but to draw money out of my business in Dunedin at the present time is really impossible . . . so you are forcing me quickly into a big Law suit on your account and mine with Calder and Taylor, to which Stout advises me we have not "a shadow of defence." I have never felt so frustrated in my life, it has completely upset me from attending to our Company's business. Surely you can get some arrangement made, either for the Company to take it over, or pay us our money and let us fulfil our bargain like honest men. I am much concerned and distressed at the accident of my little son Douglas [seriously injured in a riding accident], and trust in God that he may get all right again.[7]

On 21 May a cablegram arrived from London saying that Lora Station had been taken over by the Agricultural Company, and that £3,000 had been paid as part of the purchase price. But the Dunedin faction of Henry Driver, Stout, Reynolds and McCaughan decided that the £3,000, together with Larnach's £1,500, would best be forfeited to Calder, and they cancelled the agreement. They considered the property too far away from the company's estates, so they would rather be released from the agreement. Larnach was in the minority in the vote, and was forced to bow to the wishes of the other men, but not without feelings of great resentment. There was no talk of returning his £1,500 deposit to him. He wrote to Vogel,

If the offer is accepted by Calder, you and I ought not to be made to stand the whole loss. The extra £3,000 to be paid should be borne by the other vendors (not me) as the arrangement with Calder was entered into by us for the benefit of all concerned, and as there seems to be a suspicion here that we bought for the purpose of speculation out of the Company and would not have offered the property at what we agreed to give had the property risen in value. I wish you to have forwarded to the local Committee here, a copy of the Minutes made when we reported the agreement with Calder to the London Directors at the first meeting. . . . The fact is there is a feeling, I think with some of the Vendors that you and I have been paid too highly, and if they could, they would prevent our getting any more money, but our agreement with them is very clear, and we must see that our conditions are clearly understood and carried out.

Larnach's letters to Vogel always ended on a variation of the same theme, and, it seemed, on deaf ears: "All I ask of you in fairness is that if you are paid anything . . . I am credited with an equal amount." His opinion of Vogel is recorded in a letter to Mrs Reynolds in 1888; he regarded Vogel as a gambler manipulating several packs of cards, and considered it "a sorry day for New Zealand when such a distinguished member of the Ancient Semitic race, composing the twelve tribes, ever placed his flatted feet on the virgin soil of this young country."

In other business activities, Larnach would prove himself scrupulously honest and very loyal. However, where the Agricultural Company was concerned, he seemed to have developed a confused morality. In implying government support for the floating of the company, he had believed that not only would the company's success benefit him, it would also profit New Zealand from the flow of immigrants and capital that would result.[8] His belief in the eradication of rabbits by good farming methods was vindicated to some extent by George Bell, the only member of the syndicate who actually farmed his property, and lived on it in his commodious sixteen room sand-stone dwelling, Waimea House. George Bell refused to lower the price of his land, claiming comparative freedom from the pests because of meticulous eradication programmes, and giving some credence to Larnach's faith in the amendments to the 1877 Rabbit Board Act, which suggested that with care, the rabbits could be contained. But now it seemed Larnach was happy to extricate himself from the company that gave him little say in its running, continued to withhold information from London, and, in Larnach's view, was not exercising enough economy.

* * *

The move to the town house at Manor Place did not altogether alleviate Larnach's domestic worries. Eliza was still not entirely happy and she wrote to the children in May 1880:

> Papa expects everything to be done in a day, but the workmen are so slow in doing anything that it keeps me back in all I ought to do. . . . Fanny Jones is still staying with us, I think she goes home this afternoon, indeed I shall be rather pleased as the noise she and Aunt are making will drive me out of my mind. Ever since I left The Camp I have been suffering with sore eyes, and now my right one is awfully sore, there must be something growing in it, I hope it may not turn to cancer. . . . We have a new housekeeper at The Camp, Elizabeth says she does not know how to cook, so it will be a poor lookout for Papa, breakfast and dinner, when he goes out there alone . . . Papa will not have time to write by this mail, but he sends his three darling daughters hundreds of kisses to you all.

Larnach's greatest worry, however, was the alarming decline in his other investments, and the mismanagement of his affairs that had occurred in his two year absence. For a man who had always trusted his friends, disenchantment was now setting in. Mr A. Cook, an officer of the Colonial

Bank, while acting as his agent in his absence, had lost him several thousand pounds. Henry Driver and A.H. Morris had held Larnach's power of attorney while he was in England, and they had made many careless mistakes, such as paying for fencing and maintenance on properties Larnach no longer owned, and buying shares that had been illegally transferred from the New Zealand Newspaper Company to Larnach's name, with demands for payment now being made. But the greatest mistake was of Larnach's own making. In his haste before departing for England, he had signed but omitted to read the "small print" on a document which involved him in a large guarantee to the bank on behalf of Guthrie and Larnach, and which now had been called in. Also, in his absence, more than 2000 Guthrie and Larnach shares had been transferred to his name without his authority, and payment far beyond their present value was being demanded.

Adding to his woes was the fact that he had not been called to the Legislative Council. Before leaving for England, Larnach had left a letter of resignation with the Government on the understanding that if it was to be used, he would be called to the Legislative Council. That this did not eventuate is not surprising considering the antipathy that Sir George Grey now felt towards any member of the Agricultural Company. Not long after his return to New Zealand, Larnach wrote to Sir Julius Vogel, "The Treasurer, Atkinson, has notified me today — politely — that the Government had cancelled my appointment as one of the Agents under the Inscribed Stock, through my not being any longer a resident in England. As usual some political or underhand move is going on."

In a year that had been filled with disappointment, the ultimate blow struck Larnach on 8 November 1880. He had just arrived in Melbourne on business, and was deeply shocked to receive the news of Eliza's death in a telegram from Dr Hocken. Eliza died at the town house in Manor Place. Her death was sudden, "having been seized with an apoplectic fit at about 2 p.m. and she died about two hours later." [9] Writing to his agent in London, Benjamin Petersen, Larnach says, "You are right in saying that I have had my share of troubles since my return here. The loss of my dear

wife has been the worst setback and the heaviest to bear. I even now sometimes cannot make myself believe, and realise that she is gone forever from
me."

In an uncanny error, Eliza dated her September letter to her children
as 23 November, when in fact she died on the 8th of that month. In this
last letter she again mildly voiced her great distress at the lack of letters
from any of them.

> My own darling children, I was so pleased to receive your letters by
> the July mail a little over three weeks ago, but my heart was almost
> broken today that there were none. I hope my darlings that you
> enjoyed yourselves in Switzerland, did you see the lion in Geneva
> and hear the organ? Be sure and describe all you have seen in your
> travels. I hoped you looked after your sisters, Douglas, and did not
> tease the girls. . . . Your father is calling out for shirts and socks, he
> is unable to write as he is dreadfully busy. I feel so tired and stupid
> I can hardly hold the pen. My own Coll, I wish you many happy
> returns of your birthday which will be on the 21st of next month.
> Bless you, you darling and may you see many more. May God be
> praised we shall meet before your 16th birthday. Accept Papa's,
> Aunt's and Baby's best wishes, and most of all from your loving and
> affectionate Mother, E.J. Larnach.

Mary Alleyne broke the news of Eliza's death to the children.

> My poor darlings, my heart bleeds when I think of the blow it will
> be for you to hear that you are now motherless. Your Mother died
> after only three hours of illness on the 8th of this month. . . . Your
> Papa arrived from Melbourne last Monday and the next day the
> funeral took place. Mr Driver went and met your Papa at The Bluff
> and made all arrangements as he was quite broken down and pros-
> trate with grief. He is calmer today. I was so perplexed as to what
> to do for the best as your Papa was away, but thought it would be

kinder to write, as a telegram would have kept you in suspense such a long time.[10]

Eliza's great friend Julia Hocken wrote to Donald at Oxford,

My dear Donny, I was at your Father's house today, and as he was writing to you, I asked him to give you my love and sympathy. He begged me to write to you myself. He is dreadfully distressed. He thought as I knew your dear Mother so well, and we were such friends, that it would please you to have a separate letter from me. Your Mother often spoke of you to me, and relied upon you and loved you very much, but I think since her return from England we have been more thrown together, and you were constantly spoken of. The day she died, she was to have dined and gone to the theatre afterwards. My maid saw her just twenty minutes before she was attacked. I tell you this to show you had you been in Dunedin you could not have seen her conscious. I was with your Aunt for the first week, indeed until your Father could return from Melbourne. Dr Hocken telegraphed him at once, and fortunately there was a steamer just leaving. He had the melancholy satisfaction of following her to her grave."[11]

Among Larnach's papers was this hand-written poem:

In Memoriam.
by Thomas Shepherd, O'Connell Street, Ashby, Geelong.
December 1880.

Eliza Jane Larnach, the beloved wife of W.J.M. Larnach, Esq.
Dunedin.
Who has passed away from all in the very bloom of life, leaving behind her a bereaved and kind husband and dear children to morn [sic] their loss, which to her is eternal gain.

Of her it may well be said, a blooming flower hath fallen to death an early prey.
Death, like a mighty tyrant strong,
Has aimed a fatal blow,
And laid with the promiscuous throng,
Our lady Larnach low. [12]

(Another twenty-two verses follow in similar vein.)

Chapter XIV

A MARRIAGE OF CONVENIENCE

On 27 January 1881, William Larnach celebrated his forty-eighth birthday by writing several letters, including one to his son Donald:

My Dear Son, I duly received your letter of the 18th November last, written just ten days after your dear Mother's death, and I was glad to find that you had borne the dreadful news with becoming manliness, fortitude and resignation. No one knows how I have suffered under the severe and unexpected shock, and having to write to you all so frequently brings back the sorrow of my loss with extreme intensity. We must bear it my son, and pray to God for the everlasting rest and happiness of the soul of your dear and loving Mother. . . . Poor little baby seems to have a faint vision of what has happened, because she won't go farther than the door of the room in which her poor Mother died, and she looks at her likeness every day and says "poor Mama". I am glad to say that the dear little thing is keeping well and seems devotedly attached to her aunt, who is equally attached to baby. I never saw such a wonderfully intelligent child as Gladys; nothing escapes her observation, only she will have her own way in everything and, under the sadness of our circumstances, I must admit that she gets it. So should she grow up a spoilt child there are many excuses to be urged both in her favour and ours.

And now my son, from not having heard from you since the middle of November, I fear that you were unsuccessful in your exam. for Mods. It was too much to expect you to go up under the trouble you are carrying, so I won't consider it a failure if you did not get through. Be steady, persevering and economical, and all will come right.

You will be sorry to learn that poor Morven, Aunt Amelia's daughter, died after a short illness, last Wednesday week. Death seems busy among the Larnach name. . . . We are all well and unite in much love, my dear Donald, Your ever affectionate Father, W.J.M. Larnach. P.S. This is my 48th birthday, but not a very happy one.

The girls and Douglas also received letters written in the same melancholic vein from their father, and while letters to Donald always began "My Dear Son", letters to Douglas were much warmer, always "My Darling Son". The first of March was Donald's twenty-first birthday, and his father sent him this cable: "God Bless and prosper you, all well, practice economy." The children were causing Larnach an enormous amount of worry; a smallpox epidemic raging in London made him fearful for their health. He was also concerned that soon he would no longer be able to afford to keep them all in London.

Kate, devastated by her mother's death, pleaded to come home, and Douglas, who was not progressing well at school after his riding accident when he suffered concussion and broken limbs, also wanted to return to take up farming. The two younger girls were constantly chided by their father for their expenditure on clothes, and their poor spelling and writing. He wanted them to concentrate on embroidery and "cutting out", but mainly on their music. Colleen was learning the harp and Alice the violin. Donald, who had been admitted to the Honourable Society of The Inner Temple the year before, was becoming increasingly more extravagant, and at this stage may have concealed from his father that he had recently married a young woman by the name of Violet Mary Riddle, and that before the end of 1881 their first daughter, Gretchen Guise Larnach, would be born at Kingston-on-Thames, near London. In William Larnach's collection of letters, there is no mention made of Donald's marriage. Perhaps the letters that mattered were too painful to be kept. Nor was Violet Larnach's name ever mentioned in future letters written by William; she was only ever coldly referred to as "your wife". Did William think Violet married

Donald for his money? Donald's daughter Gretchen, years later, spoke of the animosity between her mother and grandfather, but did not know the reason why. Violet Larnach is said to have been an actress, a profession scorned in the 1880s. Was this why William was so disappointed in the marriage? Why her presence at The Camp was unacceptable to him? Whatever her profession, judging by her piano albums passed down through the generations containing the pencilled remarks by her Leipzig Conservatorium piano teacher, she was at an advanced stage of piano playing, and according to contemporaries had a fine singing voice.

The disappointment of Donald's early marriage may have changed William's mind about allowing Douglas to come home. He had been keen for Douglas to go to Edinburgh to study medicine, but when Douglas suggested farming, his autocratic father thought otherwise. "I know what is best for you my son, few people make money nowadays by farming. When you come back I will get you into a solicitor's office as I have made up my mind that you ought to have a profession."

Also written on William's birthday was a letter addressed to the chairman and directors of Guthrie and Larnach, which stated, "Gentlemen, I beg to resign my seat on your board as one of your Directors. It appears to me that notwithstanding the large interest I hold in the Company, I have not power to veto or prevent that which I disapprove of." It was obvious a rift had occurred between Larnach and Guthrie, who, although an enterprising manufacturer, proved to be a muddler and no longer confided in Larnach.

As a promoter of great ideas and a generous financial backer, Larnach was hard to beat, but there was never anything very practical about his contributions. He trusted others too much, and left the day to day decisions to them. In today's parlance he was not a "hands on" businessman. Usually his advice was respected, and he certainly had power to influence economic progress in many fields, but his involvement with the Agricultural Company had so preoccupied him that he now had no intimate knowledge of the workings of Guthrie and Larnach. Although a large shareholder, his role was little more than the average shareholder has in any business.

Walter Guthrie now ran the business himself. Nevertheless Larnach felt aggrieved that his advice had not been sought more in the running of the company and, agreeing with others on the board, considered Guthrie's policies had cost the company many thousands of pounds. The recent destruction by fire of the Pararaha Steam Mill on Auckland's west coast was another setback. He could see that the company was heading for doom and would have to be wound up, and that he personally would lose heavily. For the past three years he had not received any interest on his £60,000 invested in the firm, "and it is even probable that I not only may never get any interest again, but lose every shilling of my principle (sic) money as well."[1]

Although large amounts of capital were tied up in Guthrie and Larnach, the Agricutural Company and the Waimea Plains Railway Company, Larnach was also involved with the National Loan and Insurance Company, the Colonial Bank, the Kaitangata Coal Company, the Walton Park Coal Company, the Equitable Provident Company, the *Otago Daily Times*, the Witness Company, the Morning Herald Company, the Dunedin Exchange, the Otago and Southland Investment Company, Round Hill Company, N.Z. Loan and Mercantile, Drapery and Importing Company, N.Z. Shipping Company, the Kauri Timber Company, and The Dunedin Tram Company. This is by no means the complete list of his interests, many names are unknown. His reputation as a businessman and his experience made him a popular choice as a director. He was a floater and promoter of companies, in addition to being a director of many of them. He carried out this work on a commission basis, and was often issued shares as remuneration. Now he was about to become involved in the New Zealand Refrigeration Company, and the proposed sugar-beet industry. These last two projects interested him because, apart from the obvious advantages from both developments, he could see land prices increasing as a result.

At that time, however, the deteriorating economic situation in New Zealand and Australia was beginning to affect everyone. Increasingly critical letters from Joseph Clarke kept arriving, complaining about the management of Waimea (part of the Agricultural Company's land), the growing of crops, the drainage of swamps, and the harvesting of grain — all things that Larnach, as Clarke's agent, kept a close eye on. He visited the property regularly, anxious to protect Clarke's big investment in the Agricultural Company, and to keep it in peak condition ready to sell. He wrote to Clarke,

> Whatever I have done for you has only been in the best of your interests, and it is rather disheartening to be tried, judged and found guilty without having the opportunity of being heard in self-defence. I therefore, not knowing what influences may be at work, ask you to suspend arriving at any conclusions until you have calmly discussed the whole question with me. The weather is so unsettled that I cannot get on with the shearing. After that is over, Henry Driver and I will come your way. [2]

While Larnach was spending time supervising the activities at Waimea, Henry Driver was complaining that Larnach was not at the Agricultural Company's office in Dunedin every day. Larnach retaliated, "I have the interests of the Company at heart as you know, I therefore object to any insinuation implying such a meaning. . . . It is not easy for me to be at the office of the Company every day, as I am not a salaried manager." [3]

When in Dunedin, Larnach mostly stayed at Manor Place with Mary and little Gladys, who seems to have been the one bright star on his horizon. He wrote to his daughters in England of her constantly.

> Your dear little sister has now got a cat, which she calls "Poof Cat" for pussy-cat. . . . I have to give baby a halfpenny piece or more nearly every morning before she will consent to go out with her nurse, and then she insists that I go shopping "down town" with her and her cat. . . . We have been very quiet in Dunedin, and very dull. Your Aunt and I never go anywhere but to The Camp since the death of your dear Mother, we cannot forget her, nor the fact that she has gone away from us forever.

Early in March, William entertained his Uncle Donald and Aunt Jane at The Camp, where they were greatly impressed with all he had done. His uncle had been sufficiently interested in the Agricultural Company to see for himself the quality of the land William was selling, and had stayed at George Bell's station at Waimea on the way to Dunedin. The Depression was now really hitting the company and it was desperately short of finance. Vogel was blamed for his extravagant promises and plans, and expenditure was to be cut to the bone. Larnach felt that a much firmer hand than Vogel's should be in charge of the company, but Larnach no longer had any say in the matter.

The Larnach tomb in the Dunedin Northern Cemetery, built by Larnach in Eliza's memory. The design, by R.A. Lawson, is based on that of First Church, Dunedin.

Mary Alleyne, Eliza Larnach's half-sister and William Larnach's second wife.

Larnach's optimism in property never seemed to wane, even although he was so "slaughtered", as he put it, for money. While buying land in Lawrence in partnership with Henry Driver on the one hand, he at the same time sold several properties on the Peninsula, mortgaged Wellington properties in College Street, Holland Street and at the Hutt, and was hounding his agent in London, Benjamin Petersen, to "sell that confounded property, 74 Courtfield Place." At The Camp, he had just glassed in all the verandahs, and by the middle of the year a replica of First Church, Dunedin — a memorial chapel in the form of a mausoleum — had been built over Eliza's grave.

In September, Larnach and a Mr Robert Gillies of Dunedin accepted the offer of promoting the Westport Coal Company in Australia. Before leaving for Melbourne, William proposed marriage to Mary Alleyne, and instructed his solicitors, Sievwright and Stout, to prepare an antenuptial agreement in her favour. He put all his freehold properties on the Otago

Peninsula, including The Camp, plus all his shares, his horses, carriages, furniture, and Manor Place in her name, and authorised a payment of £5,000 to Mary Alleyne for entering into a matrimonial bond with him. His forthcoming marriage to Mary was really a marriage of convenience. It was certainly not a great romance. It was more like the re-reading of a well loved novel than the excitement of opening a brand new book.

William had known Mary since she was eight. He was fond of her, and for the last fourteen years The Camp had been her home. According to servants' gossip, Mary was not without her problems — an over indulgence in drink sometimes found her sobering up in a room on the nursery floor. William himself had been a heavy drinker; he had enjoyed a bottle-opening bonhomie with his employees at The Camp, and had been considered a bad influence on them by their wives. But by 1881, on his own written evidence, he was a total abstainer, and he advised Douglas, who was still recovering from his riding accident, "not to take any liquid stronger than water in case it should injure your brain." In spite of Mary's tendency to tipple, Eliza had considered her sister capable of being Gladys's guardian, and William, who obviously doted on the child, was pleased Mary was so fond of her. But most importantly, he needed to be married to be able to make over his property to Mary as his wife, as insurance against the very real risk he now faced of bankruptcy through the failing business of Guthrie and Larnach.

Four days after the signing of the nuptial agreement, Larnach resigned as a director of the Agricultural Company, pleading lack of time to give to the company. He left for Melbourne, taking Mary and Gladys with him, and made a point of telling people that Mary and Gladys had an apartment on the Toorak Road, while he stayed at the Australian Club. No mention was made of the intended wedding.

The promotion of the Westport Coal Company, which eventually owned most of the mines in the Buller region, proved so successful that Larnach considered staying in Melbourne permanently. He approached Mr Richard Goldsbrough, the most successful wool broker and financier of pastoral land in Melbourne, and offered his services to represent him and open new branches of Goldsbrough's business. But Goldsbrough was himself experiencing financial difficulties, and Larnach's offer was declined.

Larnach then turned his attention back to banking. Writing to his uncle, he told him of the misfortunes that had befallen the Bank of Victoria and of laxity in the management of the bank, and wrote, "I would very much like to have the task of putting matters straight in the Bank of Victoria . . . and if it was made worth my while I would go into it heart and soul for I like such work where there is room for redemption."[4] However nothing came of that either, and he and Mary returned to Dunedin in the middle of December to good and bad news. The good news was that 2050 ha of Joseph Clarke's land at Waimea had sold for £50,000, and the bad news was that Clarke was not prepared to give Larnach his full commission, nor were the directors of the Westport Coal Company forthcoming with their promises of payment either. Larnach wrote to Mr W. Dickson, the general manager of the Westport Coal Company

I cannot help saying that I feel much surprised and disappointed at the tone of the Resolutions . . . and I must inform you on behalf of myself and Mr Gillies, your proposal is declined. To accept an honorarium such as the amount recommended by your Board would not nearly compensate us for the great loss of Time, Trouble and Expense which we have suffered in the anxious work of floating the new company. . . . Why apart from the neglect of my own matters here, my expenses came to a lot over £300.[5]

Larnach and Gillies had expected to get five per cent of the floated capital, and they had sold in excess of 40,000 shares at 50s. a share. The outcome of these transactions is not known, but it shows the difficulty of extracting money that was honestly earned as the depression in New Zealand intensified.

Yet even in the midst of his own money worries, Larnach rarely refused to help others. Eliza Larnach's brother, Dick Guise, approached him for money, which again raises doubts about the so-called fortune Eliza and her brother were said to have inherited. "I don't know what to do with you," Larnach wrote to Dick Guise, "I have so often helped you and you have so often deceived me. If I do anything for you again, it will only be in memory and out of regard for your late sister. I want to know truthfully your real position and in as few words as possible, I don't like long letters." He enclosed £75 in the letter.

It is often wrongly stated that Larnach was responsible for having the Deceased Wife's Sister Marriage Act of 1880 passed (before its passing it was illegal to marry your wife's sister), but he had been out of Parliament for two years prior to the act being passed. However he did take advantage of it, and as the year drew to an end, he wrote to his close friends telling of his forthcoming wedding to Mary Alleyne.

> I write you these lines to say that on Saturday next, Jan 7th instant Miss Alleyne and I are to be married. Since Mary's return from Melbourne, she and baby have been staying with the Reverend Mr L. Stamford, at Blueskin Gorge, from whose house we will be married. I have some people who object to the marriage of a Man with his deceased wife's sister, but under the peculiar position in which I have been placed, knowing Mary from childhood, I am hopeful she will make the best Mother for my children.[6]

The wedding did not meet with all the children's approval. Colleen, then seventeen, was reprimanded by her father: "In speaking of your Aunt 'Alleyne' as you are pleased to call her in your letters, it will be sufficient to speak or write of her as your Aunt. Her name is not Alleyne any longer which you know and I cannot allow any disrespect or you and I will fall out."

The newly weds returned to live at The Camp. Only a few days after the wedding, Larnach broke his leg in a buggy crash, and it was five months before he was active again and able to leave The Camp. His mother, Emily, died in April in Melbourne, but he was not able to attend her funeral. She was buried with her husband John Larnach at the Singleton cemetery in the Hunter Valley.

The sailing ship Dunedin *which carried the first cargo of frozen meat
to Great Britain in 1882.*

Shortly after his accident, on 15 February 1882, Larnach, as managing
director of the New Zealand Refrigeration Company, had the satisfaction
of watching from the observation room of The Camp the sailing of the
1200 tonne ship *Dunedin* from Port Chalmers. She carried 130 tonnes of
meat which had been frozen on board in specially insulated refrigerating
chambers. This was the first enterprise of its kind in New Zealand, and only
the second in the world. This company was perhaps the most important for
the future farmers of Otago, and Larnach, together with James Shand and
R. Crawford, had put much preliminary work into it. The trial voyage was
not without its moments of anxiety. Sparks from the refrigerating plant's
funnel more than once set fire to the sails and when something went amiss
in the freezing chamber, Captain Whitson, while investigating, nearly
became frozen meat himself and had to be hauled out of the chamber by a
rope tied round his legs. The cargo arrived in London after ninety-eight
days in perfect condition, and was sold at a good price. From that time, not
only the fleece but meat from the sheep became a marketable product,

instead of being sent to boiling down works. It also raised the value of the cow to that of the sheep as markets opened for dairy products, and this greatly assisted small farmers.

* * *

The arrival home of Douglas and Kate, Larnach's favourite son and daughter, helped cheer the winter days as he slowly recovered from his buggy mishap. But he was shocked by the ill-effects still suffered by Douglas from his riding accident of two years ago, and disappointed that Kate had managed to lose all her music on the voyage home and was quite incapable of playing a note on piano or violin without it. Her scant knowledge of French and German did not impress him either, and doubts about the teaching ability of Miss Visick surfaced. Nevertheless, all was forgiven. Kate's pleasant nature had always made her a favourite with her father, and William and Mary were delighted to have her home again. Gladys was confused by these two rivals for her father's affection, and refused to allow them to call him Father, while Mary was pleased the older children's homecoming had helped relieve the boredom suffered by the recuperating William.

By August, Larnach had finally persuaded the directors of Guthrie and Larnach to go into voluntary liquidation in order to officially wind the company up. The employees were to be paid in full, but the shareholders would suffer, "and as I am much the largest, small holders will not have much to complain at all sharing alike." At a shareholders' meeting, Larnach was absolved from any blame. It was found that Larnach had not meddled, whereas others had adversely affected the running of the company. Larnach was elected to be one of three liquidators. "I feel much more comfortable having no business running under my name," he wrote to a friend.

His interest in politics resumed again, more to occupy himself than for the love of it, although the opportunity of helping the Agricultural Company, in which he still held debentures, may have been a reason. In January 1883, after the death of James Seatoun, who had been the House

A cartoon depicting Larnach wooing the "Peninsula dairymaid" in the Peninsula district elections in 1883, when Larnach defeated Bishop Moran.

of Representative's Peninsula member, Larnach contested the by-election. The surprise of the campaign was the other candidate, the Catholic Bishop of Dunedin, the Rev. Dr Patrick Moran. "What next?" declared the *Otago Daily Times* on 10 January. "We admire the pluck and boldness of the doughty Bishop more than we can admire his discretion . . . he is determined to fight out the education issue to the bitter end . . . but the Bishop's rash step is likely to give an easy victory to Mr Larnach, whose views are equally obnoxious to the fiery prelate."

Bishop Moran wanted state funding for private schools in the form of tax relief for those parents who chose to educate their children in private or religious schools. Larnach's views were that all parents should pay for their own children's education, as "it would relieve the country of a monstrous load of direct taxation." He considered the colony was made a laughing stock for providing free education to children of parents who could well afford to pay for it, and only in cases of extreme poverty should the State contribute. However, as this idea raised little enthusiasm, he decided to remain with the status quo, agreeing to free, secular and compulsory education for children aged from five to fifteen years. Larnach personally believed sound education was based on religious principles, and hoped the matter could be settled by introducing Bible reading into schools. He even hoped to bring back the old Presbyterian Otago system, which compelled Catholic children to read the Scriptures or face the alternative which, according to Bishop Moran, was "to remain outside shivering in the cold . . . while the other scholars were seated round the fire provided by the taxpayer, both Catholic and Protestant." Larnach seemed oblivious of the fact that the Catholic Church for many years discouraged its members from reading the Bible, in case they misinterpreted the meaning. The Church interpreted the Bible for its members and made the meaning clear in Church teaching, and a Catholic parent in all conscience could not allow his child to attend Protestant Bible classes.

Dr Moran spoke convincingly of the need he felt to represent the 70,000 Catholics of New Zealand, and received a warm hearing from the crowd of mostly Irishmen from the electorate of South Dunedin.

Another controversial issue was the Chinese question. Introducing Dr Moran to the electors in Naumann Hall on the evening of the nominations, Mr Gourley, unhampered by the hypocrisy of political correctness, in referring to Dr Moran's views on the Chinese question, said that "if the influx of Chinese was not speedily stopped they would become as big a pest as the rabbit . . . Liberal members would have to table a motion in the House to exterminate the Asiatic intruders in the same way as the objectionable quadrupeds."[7]

It was rumoured that Larnach was all for Chinese immigration as a source of labour, but this he strongly denied.

A bogus has been raised to deprecate me in your eyes on the Chinese question. It is all claptrap. I can only tell you plainly that I was very much grieved to hear a gentleman whom I respect very much comparing the Chinese to rabbits. I say it is humiliating and degrading for a white man who has had a respectable education to compare a portion of God's people to beasts like rabbits. If I lose my election in consequence of taking the stand I have, I will come out with respect. I am in favour of the Chinese being treated in a proper way, as a portion of God's people, as I am in favour of Maoris or any savages being treated in a proper way.[8]

He went on to say that he was not in favour of Chinese coming here in large numbers, but that those who were here should be allowed to bring their wives, and be treated fairly. As a poll tax had now been imposed, the numbers were decreasing, and he would do nothing to disturb this arrangement.

The contest was clearly between Larnach and Dr Moran; the other two contenders, one of whom was a Catholic, were clearly not in the running. The election day result was reported by the *Otago Daily Times*, "Probably no contest for the representation of a single constituency has . . . caused such general excitement as the election which has been a pronounced victory for Mr W.J.M. Larnach C.M.G." The most surprising result was Larnach's huge majority over Dr Moran in that stronghold of Catholicism, South Dunedin. There, the *Otago Witness* described the men as

a good many rough diamonds among the free and independent electors of South Dunedin. Indeed they are worse as supporters than opponents. . . . As supporters, the sturdy democrats of the Flat are not altogether indifferent to the privilege of slapping with genial force, a C.M.G on the back or poking him in the ribs. Mr Larnach periodically descends from the castle to the cottage and harangues the plebes on the Flat in their vernacular, he never talks like a book, and certainly not like a copy book . . .[9]

At one meeting when interjections were getting too noisy and out of hand, Larnach shouted, "Kennel up, you curs!" The electors loved it and order was restored. It was not his manifesto they liked, but the man himself.

There was no denying that everything Larnach stood for was for the promotion of capitalism. He supported capitalist immigration and the removal of property tax; in fact he was absolutely opposed to direct taxation in any form. In his view, taxes should be raised through stamp and customs duties, and everyone should pay for improvements such as railways. He was a puzzle to the *Evening Star*, which reported

> . . . it is absolutely impossible to comprehend why a man of genial character and comfortable circumstances troubles himself with politics in this democratic community, whose ways are not his ways and whose aspirations are utterly beyond his sympathies. The electors of the Peninsula must surely reverse the ordinary rules and go in for men, not measures. [10]

The article even went so far as to forgive Larnach for leaving Sir George Grey's Government so prematurely to promote the Agricultural Company.

> In the interests of the community, we believe that it would have been better had he remained at his post . . . for no Ministry required so stringent a check upon their doings as that of Sir George Grey, and a man of large business experience like Mr Larnach was absolutely essential to keep them from doing the mischief they worked. . . . The affair is long past . . . the business of the electors is with the present, not with the past.

After his successful return to Parliament, Larnach kept a very low profile for the rest of the Session, as other worries were again occupying him. His younger brother, John Larnach, a shareholder and accountant of the Sydney and Country Bank had written to William asking his opinion on Mr A. Cook, who was applying for the position as manager of the Sydney and Country Bank. Cook, of the Colonial Bank, had acted as Larnach's agent while he was in England, and made serious errors in managing his affairs. John Larnach, in his capacity as a shareholder of the bank, showed his brother's reply to the directors of the board, and they decided against employing Cook.

Cook then embarked on a lawsuit against William Larnach. It proved to be a long and expensive exercise for Larnach. He was forced to give evidence to a commission in Wellington, then go to Sydney, employing a solicitor from Melbourne to defend him, who later charged him "outrageous fees". The plaintiff Cook had the clever solicitor Sir Archibald Michie, whom Larnach had already faced when Sir Archibald so successfully defended Robert Alleyne. The case was fought not on whether Larnach's letter was libellous — that was not in question, as Larnach had only stated the truth — but whether he had sent the letter to his brother out of malice, thus taking away Cook's chance of employment. The jury could not come to a decision and asked to be discharged, with eight of the jury in favour of Larnach. Nevertheless he was faced with hefty costs, and wrote, "I have my hands pretty full of troubles just now, but my head is cool and my heart will never fail me under any circumstances." Despite his words, tensions were beginning to show in his nature. He had greatly overextended himself in every way, and hints of irascibility started to appear in his normally jovial character.

Chapter XV

THE MINISTER OF MINES

The rapidly declining Agricultural Company would once again become intertwined with politics in 1884, but not before another parliamentary election was fought. In fact fighting was what the main players in the company were now doing. Larnach had distanced himself from the Agricultural Company, annoyed by the refusal of the London directors to reveal to the British public the dismal prospects of the company's land, information Larnach had given them on his return to New Zealand. He had cashed up some of his debentures, and relations between Larnach and Henry Driver were now strained. Joseph Clarke was taking George Bell to court, Sir Julius Vogel and the London manager Mr H.S. Valentine were arguing over whether to wind the company up, and Vogel, in his endeavour to pacify both the London directors and those in Dunedin, complained that he had forfeited the friendship of both Driver and Larnach.

Even the Waimea Plains Railway Company, set up to facilitate the Agricultural Company, and through whose land the railway ran, was now forcing a further financial crisis on the Agricultural Company by demanding payment of rate arrears of nearly £10,000 from the settlers. Larnach, the chairman of directors of the Railway Company and a large shareholder, made it clear that the non-payment of rates meant no dividend for the Railway Company shareholders and no fees for the directors, so he had no option but to force payment by using the legislation of 1883.[1] Anger was now widespread among the few Waimea Plains settlers, one of whom was imprisoned for shooting at a rate collector. A meeting was held at Gore of the settlers and Agricultural Company managers, and all agreed to resist payment of the rates.

In Melbourne, the court case Bell v Clarke was in session. Joseph Clarke, acting on behalf of Larnach, Driver and all who had sold land to the Agricultural Company, and who had accepted a lower price because of the rabbits, denied there was any agreement with George Bell that he should receive a higher price because he maintained his land was free of rabbits. Clarke alleged Bell owed the company £90,000. The litigation was to continue for a number of years.

Sir Julius Vogel felt it was time to come to New Zealand to smooth all the ruffled feathers. Always the great spender, Vogel, since joining the company had done nothing to curtail his gambling, or his lavish lifestyle. He had extravagantly remodelled his London house in anticipation of the great expectations he had of the company, and was now cash-strapped, crippled with gout and sick with worry.

He arrived in New Zealand in April 1884, confined to a bath chair, and hoped his crippled plight would arouse the sympathy of the Government when he asked them to reward him financially for his past services to the country. Officially this request was the object of his visit. He was very careful to conceal the real purpose of it, which he admitted in a letter to Joseph Clarke: "It is of great importance both for the success of my mission and the good of the Company that the purpose of my mission be as much concealed as possible."[2]

Vogel had originally intended to arrive in New Zealand, sell 12,300 ha of Waimea land at bargain prices, and return to England. However, the publicity about the high railway rates had killed that idea. The only possible way to help the company was for Vogel to return to politics, and he was encouraged to do so by Robert Stout, Henry Driver and Larnach, the latter having buried his personal animosity towards Vogel for the good of the company. Before entering Parliament, Vogel resigned from the London chairmanship of the company, explaining in his letter to the London directors, "I want to impress on you to be careful how you speak of anything I do . . . it would not do to attribute public actions to private motives . . . but it all comes back to the point I am anxious to save the company and I have taken the most effectual steps to do it but you must not compromise me."[3]

In the general election held in July, Stout and Larnach were also returned to Parliament. Larnach did not have to announce any new policy to his Peninsula electorate; eloquent speeches were not his forte, and his very outspokenness disarmed the opposition. "I did not come to bore you with any silly twaddle — just to ask for your support on the ground of past services. . . . If you were to vote for any mountebank politician who presented himself and sent such up to Wellington, then I say God help New Zealand." (Great cheering, hooting and cries of "kennel up" followed this statement.) "But I give you credit for more sense . . . and no doubt on Tuesday will find myself at the head of the poll."[4] This was followed by great applause, groans and uproar. It was another massive victory to Larnach. The unsuccessful candidate for the South Dunedin seat, Mr Hodge, blamed his defeat on Larnach's popularity. "I believe I have had to fight more against this personal popularity than against political principles."[5]

Vogel also had a strong personal following. His arrival in the country had sparked a feeling of nostalgia for times past, when money had been plentiful. When Parliament met after the elections, and following the resignation of Atkinson, to the amazement of many it soon became clear that — in a strange alliance of two men of very different characters — the respected, seemingly principled Stout and the wily opportunist Vogel hoped to form a government, in cohorts with John Ballance, James Macandrew and William Montgomery. When Sir George Grey heard of the old combination of the Agricultural Company partners, who in his opinion had previously so cleverly hoodwinked him and robbed him of his return to power, he was appalled. In a strong speech to the House he tried to expose their antics, even "if it costs me my life — if it costs me my reputation."[6] He described the men as "The Agricultural Company ministry coming back to office."[7] But his accusations fell on deaf ears, as the rantings of a disappointed man. It would be many years before historians discovered the truth of his words, so skilfully did Stout and Vogel conceal the reason for their alliance.

To the country, Vogel seemed the obvious choice as premier, but claiming his health as an excuse, he promoted Stout as premier, on the understanding that Vogel take over the reins should his health improve. In a letter to son Donald, William Larnach wrote from Wellington, "Sir Julius

Vogel is here again in Parliament, he was recently sent for to form a new Ministry, but I think he has made a fool of himself and lost cast, as I have told him, by agreeing to accept a subordinate position to that of Premier, and Stout, who has seen nothing of the world to assume that position. I will not be surprised to see them, the new men, kicked out before many days."[8]

Larnach was quite right. Three days later the Stout-Vogel Ministry, opposed by the Grey faction, was defeated. But after much grouping and regrouping of various members in an attempt to form a stable government, the second Stout-Vogel Ministry, to be nicknamed "The Government of Railways", finally came into being on 3 September 1884. Its main aim was "the basic but carefully concealed purpose of rescuing the Agricultural Company, and railways provided the strategy for this rescue."[9] Exactly six days after the new Ministry was announced, a bill was brought down for the purchase by the Government of the Waimea Plains and other district railways.[10]

Larnach was in no hurry to take a place in the Ministry. Again he wrote to Donald, "Sir Julius Vogel is again in the Government and perhaps I may join him later on if his Ministry lasts through the Session. At present I prefer standing out."[11] Ironically he was busy as chairman of the Waimea

A cartoon portraying Julius Vogel as the driver, with Robert Stout the lead horse, and William Larnach behind him in the Stout-Vogel Ministry of 1884-7. The picture was originally captioned, "The Road to Ruin".

Plains Railway Company, fighting the Government's paltry offer to buy the company, an offer which, if accepted, would mean a considerable loss to shareholders. His involvement with the Railway Company was an embarrassment to the Government, which Stout was anxious to remedy. In a letter to Vogel, Stout insisted Larnach resign his directorship of the company "absolutely at once. . . . He is to do so and when that is done we will fix his position up. There are only left to him 'Mines' and 'Marine'. But I suppose we can rearrange offices."

Early in 1885 Larnach resigned from the chairmanship of the Railway Company, and in compensation of any loss of director's fees, he received a minister's salary. He was appointed Minister of Mines, Marine and Customs, but not without some resentment at Stout's dictatorial ways, and he was later to openly oppose Stout on land and educational policies. Even after this appointment, Larnach continued to work behind the scenes to get a substantial Government offer to buy the Railway Company, and it was not until 1886 that negotiations were completed to the satisfaction of everyone.

For unknown reasons, Larnach was not keen to accept the office of Minister of Mines. The *Cromwell Argus* and the *Lyttelton Times* objected strongly to his appointment. "Mr Larnach represents nothing but the Waimea Plains Railway," reported the *Lyttelton Times*, while the *Argus* called him a square peg in a round hole.

> We could name a dozen gentlemen far more suited to the portfolio . . . it certainly seems a most strange thing that the government should have passed them over in favour of one whose only claim to the position appears to be personal influence. In many respects we admire Mr Larnach as a public man, but we cannot for the life of us see wherein lies his fitness for the position.

Perhaps their criticism goaded Larnach, for it was said of him that "he had enemies who declare that it is only necessary to inform him that a thing is impossible in order to ensure his attempting it forthwith." [12]

In accepting the portfolio of Minister of Mines, Larnach demanded that he was given a free hand to develop the mining industry. It was to be a challenge that he would enjoy, and one that would prove beneficial to the country. In spite of the fact that Vogel was confident of finding gold and coal on the Agricultural Company's land and hoped that the Government could aid the search, this was a portfolio to become dear to Larnach's heart, and one that he worked on with enthusiasm in a genuine desire to aid the mining industry without granting any favours to the Agricultural Company. "It has been said that Larnach's ability as Minister of Mines has never been exceeded." [13]

He was now able to leave the running of The Camp in Douglas's hands, while Mary, Kate and Gladys joined him in a Wellington apartment. Kate chose to do voluntary work at the hospital, and although Douglas was put in charge of The Camp, his father was constantly writing to him with advice, even on how to sign a cheque. Larnach allowed Douglas to keep all the rents and income generated from the farm as his salary.

During this time Larnach's dealings with the London board of the Agricultural Company were at a low ebb. The company was trying to get son Donald to pay up on the shares his father had given him. His father, to protect his son, wrote,

He has not got a sixpence to pay further calls, nor will I pay for him . . . I might be looking to give the Company two or three thousand pounds in Debentures . . . but if they once fire a single shot to worry him in any way, they shall go through the Court . . . and the Company will get nothing, so Mayne [the chairman of the Company] had better watch out, and not bang his head against a wall . . . I have been working for months with all my influence to get the Government to agree to take over the Waimea Plains Railway and so save the Company in Rates, which the London people don't seem to recognise who their real friends are. If they get my back up I can make it pretty warm for them in another direction they little dream of. I have lost money by the Company, and so has Donald and I am not going to be bounced, and I will refuse absolutely to do anything.[14]

To those less well off Larnach was not so threatening. In a letter to an agent about his tenants, Larnach said he was "sorry to learn that the poor woman has been ill. Better have done what she requires in the way of repairs to her cottage and write 30/- off her overdue rent to keep her in good heart, and you may write off a similar sum from the other tenant, Mrs Larkin, to encourage her to pay the balance due."[15]

Nor was Larnach frightened to right an injustice when he saw fit. An undated newspaper clipping reports that bailiffs levied a Mr Anderson the sum of £472 15s. 6d. and that afternoon seized 145 head of his cattle. Between 3 a.m. and 4 a.m. the next morning, William Larnach, Henry Driver, John McLean and a drover named Wingfield forcibly rescued the cattle from the custody of the bailiff, returning them to Mr Anderson. Larnach and his friends then appeared in court to show cause why they should not be charged with contempt of court. Unfortunately the outcome is unknown; Larnach neglected to paste the court's decision in his clipping book.

Larnach's elevation to Minister of Mines was in contrast to his rapidly declining fortune, yet he remained philosophical, writing to his uncle, "I have had my share of troubles and losses caused no doubt by errors of judgment on my part, but chiefly by the great depression . . . particularly in this Colony."[16] The children in England seemed unable or unwilling to comprehend his pleas for economy, and his letters to them alternated between bossiness and benevolence. Hoping to save money with the cheaper living conditions on the Continent, he had sent them all to Leipzig to study German, and they all, including Donald's wife, Violet, studied music at the Conservatorium, where Alfred Hill, the conductor and composer of many Maori songs, the most popular being "Waiata Poi", was also a student.

Donald, who had been unable to live on the £600 per year plus dividends from the many shares his father had put in his name as a single man, was now the father of two daughters, Gretchen and Olive, and expected his father to provide for them all. At that moment, Donald was in his father's good books, having passed all his law exams. Donald's idea of economy was a large apartment at Rosa Platz, accommodating not only Donald's family and his sisters, but his two children's nurse, Donald's valet, and a maid for Colleen and Alice. Donald had brought his piano and library from England, and Colleen her harp. The long-suffering father wrote "we were glad to hear that you were all settling down with your sisters [in Leipzig]. Your quarters appear to be of a rather palatial kind, but I suppose it is prudent to pay a little more for rent for a healthy habitation than to run the risk of being laid up in sickness and having to pay doctor's bills."[17] Trying to impress on them the delicate situation of his finances, William kept reminding the girls to "make great progress with your Music and Languages," telling them they may yet have to use their education and musical accomplishments to earn a living.

Chapter XVI

OF MINES AND MINERS

Early in 1885, as one of his first duties as Minister of Mines, Larnach left Dunedin by steamer for Hokitika on an inspection tour of the mining industry. It was a gruelling trip, according to the many clippings carefully pasted into Larnach's scrap book, yet one that Larnach thoroughly enjoyed. Every mode of transport was used including buggy, boat, coach, dray, trap, train, horse and shanks's pony, on roads varying from steep slippery trails over mountain ranges to boulder strewn beds of shingle marked only by the occasional post to indicate the direction on the flood prone river flats. On this trip to Westland, his son Douglas travelled with him, and Larnach also persuaded a world authority on mining, Professor Black of the University of Otago School of Mines, to accompany him.

For years thinking men had been eager to establish schools of mines throughout the colony, but the answer had invariably been the same as that in the *Lyttelton Times*: "Look at Otago, splendid School Of Mines, splendid Professor (Professor Black), best mining expert south of the equator (Professor Ulrich), but only two students! Why another School of Mines?"[1] With no diploma of commercial value available at the end of the three-year course, there was nothing to encourage students to study mining. Yet the university sat there waiting for the mountains to come to Mohammed, until Larnach pointed out the impracticality of miners coming to Dunedin to study. He wanted lecturers to visit each mining district annually and instruct these hardworking men in some scientific knowledge, so that they could become informed prospectors.

Professor Black was surprised to find over 1600 men willing, anxious and ready to study mining. They had formed associations, pooled their money to buy books and equipment, but lacked instructors. In a period of eight weeks he delivered forty-four lectures at fifteen different places, on geology, the chemistry of gold, mineralogy, the extraction of metals from their ores, and how to identify many valuable minerals that were being tossed aside because of ignorance. His lectures were usually accompanied with the inevitable flash, bang and disagreeable smell of chemical experiments, but here at last theory was being joined to practice.

A strong friendship between Larnach and Richard Seddon developed on this visit. Seddon, a politician whose presence was beginning to be felt in the House, was the member for the West Coast town of Kumara, and the owner of the Queen's Hotel there. He was a dominating figure, both in size and personality, and enlisted friends by "favours, threats, promises, cajolery and good fellowship."[2] He was not above using his fists to solve an argument, something Larnach would not have dreamt of doing, but then Larnach was of only medium build compared to Seddon's gargantuan figure. Seddon was drawn to Larnach by his lack of pomposity and his forthright manner, and although the friendship was often tested through the years by the machinations of politics, it survived.

The presence of the premier, the Hon. Robert Stout, lent lustre to the entourage in Westland. At a meeting of miners at Dillmans, Richard Seddon presented the ministerial party with petitions, chiefly concerning the price of water used for sluicing. In Kumara, miners each paid £3 a week for water, more than most other districts, and this was a bone of contention. The Kumara Sludge Channel, as it was known, had been Seddon's idea, but at that time, through faults in design, it was incapable of supplying all the claims with enough water, thus halting work and annoying the miners. They were holding Seddon responsible, which was prejudicing his re-election; almost as serious, his tavern takings were dropping as fast as his popularity. Larnach's sympathies were with both the miners and Seddon, and he promised to do his best to reduce the price of water, at the same time listening to the many other petitions unrelated to mining that were foisted on him.

It was not all petitions and promises. On 14 February a banquet in honour of the ministerial party was held at the Hokitika Town Hall, where hosts and visitors alike tossed compliments about like cabers on a Highland sports day. The premier stated that this was the largest banquet they had attended, "the best got up, the best served, and it showed him that Hokitika still remained the capital of Westland."[3] As the evening wore on, formalities relaxed. Toasts were made, and replied to in song. The premier proposed "Prosperity to Westland", to which Richard Seddon replied by singing "The Wearing of the Green". The Hon. Mr Bonar proposed a toast to "The mining industry", to which the mayor of Ross, Mr Malfroy, sang "The Marseillaise". "The Maid of Athens" was sung in response to a toast to "The commercial and agricultural interests". Toasts of ever diminishing relevance begat songs equally inapt, it was an evening of bevying and boisterousness, the only two sober people present being Robert Stout, who had never imbibed, and William Larnach, a recent abstainer, who was advocating the building of inebriates' asylums in large towns with all the fervour of the newly converted. At the end of the festivities a final round of applause went to the exhausted musicians, Mr Gossens (piano), Mr Linn (cornet) and Mr Sargison (violin).

Two nights later, a packed audience filled the Duke of Edinburgh Theatre where "the front row of the Dress Circle was fairly sprinkled with ladies."[4] Robert Stout and Larnach both addressed the crowd, affirming all the assistance they hoped to be able to give the mining industry. Stout, never one to grapple with realities, spoke on the importance of studying politics, from primitive man to the Plantagenets to politics of the day. "Young men," he preached, not noticing the glaze of boredom masking the eyes of his audience, "would then enjoy a great intellectual repast."[5] Polite applause followed, then Larnach, with tongue in cheek, extoled the virtues of Sir Julius Vogel, assuring his audience that in spite of the accusations of some vicious writers, Sir Julius really had the welfare of the country at heart. To work with the Hon. Robert Stout and Sir Julius Vogel was most satisfying, and he wanted everybody to know there was not a member of the Government who wanted anything but the welfare and progress of the colony. Unable to forgive Stout entirely for removing him from the Waimea Plains Railway Company, Larnach couldn't resist a small dig, and it wouldn't be the last time he would do so. He ended his speech disagreeing with the premier about Stout's rejection of the need for a Hokitika-

Grey railway. Larnach felt Hokitika needed a railway to bring commerce to their port. This of course endeared him to the audience, brought light to their eyes, and the meeting finished with great cheering.

Wakamarina Gorge near Nelson about 1890. Miners using massive steam-driven pumping gear expose the river bed below a timber dam.

The next port of call was the isolated town of Collingwood at the remotest end of Golden Bay. The party left Hokitika by steamer for Nelson, Robert Stout went on to Wellington, and the others, through the kindness of Mr John Kerr in offering his steam launch, *Tainui*, were conveyed to Collingwood. This far-flung community, with an abundance of metals, had no roads, not even to Takaka, and no deep water anchorage, pack horses being the only means of getting products to the markets. Larnach spent three days visiting huge deposits of iron ore at Parapara, then travelled up the Parapara Creek to a sluicing claim at Glengyle, where hospitable miners produced homemade currant cake and tea. A silver mine at Richmond Hill, and finally the Collingwood Coal Company's mine at Ferntown completed the tour, but not before the usual requests unrelated to mining were aired.

Saddle horses were arranged for the party to ride back the 135 km to Nelson, on the way crossing over the Takaka hill, which even today is a many corkscrew-cornered road carved into the marble mountain. If the ministerial party thought the going rough so far, there was much more to come in Canterbury. But on arrival at Christchurch, they found a delay was necessary to arrange an expedition to the Wilberforce River to visit reefs so far into the Southern Alps that Hokitika was only 35 km away as the crow flies. Rather than waste time waiting, Larnach took off for Otago, where he was reported by the *Otago Daily Times* as "flying meteor-like over the Otago mines."

The tour party of the Otago goldfields consisted of Larnach's secretary, some directors of the various mining companies, reporters and Mr Vincent Pyke, the member for Dunstan, a man with a strong objection to the appointment of Larnach as Minister of Mines, as he had been led to believe the position would be his. Pyke, thoroughly conversant with the minefields, joined the tour party at his own expense. He gave the impression that he would be a "wet nurse" to Larnach on the tour, and hoped to show the Government what a capable fellow they had overlooked. He was unaware that Larnach had already immersed himself in the mysteries of mining and was fully conversant with Gilbert and Sullivan sounding words of matters metalliferous, carboniferous and auriferous. He had also absorbed details of mineralogy and geology, of head and tail races, extended claims, mining leases and miners' rights, so Mr Pyke found himself swept along in Larnach's shadow on a tour of triumph never before seen on the Otago goldfields. Normally a genial man, Mr Pyke was not pleased. He was later to tell the House,

> In the most kindly manner I gave up three weeks of my time to "coach" the Minister through the goldfields. I paid for my own expenses for everything I ate, drank and used, to the utmost far-thing. The Minister was not courteous to me; on the contrary he sent me a claim for 15/- as my share of his wine bill, though I never saw a glass of wine on his table except when he entertained some of his friends at Invercargill.[6]

On a wet, bitterly cold windy day, the ministerial party rode up a steep, slippery road over the hills to Waipori, 27 km from Lawrence, the first stop on their tour. Though they were vastly fewer in numbers than in the great rush of 1862, the depressing little semi-deserted, corrugated-iron town, battered by the harsh elements of twenty years, housed enough enterprising gold miners to warrant a visit from the minister. As had been the pattern at every place he visited, a deputation waited upon him with requests. Had all been granted, the Government's deficit would indeed have been large. One man requested 27 km of railway at Government expense to open up a private mine, another that a water race he had almost finished be at public expense.

Next the party descended into the workings at Gabriel's Gully and saw the enormous hydraulic force in operation there. From there they travelled to Invercargill, by train to Kingston, and by steamer to Queenstown, arriving at eleven o'clock on a wet night in a strong westerly wind. The best accommodation had been taken over by brass bands from Cromwell, Invercargill and Arrowtown, in town for their annual band contest, so the jaded tour party had to rough it in fairly cramped quarters. The next morning, in even worse conditions, the party, with the exception of Mr Pyke, took off on horseback in driving rain for Skippers and the Shotover area. The road to Skippers was far from completed and the mayor, who commandeered the minister's ear on the steep climb, lost no opportunity to place its completion high on the agenda of requests, coupled with the planting of forests, the mail service, the telephonic communication between Queenstown and Glenorchy, and the construction of tracks to outlying diggings.

It was the miners themselves that Larnach enjoyed meeting, and one who greatly impressed him was a man who had mined at Skippers for twenty years.

> He was a most enterprising fellow, had taken everything there on pack horses, and now carries on his work in a most systematic manner, sluicing away some 60 feet [18 m] on the banks of the Shotover River. He has immense water power . . . teaching himself blacksmith's work, making his own water pipes from plates that have been pack-horsed in. He employs six to ten men, and pays them handsomely. . . . He has only an acre of freehold, but he manages to grow sufficient vegetables for his own use. He has built a very fine house, and is raising a very nice family. [7]

A visit to the Arrow fields followed, then the party zig-zagged over the Crown Range to Cardrona and on to Pembroke (Wanaka), before heading back to Cromwell. There, the visit of a minister of the Crown was a rarity, and the mayor and councillors with great alacrity opened fire with a volley of more requests. The dangerous condition of the Cromwell Bridge was pointed out, along with the need for a house for the gaol warden, and the building of a new post office — all subjects the minister adroitly evaded as not being his department, but promised to pass the information on to the appropriate authorities. The *Cromwell Argus* reported that "The miners and others have discovered that the newly created Minister of Mines is not a square peg in a round hole, he showed a large knowledge of mining matters." [8]

174

The party travelled by coach through the Cromwell Gorge to Clyde, along the perilously narrow road hewn out of rock above the mighty Clutha River. Little stones edged the rim of the road like piped icing on a cake, and would be about as much use should the horses take fright at the constant danger of falling rocks from the slopes above. Larnach was indefatigable in visiting every mine possible; Clyde, Ophir, St Bathans, Naseby and others, then back to Lawrence. More requests were noted and promises made. The *Otago Daily Times* likened Larnach to an overladen beast of burden bowed down with information and promises. There had not been any official inspection of mines since the abolition of the post of goldfields secretary in 1867; previous governments had been content to allow the goldfields to be administered by under-secretaries. But now Larnach was raising mining to the status of other portfolios, and the *Cromwell Argus* and *Lyttelton Times*, both of which had strongly denounced Larnach's appointment just three months ago, were having to eat their words.

* * *

Three weeks later, back in Christchurch, all was in readiness to continue the expedition to visit the mines in the high country of Canterbury. The retinue comprised some of the directors of the twenty-three companies involved in the Wilberforce reef, who were looking forward to a jaunt in the mountains. Others were the mayor of Christchurch; shareholders; reporters; the inspector of mines, Mr Binns; and mine host of the Commercial Hotel, Mr C.F. Warner — a substantial shareholder who had organised the provisions for this ministerial picnic. To Larnach and the inspector of mines this was to be a continuation of the six weeks hard work they had already undertaken in Westland and Otago, but to the rest of the party this was a novel undertaking, as gold had not been found in Canterbury until the newly discovered Wilberforce reef some months pre-viously, and gold fever was a new malady for Cantabrians.

The first leg of the journey was by train to Springfield, enlivened by the wit and entertaining anecdotes of Mr Warner. Then a coach was taken over the rather rough and steep Porters Pass road. It took about four hours to reach Lake Coleridge Station, where they were hospitably entertained. The next morning the mirth which had been so evident the previous day soon disappeared in the closely packed coach, where, in addition to cramps and stiffness, queasiness overtook the passengers. The road was described as "nothing that need frighten the nerves of an elderly lady in the habit of taking pony carriage exercise, except for two steep cuttings, and imaginary terrors are reduced almost to nothing with a good brake on the wheel and a skillful hand on the ribbons."[9] No one was sorry when a hut was reached 13 km beyond the Harper River, and after a meal which did credit to Mr Warner, everyone turned in. The hut had only two bunks, so for most of the party it was a long uncomfortable night. Very audible snoring disturbed everyone except the offender, the Hon. Minister of Mines.

Now began the more difficult part of the journey. The Harper River had to be crossed by going downstream, in what seemed an interminable waste of big boulders and small tributaries. The heavy, well-laden coach bumped, wound and splashed its way to the woolshed of Glenthorne station, where feeding and rest for the horses took nearly four hours. Another night was spent in an equally uncomfortable hut, and the next morning, light Yankee wagons conveyed the minister and pleasure seekers across the river and onto a tussock-clad flat. After a further 19 km of boulder-strewn river bed crossings, and high ridges that gave expansive views of mountain ranges, the party reached the North Creek Company's huts about midday.

After lunch, the party set out on foot to climb to the tunnel being blasted out of the hard rock by six men. This tunnel was 1113 m above sea level. They then climbed another 183 m to the highest outcrop on the snow line. The evening was becoming chilly, and after they had admired the view, a race down to the gully began. One reporter wrote, "the Hon. Minister of Mines astonishes his companions, indeed he is in splendid fettle, both in nerve, wind and limb, and is generally among the first to accomplish a long climb. No one seeing him would credit him with fifty years which, in a half proud, half regretful tone, he claims to have spent in the world."[10]

Next morning, because of a shortage of horses, only Larnach, Mr Binns and a guide set off for the pass at the head of the Wilberforce to the Browning's Pass reef. Three men, Messrs Pullar, Lockwood and King, had lived there for a year since Mr Pullar discovered the reef. In spite of a hard frost, which was then thawing, Mr Pullar took them on a bridle track which had been formed in the loose-moving shingle that covered the passable side of the gully and ascended about a thousand feet until the traveller could land on the glacier. This was slippery but not steep, which made the ascent easier. Three hundred metres further on, the gully with the reef was pointed out to them, cropping out some 330 m above. This gully was also filled with a small glacier, down which there was a continuous rattle of small stones. Only experienced climbers went beyond this point .

Mr Pullar explained how three tonnes of auriferous quartz were obtained there, under enormous difficulties. The two men working the reef had to begin their day with a rough climb of 914 m. Then, surrounded by ice and up to their knees in water, they blasted three tonnes of quartz, packed it into bags, and sent the bags sliding down the glacier at a great rate; the men had previously removed from the glacier large boulders or stones that could tear the bags. At the foot of the glacier, the quartz was packed down the bridle track of the continually moving shingle slip, back to the Browning's Pass camp. The proposition to the Minister of Mines was that the reef would be much more accessible if a well-graded road was put in from Hokitika, only 37 km away. All this was carefully noted down for future reference. It was late in the evening before the party returned to base camp, and two more days with other mines to inspect before they would be back in Christchurch.

So ended Larnach's first tour as Minister of Mines, and he returned home to set out a complete record of mining operations in the colony, confident that mining would be of great benefit to the country. He considered the quality of West Coast coal, used so extensively for steamships and trains, to outclass coal from Newcastle.

There can be no doubt that there is an enormous store of wealth in the minerals of New Zealand. The agricultural and pastoral interests I do not wish to detract from . . . the value of them is enormous to the country . . . but it is the mineral product, the development of which will cause this country to stand in a fore-most position in this respect in Australasia. [11]

In 1886 Larnach introduced a mining bill which was a consolidation of six-teen other measures and met with the approval of the House, with the exception of Richard Seddon. His criticism was that it would confuse the miners, who were used to working under the old 1877 Act. In spite of his objections, the bill was passed and was hailed as a progressive piece of leg-islation. Larnach advocated reducing miners' licence fees from £1 to 5s., strongly criticised the threat to human life caused by the laxity with which the supervision of mine safety had been conducted, and wanted improve-ments to the Hokitika and Greymouth harbours. In spite of his own inter-est in the Westport Coal Company, which he had promoted so assiduously in Australia, he also recommended strategies that would lessen monopolies of mining companies and shipping companies, in particular the Union Steamship Company, which had virtual control of all cargo from Westland. As well as establishing the mining schools, the University School of Mines established a three-year course qualifying men to go onto the minefields to instruct at the new schools. Another achievement was "The Handbook of New Zealand Mines", compiled under Larnach's direction, which supplied a mass of information dealing with every aspect of mining and a compre-hensive history of the industry. The book was used for study purposes up until the 1920s.

Chapter XVII

MISFORTUNES MULTIPLY

Towards the end of 1885, the full impact of the liquidation of Guthrie and Larnach was published. After clearing all debts, the company was able to pay shareholders 5s. per share. For Larnach this meant that from his £61,480 invested, he received only £3,074. With the inside information available to him, he could have minimised his losses by selling much earlier, but he felt a responsibility to the smaller shareholders and, like a captain of a sinking ship, chose to go down with it. Sir William Russell once said in the House, "There is possibly no man in New Zealand who is more above suspicion of doing a mean or dishonourable act." Walter Guthrie also took a heavy loss, although he had managed to sell 1700 shares earlier at a better price. Two years later, Walter Guthrie Ltd went bankrupt in Invercargill.

Bankruptcy was now a very real worry for Larnach. He arranged to borrow £15,000 on the strength of his Agricultural Company shares. He became meticulous about every penny, and writing to Douglas from Wellington he chided,

You have never acknowledged the cheque I sent you to pay the premiums on your life policy. . . . Now you can't be too particular in answering letters where money is concerned. Last Saturday I wrote to you and your Aunt, in your letter I sent you a cheque for £5. In your Aunt's letter I sent her a cheque for £3 for her and your sister's expenses coming up from Dunedin by Steamer, and your Aunt should have received this letter before she left Dunedin on Wednesday . . . unless the letter comes to hand I will put the matter in the hands of the police.

Although pushed for money, he still felt able to donate a building site for

179

the Masonic Hall at Portobello. But he could no longer keep the other children in Europe. "Get Donald and the girls ready to return to New Zealand without delay. I can no longer afford Germany," a worried Larnach wrote to his London agent, Petersen. To Colleen and Alice he warned, "on board ship is a fearful place for scandal. . . . Your governess may return with you, but it will not be necessary for Donald to bring any servants." For some unknown reason, Donald's wife and two children were to remain in England. Perhaps William still had not accepted Violet into the family.

After eight years in England, the arrival home of Donald, Colleen and Alice was not the happy reunion Larnach had expected. Kate and Douglas had settled back happily with Mary and their father, but Colleen and Alice, bored and discontented, disliked the isolation of the Peninsula and particularly resented Mary taking their mother's place. Their musical prowess was an improvement on Kate's, and in an old programme of a concert held at the Highcliff Drillshed, the two girls played piano duets. Colleen then gave a harp solo, while Alice played the violin. One item consisted of violin and harp played by the girls, the pianist being Mr E. Towsey, while his brother Mr F. Towsey sang. There are stories of Alice wishing to become a ballet dancer, and dancing on the top of the billard table to the amusement of her brothers and sisters. Although their father encouraged them to entertain their friends at The Camp, they found the place dull, and after a time Colleen and Alice left to live in Christchurch. For Mary, also, The Camp held little charm. She missed Eliza's company, was unpopular with the staff, and remaining at The Camp for long periods while William was in Wellington did not help her drinking problem.

The building of the ballroom had already started at The Camp before the arrival of Donald, Colleen and Alice. The ballroom was equipped with three fireplaces, a sprung floor, and windows recycled from the first Bank of Otago. It is often recounted that it was built for Kate's twenty-first birthday, although she was at that stage twenty-four, but it seems more likely to have been built for Colleen who was to come of age in October the following year, and was perhaps devised in the hope the children would enjoy The Camp more.

In March 1886, as an antidote to his worries, Larnach made another

*A group of friends at The Camp being entertained by Douglas Larnach, standing
at the back wearing a black hat, and Donald, with black hat askew.*

excursion to the West Coast, again accompanying Professor Black who was
visiting the mining towns on a lecture tour. This time, instead of going by
boat to Hokitika, the party travelled through the Haast Pass. So few travellers had been that way that the journey took on the aspect of an adven-
ture, and it highlights Larnach's love of a challenge coupled with a strong
streak of stubbornness in his intrepid nature. He was very enthusiastic
about the area and in later years he invited Sir William Clarke, who was
suffering from acute rheumatism, to come to New Zealand and join him in
an expedition on horseback to the Coast, saying he could "guarantee his
health would improve."

As well as the usual reporters and civil servants joining these tours, on
this trip Donald accompanied his father, after packing his saddle bags, to
the great amusement of a reporter, as if he were spending a weekend at an
English country house. He carried his Saville Row dress suit (the subject of
a large and acrimonious overdue bill from the London tailor to his father),
evening shirts, a bootjack, novels, boxes of cigars, eau de Cologne and

white gloves. He hadn't counted on the obstinacy of his father in travelling against all odds, which would be the ruination of his fine clothing.

The head of Lake Wanaka was reached by boat, and the party climbed to the summit of the Haast Pass on tracks that were "so steep and rough that the horses could barely scramble up."[1] After spending the night there, and breakfasting on anchovy toast and devilled kidneys, they descended the western side of the Pass, following an elusive track, where in some places they had to dismount and lead the horses down precipitous slopes. Eventually reaching the coast, they met people sluicing the sand for gold, who gave them the benefit of their experience in swimming horses across rivers. At the Clearwater River the ferryman was reluctant to take them across the flooded watercourse, but Larnach ignored his advice and, with Donald dutifully following him, attempted to cross, while Professor Black and Professor Mainwaring Brown[2] and the rest of the party prudently stayed behind. Such was the force of water that the horses were swept off their feet, and father and son, luckily both good horsemen, had to calm the horses and head them down river until reaching a bank, where with difficulty they regained their footing. They found themselves stranded on a shingle island between two fierce torrents, with horses that refused to budge. The marooned Minister of Mines and his elegantly attired son, tentless and strafed by sandflies, had to spend a miserable night on the island; monuments to perversity and derring-do. The rest of the party, cosy under canvas, kept sandflies at bay with liberal smearings of lard on hands and faces. They waited until the river went down next morning, then caught up with the stranded pair. In pouring rain, the party had trouble finding the track, and it was 9.30 p.m. before they reached the next shelter, wet, cold and hungry.

Writing to Sir Julius Von Haast, Larnach recounts the trip.

I have made a great ride through a large part of the West Coast. We rode through the Haast Pass to the junction of the Landsborough and Clarke [rivers] then down the Haast to the mouth, then to Jacksons Bay — very nearly got drowned in the Clearwater River . . . in fact it was in heavy flood, after a time we got out of the river safely, wet from head to toe. After leaving Jacksons Bay, I rode up the Coast to Ross, crossing the Haast at its mouth. I saw a great deal of the country, which before the present time is very little known, and I have a greater opinion of its mineral resources than ever I had before. I am now getting up a party of nearly 200 future miners equipped with government tools for them to use. . . . I hope the experience will bear fruit. I have instructed the Mines Department to send you, as the Agent General, the mining statement of the year.

The journey up the driftwood-strewn coast to Ross, which Larnach mentions with such nonchalance, was nearly 320 km, past Bruce Bay with the wonderful white egg-like stones, the seal colony at Gillespies Beach, and the white heron colony at Okarito. There were numerous hazardous river mouths to be crossed, the reckless gallops round rocky bluffs timed to each receding roller, one of which nearly swept a party member out to sea. At one stopping place the local policeman warned Larnach that unless a start was made before nine o'clock in the morning, Okarito would not be reached in daylight. Larnach obstinately procrastinated until ten, when the policeman uttered his final warning that the ride would be impossible. This determined Larnach to wait another half hour, after which he led the way at full gallop and reached Okarito in safety.

After their tour, the Hokitika paper contemplated that in the event of the present member of Parliament being called to the Legislative Council, Mr Donald Larnach junior could be a candidate for the Hokitika seat.

He is a well grounded scholar, fluent speaker, and has had a large commercial experience. Why should it not in deference to "the power that be" and in return for the favours received from the present Ministry return a "Cabinet Minister's Son?" Mr Larnach jnr. accompanied his father on the last trip through Westland and during the visit made himself very agreeable and took exceedingly well with the residents. [3]

183

But Donald Larnach, whose only commercial experience had been in squandering his father's money, had since departed for Auckland, where he was acting as associate to Mr Justice Ward, while he waited to be called to the Bar of the Inner Temple. To Petersen, Larnach wrote, "I hope you have been able to induce those Old Benchers at the Guild to call Donald, although absent from London. The chap worked hard at the Temple, and passed all his Examinations and because he failed to eat three dinners there, they have not as yet called him." [4] Donald was finally called to the Bar of the Inner Temple on 22 June 1887, and he returned to England and to Violet and his daughters. They then moved to Melbourne, where Donald practised law, reading in the chambers of the Hon. John Madden. A third daughter, Margaret Emily, was born in 1889.

*   *   *

Back in Wellington, politics were beginning to pall for Larnach.

> One must do something for a living and so, for the present, I am in Politics, but directly I can see a chance of throwing them aside, I will do so. . . . The worst of having to live here [Wellington] is a divided household, for the wife has generally to remain South to look after the place and I have to content myself with apartments while here. . . . I have not been South for five months. [5]

Larnach's opposition to many of Stout's political views was attracting attention from the press. While Stout wanted to stop the sale of Crown lands and substitute perpetual leasing, Larnach diametrically opposed, ridiculed and condemned the idea. He considered everything should be freehold. On the question of free, secular and compulsory education, of which Stout was a great supporter, Larnach pushed the view that the state was

> despotic when it says that children shall not be taught to read the Bible, or that it shall not be taught a religion. . . . The state ought

to insist that every child in the Colony shall be educated . . . and every sect should receive alike from the Government in capitation fees for every child educated. . . . The matter of religious instruction should be a matter left between parents and children and the State improperly interferes when it says that children shall not be taught religion in schools.[6]

Bishop Moran must have been puzzled but pleased by Larnach's new views, but the motive behind his reasoning was not a born-again religious zeal, but an economy in the price of education for the State by throwing the responsibility on the different sects to educate their children, with some Government help. Larnach's views were described as "sectarianism run mad", but nearly a century later they were put into practise.

Larnach still hankered after a title, and his vanity surfaces in his letter to Sir Julius Von Haast.

My Dear Doctor Von Haast. Pardon, I had written the above without thought, and before remembering that I ought to have written "My Dear Sir Julius," but then I write that title so often, in another direction, but now my dear friend let me first thank you for your kind and valuable letter of the 4th April. . . . I was exceedingly glad to learn of their bestowal upon you — I suppose there will be some little trifle of decoration left over for the Minister of Mines on so auspicious a year as the present one . . . I have been informed that the mining portion of your exhibits (at the Canterbury Museum) is looking very creditable. By the way, the latter only requires a portrait of the Minister of Mines to set off the whole collection. If I can find a photograph of the Gentleman, before the mail closes, I will send it to you.[7]

Sir Julius Von Haast was about to leave for London, and Larnach advised him to get in touch with Benjamin Petersen, "you will find him the best in London where to procure anything and everything." He also gave Sir Julius a letter of introduction to his Uncle Donald, and for the first time a hint of rancour between uncle and nephew appears. "He is a very wealthy man, and it would not hurt him if he spent a little of his money in entertaining you."

Even stronger antipathy to his uncle emerges in a letter to Larnach's recently widowed sister Amelia:

> I notice that your fond and liberal Uncle had paid you a visit. Is it possible that at his age, when he cannot be very long distant from his Grave, when he will be called to account for the Ways he has Profited on those whom he had a right to help, could he have had the audacity to make the proposal he did? I begin to have my doubts that anyone will prosper thereafter, who may have to rely on him in the future. Did he express the Slightest Sympathy or Sorrow for any of us or was his cry all miserly fault finding?[8]

Larnach was accusing his uncle of enriching himself and ruining Larnach's father, John Larnach, by buying John's valuable station properties in Australia during the depression when John was unable to pay the interest rates. These remarks were made in spite of the fact that until Uncle Donald died, he sent a regular allowance to a large circle of relatives. But it shows how cantankerous Larnach was becoming.

Mary Alleyne Larnach's death on 10 January 1887 was the next misfortune in Larnach's life. He writes,

> I have had my share of troubles. My last blow was the death of my dear little wife Mary. I find it terrible and her death came so sudden and unexpectedly upon me that I can hardly realise that she has gone from me. The poor little thing was suffering from a fibrous tumour in the Womb, and it was operated on in an attempt to remove it . . . but blood poisoning suddenly set in and quickly ran its deadly race.[9]

The funeral, attended by the Premier, Sir Robert Stout, was large. The coffin was borne by settlers from the Peninsula to the handsome family vault in the Northern Cemetery, where Mary was placed beside her half-sister Eliza. Apart from William, his youngest daughter Gladys was the only member of the family to really mourn Mary.

Having made his estate over to Mary in the marriage settlement of 1881, Larnach now found himself, upon her death, with no control of his own affairs. He was unable to collect any interest or rents on his investments, everything being in trust for his children. Because of the children's fear that Mary would inherit their father's money in the event of his death, she had informed them of the settlement, assuring them that they were the beneficiaries.

Within ten days of Mary's death, Larnach instructed his solicitors to prepare a deed of assignment from his children relinquishing their interests in his estate. Without revealing the contents, he got Kate, Douglas and Colleen (Alice and Gladys were not yet twenty-one) to sign the document. He had as a witness a Mr Kettle, and he called the children into the dining room at The Camp, and told them, "I want you to sign a paper giving me the power to collect the rent of The Camp during my lifetime, and it will be yours after." [10] (In an unsigned will among Larnach's papers his estate is left equally to his children.) He then travelled to Auckland, where Donald, not aware his father was in Auckland, was in the smoking room of the Northern Club when his father unexpectedly appeared. William appeared to be in a great hurry, complaining that he had been looking everywhere for Donald, and that he was in a hurry to get to Coromandel, with a cab waiting at the door. "I have brought a paper with me I wish you to sign. It is merely an authority to collect rents at The Camp." Donald then asked if he could read it. "I have already told you what it is about," replied his father, but Donald again said he would like to see it. His father became angry and said, "How dare you doubt me if I give you my word of honour." Donald then replied, "If you give me your word of honour, of course I believe you," and signed the deed, witnessed by a member of the club. He thought no more about it until after his father's death, when he became aware of the consequences of the deed they had all signed, a consequence their father had not anticipated. Neither had he anticipated the quarrels it would cause among the Larnach family.

Having obtained Donald's signature, Larnach now set off for the Coromandel. This time his favourite son Douglas was with him. Unlike Donald, Douglas was undemanding and caused no problems. He completely lacked the enterprising nature of his father, and in later years preferred to live in genteel poverty on the meagre income from shares his father had settled on him, rather than turn his hand to work, while all the time complaining of the hardships life had dealt him. But at that time, he pleased his father by choosing to remain at The Camp and manage it.

Their journey covered all the mines and townships of the Coromandel peninsula. At a gathering at the Royal Hotel, Thames, he told the miners to be self reliant, ". . . do not expect the industry to be nursed by Government money. A great deal depends upon yourselves. I will see no injustice is done to you . . . now boys it is a case of 'root hog or die'."[11] The miners took his advice, and he arranged for private English investors to finance the Coromandel claims, thereby doubling the mining population in twelve months.

In July 1887, the frail combination of the Stout-Vogel Government began to disintegrate and they were granted a dissolution. Larnach believed they would "come back to Parliament stronger", and he returned to Dunedin to fight strong competition from Mr T. Begg, who was contesting his seat. It became an acrimonious contest. Larnach attacked Begg for using his name "with the intention of disparaging it". He denied a number of allegations of misconduct, including using his position to secure a position for any relative, which he quite patently had done for a young cousin when, as Minister of Mines and Marine, he had been able to speed the granting of his cousin's Mate's Certificate and arrange an appointment for him as a second officer with the Union Steam Ship Company. The public's reaction showed in the polls: Larnach won, but only by six votes. He conceded his return was a vote for the Government rather than a personal one. The Government, however, was not re-elected, and in October Sir Harry Atkinson led a new ministry. Once more Larnach was simply an ordinary member. In recognition of his work as Minister of Mines, he was allowed to retain the title of "Honourable".

Chapter *XVIII*

NEW BEGINNINGS

By the middle of 1887, New Zealand was deep in recession. In Parliament, Larnach urged the Government to limit the high interest rates inflicted by the financial institutions. [1] He could see no solution to his own financial problems in New Zealand, and with no standing in Parliament and no wife to welcome him home to The Camp, he decided to leave the country for some time. With Colleen and Alice living in Christchurch, Kate preferring to spend most of her time in Wellington, and Douglas at The Camp, there was only nine-year-old Gladys to consider. Larnach contemplated going to South America, but finally settled for Melbourne, where he was well known and had the company of Donald's three children for Gladys. Obviously intending his absence to be temporary, he neither resigned from Parliament, nor made any arrangements to sell The Camp, but he did sell his shareholding in the Colonial Bank to finance his new ventures in Australia.

A succession of farewell dinners took place; the citizens of Dunedin held one at Watson's Hotel, and the residents of the Otago Peninsula at the Highcliffe Drillshed. On 18 August the members of the Legislature hosted a dinner at Bellamy's. After roast turkey, braised duck and olives, saddles of mutton, fillets of beef with Madeira sauce, quail on toast and nougat à la crème, Rhine wine jelly and diplomatique pudding, Colonel Fraser, Member of the House of Representatives for Thames, presented a spontaneous contribution from the Thames miners expressing their gratitude for the interest Larnach had taken in their district. Richard Seddon, on behalf of the Kumara miners, gave him an illuminated address with all the miners' signatures engraved on it. Larnach was deeply touched. "Nothing they [the miners] could have done could have given me more pleasure than a testimonial of this kind, something I can hand down to my family. . . . All I regret is this, that the originals of these signatures have been copied by the engraver . . . I would prefer the original manuscript with the original signatures that have been written by those horny hands I have so often shaken." Further praise was given to Larnach by the Hon. Mr G.F. Richardson, who said that "the style of his administration so struck the miners' imagination that, never mind who came after him, round the campfires on the mining fields for many years to come the talk would be of the good old days when Larnach was Minister of Mines."[2]

Larnach's departure for Australia was marred by information given to the *New Zealand Herald* by the member for the Bay of Islands, Mr R. Hobbs, who accused Larnach of being absent from the House and attending to his private affairs while still drawing an honorarium. Mr Hobbs was under the impression that Larnach had returned to Dunedin to arrange his departure for Australia, when, in fact, Larnach had been called home and detained until a "serious and dangerous operation was performed" on an un-named member of the family, presumably Douglas, as he was the only family member at The Camp at this time. As many members from both sides of the House sprang to Larnach's defence, deploring the "gross and scurrilous libel" printed in the *Herald*, it is clear that the Australian trip was organised before the House sat and so in Larnach's own time. Glowing tributes to Larnach's character echoed round the House. Sir Harry Atkinson stated, "I am sure that I am speaking the views of the House when I say that this House has perfect confidence in the integrity of the honourable gentleman." Wrath was showered on Mr Hobbs and the *Herald*, and deep consideration was given to bringing them both to the Bar for breach of privilege, but with practically the whole House on Larnach's side, and the ramifications of charging the guilty parties so complicated, it was decided to let the matter drop.

Mr Hobbs sent a telegram to Larnach: "Very sorry for my hasty remarks of yesterday. Made under misconception. Accept my regrets. Sorry to hear of your family troubles." Larnach replied, "Sir, whether on public or other grounds, your reference to my short absence was unfriendly, unmanly and contemptible; but reflecting that a shadow of delicacy has come over you, I accept your apology." Larnach sued the *Herald* for libel, seeking to recover £3,000. The case was heard before His Honour Mr Justice Richmond and a special jury. Sir Robert Stout and Mr P.A. Buckley acted for Larnach, Mr Gully and Mr Skerrett for the defendants. The jury returned a verdict for the plaintiff for £500 damages and £250 on each count.

The most worrying aspect of the *Herald* article to Larnach was that the Australian press might print it, which would blacken his name just when he was about to start up in business there, but he need not have worried; Larnach found a paucity of New Zealand news in the Australian papers, and on returning to New Zealand, proposed to the Government that a sum be provided for the telegraphing of important news to Australia, but the idea was not taken up.

In Melbourne, the office of Larnach and Pym opened at 333 Collins Street West. Montegue Pym, an auctioneer from Dunedin, was Sir Julius Vogel's brother-in-law. The firm dabbled in stocks and shares, but concentrated mainly on land speculation. "The whole secret of floating a property," Larnach advised Pym, "is firstly, not to be too greedy by asking too large a sum for it. Secondly, show your confidence in the venture by agreeing to take one half or a third interest in shares, and thirdly, have full particulars and details lawfully prepared, *concise, clear, and to the point* so that enquiries may be met by the promoters *consistently* on every question without any show of equivocation or evasion." [3]

Larnach also became co-director with Messrs Runting and Wright in another Melbourne land company, the Royal Standard Investment Company, in which he invested heavily. But within six months he was back in New Zealand, shattered by a scandal in the Royal Standard Company. Although Larnach had no part in this scandal, it sent him into deep depression.

Larnach had only just arrived in Melbourne, when the first public meeting of shareholders of the Royal Standard Company took place. The unenviable task of revealing to the shareholders that they had been swindled was left to the only director free from blame, William Larnach. The *Melbourne Argus* reported on 7 January 1889, that

> a twentieth part of the company's money has gone to Messrs Runting and Wright in brokerage fees, even for shares yet unsold.

But this is the smallest item of the allegations brought against the directorate. The managing director Mr W.T. Runting admitted that the vendors of the properties bought on behalf of the company were mainly directors, except Mr Larnach. No sooner was the company duly formed, according to the outspoken testimony of Mr Larnach, who was in New Zealand when the company was formed, than the directors transferred to it large properties which they owned themselves, or in which they were directly interested, without consulting the shareholders. Mr Larnach asserts that on the very day after the company was registered, they purchased for the Company £330,000 worth of property owned by Messrs Runting and Wright, a substantial profit accompanying the transaction, it is said, of up to £50 per acre, thus relieving themselves of liabilities at a very handsome profit.

Six months after his return to New Zealand, Larnach wrote to Pym.

I feel very much better in health and spirits than I did when I returned from Melbourne last April. I think had I not returned when I did from the way I was constantly worrying and fretting myself about having been drawn into those land swindles by men whom I thought above reproach, I would not now be alive. No one will ever know what I suffered when I discovered what my co-Director had done with the Royal Standard's monies, and it was not for the money I had put in the concern, but for the position in which I found myself and so helpless to get out of it. Had I been a coward I would have committed suicide. [4]

Later he wrote to Pym,

I hope that William Clarke and Joseph are doing well, it is the old style of "out of sight out of mind" with them, as I never hear from any of them nowadays, but I suppose I will get over that as I have got over greater cases of Extremes in human ventures and habits before this. . . . Had I not left Victoria when I did, I believe that I would really have been dead long ago for the troubles that I was suffering mentally and the very sense of wrong I felt was killing me.[5]

Larnach had left Pym in charge of their business in Melbourne, but it was not long before breaches appeared in the relationship. Pym, without advising Larnach, put a notice in the *Melbourne Argus* in January 1890 of the "dissolution by mutual agreement of Larnach and Pym." Larnach was annoyed at not being consulted, but the two men finally parted amicably.

Troubles had followed Larnach back to New Zealand with a vengeance. Melancholia, misjudgments and misfortunes all jostled to undermine his sanity. The Agricultural Company was wound up in 1890, although the last of its land was not sold until 1909. Larnach, who still held debentures in the company, wrote anxiously to Petersen: "I am sending you an order to get all my Debentures from the Bank, I think I still hold £1100 pounds. Kindly get them and take whatever steps that may be necessary to protect me in connection with Liquidators."

Sir Julius Vogel, then back in London, had just published a novel *Anno Domini 2000; or, Woman's Destiny*. In the novel he reveals a utopian dream of draining the Clutha River dry, and exposing rich deposits of gold on Agricultural Company land; he shares the spoils with Sir Central Vincent Stout, "a young though very able lawyer", and Lord Larnach, "one of the wealthiest private bankers in the Empire", the two characters based on Robert Stout and William Larnach. In real life, however, Sir Julius Vogel eked out his last years in relative poverty. He died in 1899, and the huge commissions for Larnach and Vogel from the Agricultural Company never eventuated.

Having fled the Melbourne swindlers in April, seven months later Larnach was the innocent victim of another swindle. He was called on to front up with money on land that the Bank of New Zealand and the New Zealand Loan and Mercantile claimed Larnach owed them. Back in 1878, on the eve of his departure for England, he had been persuaded against his better judgment by the manager of the Bank of New Zealand, Mr Roberts (later suspended from the bank and from any control of the loan company), to put his name down as a shareholder on land at Hakataramea which Larnach was unaware Roberts was fraudulently representing. Roberts had persuaded Larnach to give him, Roberts, his power of attorney in connection with the property. While Larnach was in England he was ignorant of the fact that the devious Mr Roberts was buying more shares in Larnach's name by transferring Larnach's deeds of land at Palmerston and Caversham, held by the bank, to the N.Z. Loan and Mercantile Company. At the time of Roberts's downfall, Larnach was assured by the loan company that his investment was more than paying its way, and "under the worst aspect of things, the two parcels of land were to be in full satisfaction in connection with any liability . . . at that time I would have taken proceedings against Roberts but as he had been suspended from the Bank and Loan Company, I did not wish to make his troubles worse." [6] By 1890 the Loan Company had conveniently forgotten their assurances and there was nothing in writing. Larnach writes in a letter that, "With the fall in land values the company want to squeeze more money out of me." [7] It was to be another hard lesson for Larnach, who so often had placed too much faith in gentlemen's agreements.

The Loan Company's actions were symptomatic of the effect the two-month long Maritime Strike of 1890 was having on the country. After ten years of unemployment, falling wages and rapidly declining land prices, everyone was looking out for themselves and Larnach was caught in the crossfire. This caused him to write to his friend P.K. McCaughan of Melbourne:

I am now writing to ask you a small favour, and there is no use in beating about the bush in doing so. The fact is that the "Strike" has helped to deprive me of about £400 of my usual income from Coal Mines, through the actions of the Miners. The Westport Coal Company has been unable to pay my dividend since December last, and other companies in which I am interested are in a similar position, and it not only becomes hard on one, but very inconvenient as one's position won't wait for these Monies. Well the Great Northern Gold Mining Company of Victoria which our friend Joseph Clarke introduced me to . . . has suddenly gone into Liquidation and shareholders are called on to pay up balance of uncalled capital before 31st of next month. I believe my liability to be £253 7s. 5d. The amount is not a very large one unless to a person hard up, and no one knows better than you do what it is to be hard up . . . I need hardly assure you that it goes much against my grain to ask you or anyone to do this favour for me. I have also had to defend an Equity case brought against me and Brian Haggitt by Mrs Robertson, as Trustees in her husband's will. Over ten to twelve years, land values had fallen and she wanted us saddled with them — Judge gave them a swinging verdict as against her, although I fear we will get none of our money back again from her — about £320 each. Hard lines for doing a friendly turn![8]

In writing to his daughter Alice, in October 1890, who was then staying in Melbourne with Donald, Larnach describes how "the strikes are playing old Harry with everything and it will take this colony a long time to recover. . . . And so you want to teach Music about Melbourne. My dear Chook, I hardly know what to say about it. I think it would be wrong of me to prevent any-one of you earning Money, but it appears to me a difficulty exists with you unless settled permanently in a place to take pupils and then rush off and leave them."

The strike was having an effect not only on Larnach's finances, but also his political future. He was tired of politics, and had decided not to stand at the next election, but "when one looks at the attitude of the working classes just now, it behoves everyone, with any interest in, and respect for the Country to stand by his gun and fight to the last. I am contesting my old seat and fighting against one or more Labour candidates."[9] At an election meeting at South Dunedin he aired his views: ". . . in some cases where peo-ple are downtrodden, and no other remedy is possible, a strike is perfectly legitimate . . . but they should be most prudent and guarded before taking such a step." Asked for his opinion as to whether employers should have boycotted a conference with the Maritime Union set up by the Government, he replied, ". . . as to the boycott, I say there is no excuse for that. It can only be done by the exercise of might, and those who have the might may not always be in the right — the minority may be in the right. I say that the boycott is of a savage nature, and not fair." [10]

When the question arose on votes for women, Larnach said he didn't believe women wanted the vote, but was happy for a referendum to be taken throughout the country, and if the vote was what they wanted, they should have it. Yet his thoughts about women entering the House were not so liberal: ". . . you all know that they have got many natural disabilities that would not fit them for that." [11]

Although Larnach classified himself as a Liberal, his charisma with his South Dunedin voters had disappeared in the aftermath of the strike, when loyalties were now to the party rather than the man. Larnach was thrust aside by William Earnshaw, the Labour candidate. He accepted his defeat graciously, saying he found no fault with anyone voting for Mr Earnshaw. Unlike his earlier triumphant meetings in South Dunedin, the crowd gave him a rough time, booing and hooting his every word. Mr Earnshaw told the crowd "the victory would have been greater had you given the defeated candidate a fair hearing." [12]

*　　*　　*

The prospect of marriage softened the disappointment of the election defeat. On 27 January 1891, Larnach married Constance de Bathe Brandon, daughter of Lucy and Alfred de Bathe Brandon of Wellington.

Back in 1840, Alfred de Bathe Brandon had arrived from London and set up practice as a lawyer in Wellington, despite some locals questioning his credentials. Ignoring the tittle-tattle of the small community, he founded the firm that is still in existence today. He entered Parliament in 1858 and remained there until 1881. Although twenty-four years older than Larnach,

Alfred de Bathe Brandon jnr, brother of Constance Larnach.

the two men developed a great friendship in Parliament, de Bathe Brandon being an exuberant man and a great prankster, something Larnach was partial to himself. Brandon was also connected with many substantial companies in Wellington, and took a great interest in education.

The de Bathe Brandon household, consisting of three sons and four daughters, was an unconventional one, and the daughters were given much more freedom than was generally the custom. The girls were well read, outspoken, opinionated, musical and a touch eccentric — one daughter, Annie, wore a bright orange wig all her adult life. While in Wellington Larnach had been a near neighbour of the family, and after Alfred de Bathe Brandon died in 1886, he continued to visit them frequently.

Constance, the eldest daughter, was by far the best looking. She was intelligent, charming, musical and petite, and was favoured with an attractive face full of character, with well spaced brown eyes, a straight nose and a mouth that had a certain firmness about it. It was not surprising that

Bridesmaids at the marriage of Alfred de Bathe Brandon.
Constance de Bathe Brandon is seated on the left.

Larnach fell in love with her. The wonder is that she, at thirty-five, fell in love with Larnach. At fifty-seven, time and worry had left its mark on him; middle-age had thickened his waistline and rounded his once slim face, which was now festooned with a droopy grey moustache. A Scotch bonnet hiding his grey balding head was almost a permanent fixture. A contemporary described him as "rubicund of visage and slightly horsey in attire."[13]

Could it be that the unusual de Bathe Brandon girls frightened off younger suitors? Constance was the only sister to marry. Her family were not without means, so marrying for money would not have been a consideration, and Larnach's financial setbacks had received plenty of publicity. Constance's brother, Alfred jnr, now senior partner in his father's law firm, had studied at Oxford, and been called to the Bar of the Inner Temple a few years earlier than Donald Larnach. Like Donald, he had returned to New Zealand convinced of his social superiority, and considered his sister's marriage to an ageing land speculator as beneath her dignity. Before the wedding,

William and Constance Larnach shortly after their marriage in 1891.
The initialled silver frames were made by Dunedin jeweller John Hislop.

Alfred asked Larnach what money he was going to settle on Constance. Larnach was taken aback; he was not going to be compromised financially again. He was happy that any property Constance had under her late father's will "should be hers to do as she liked with, that it would make her no less esteemed and respected by him had she not a cent, nor would he be less anxious to make her his wife if she only possessed a print dress." [14] He went on to say that he had not been asked to settle anything on his first wife, that he would look after Conny, as he called her, during her lifetime and in his will, but that was all he was prepared to do.

The wedding took place at St. Paul's Pro-cathedral. The bride, who was given away by her brother Alfred, wore a gown of cream satin, embossed with sprays of lily of the valley, fashioned at Kirkcaldie and Stains. Her tiny waist was cinched in by interlacing of fine cord, which was tightened across the back of the bodice to well below the waistline. Over this she wore a short fitted jacket with a mandarin collar and puffed sleeves. The straight skirt formed a small train at the back, which was held by her two nieces, and on her light brown hair, she wore a circlet of flowers. There was a large congregation present, but it was reported that no music was played in the church. After the ceremony, performed by the Rev. J.C. Andrew M.A., the guests returned to the Brandon home for afternoon tea before the honey-mooners left for the west coast of the North Island.

Larnach's pride in his new wife was evident, he took her everywhere with him. The happiness that had eluded William for so long now returned. To give the newly weds more time on their own, Gladys, now thirteen, was sent to board at Saint Dominic's College, Dunedin. Kate was nursing in Wellington, and Alice and Colleen drifted between Australia and New Zealand. They stayed with friends and relations, avoiding home as much as possible. This was a blessing for Conny, as they were as hostile to her as they had been to Mary Alleyne, and for the same reasons. Douglas remained at The Camp, and Donald, unable to support his family as a lawyer, blaming the depression in Melbourne, had applied to the Lord Mayor of Melbourne for the position of town clerk. His application, although backed up with references from his father's friends — including Sir Robert Stout, Sir W.J. Clarke, and managers from all Melbourne's major banks — was to no avail, and he still relied on his father's generosity. In fact, all the children depended on their father for income.

On his return from the honeymoon, Larnach bought a house at 45 Molesworth Street, Wellington. He was appointed chairman of a royal commission in Wellington to investigate the workings of the Public Trust Office, which had been in existence since 1872 and was now the subject of startling allegations of "active malpractice and passive neglect." The office was committed to the management of estates entrusted by wills, those dying intestate, and those with mental illness.

The commission's revelations were astounding. To begin with, the auditor general had certified the department's annual audit without any investigation, which would have revealed eighteen years of incompetency, corruption and criminal neglect. Little or no effort had been made to find next-of-kin; thousands of pounds which should have been distributed to beneficiaries had disappeared into the Consolidated Fund; and watches, jewellery and clothing coming into possession of the Public Trust was bought by the staff at vastly undervalued prices. Even the public trustee himself, Mr R.C. Hammerton, admitted acquiring watches and binoculars.

His chief clerk, the Rev. Charles de Castro, had a penchant for watches, rings and clothing, collected over many years, and argued that they were just trinkets and of little value. To minimise his own sins, de Castro told of taking watches to Sir Harry Atkinson, then prime minister, who was also eager for a bargain. Reluctantly de Castro admitted that anything valued at £20 they usually bought for £5 or £6, with the head of the office, Mr Hammerton, having first choice and the rest of the staff in order of hierarchy.

Summing up the findings, the commission found that the trustees had "displayed a total absence of capacity and knowledge of how estates should be managed." Larnach and the two other members of the commission, Mr Andrew Loughrey, a solicitor, and Mr. T.K. Macdonald, Member of the House of Representatives, were likened by a member of the House to the Spanish Inquisition, because they asked questions of the Public Trust officers that "bristled with brutality". But Larnach argued that the only evidence available to the commission had to be wrung out of the officers of the department, whose "conduct was not only improper and open to grave suspicion, but utterly indefensible and illegal." [15] No one was surprised that the Public Trustee had gone on an indefinitely extended leave of absence as a result of the inquiry, and was followed by the chief clerk and office solicitor.

The commission had lasted from 16 March to 22 June, sitting all day and often from 8 p.m. to midnight. For this service, the commissioners received £3 3s. per day.

Barely had the commission finished with their findings, when Kate, so cherished by her father, became seriously ill with typhoid. After five weeks, during which Larnach was filled with anxiety, Kate died on 24 July 1891. With resignation, he wrote to Petersen,

> . . . money and business troubles are not much to me so long as my health continues good and my heart large, which in that respect I have nothing to complain of. Family troubles knock me over more than anything, and I have had a big one to face and bear of late by the death of my dear good little daughter Kate . . . her death has been a great blow to us all, but God's will be done, I must bear it with good Grace. [16]

Kate Larnach photographed in London at the age of eighteen.

After Kate's death, Nurse J. Duggan wrote to Colleen,

Although I am a stranger to you, on several occasions when your
dear sister felt she could not get better she said to me, "Nurse, if I
die will you write to them at home, give them my love and tell
them to look after Father just the same as before he married". Dear
little girl, she was always thinking of him and no matter how ill she
felt, always greeted him with "I am better Father," her only desire
not to worry him, and her great anxiety was on his behalf for fear
he was not properly cared for . . . I said you are fond of your father
and her reply was, "I love him more than anyone else on the
earth." To me she became very dear indeed, and I can never forget
her utter selflessness and thoughtfulness. [17]

Kate's coffin was borne through the streets of Wellington, followed by
friends and members of the Legislature, to the Government steamer S.S.
Hinemoa, where William and Conny boarded the ship for the voyage to

Dunedin. Kate was buried in the family mausoleum beside her mother and aunt in the North Dunedin cemetery.

Conny's arrival at The Camp should have been a triumphant moment for William, as he showed his bride the home that was his pride and joy, introduced her to his Dunedin friends and looked forward to the prospect of their years together. Instead, the place was once more plunged in gloom. Kate had been popular with the staff. And Gladys, desolated by the third death of close family in her young life, left boarding school for several months and returned to The Camp to seek solace from her father. William explained "It is best I take to look at things in a philosophical manner . . . grumbling and fretting over them will not cure them, nor make us any happier, and people should always bear in mind this, that no matter how great the troubles of some are, there are others in this world suffering greater troubles." Yet it was to be several months before Larnach could bear to resume normal life again.

One of the first things he did was write to the prioress of the Dominican Convent, Sister M. Gabriel, deducting fees for the time Gladys had missed at school and asking that the charges for "Pinafores, Harp, Drawing and Painting and Sundries" be modified. He also warned that if Gladys did not make progress, he would give one month's notice before withdrawing her.

Larnach began to make some extraordinary decisions. He sold his valuable Kaitangita Coal Company shares for half their value, then bought shares in the Colonial Bank, becoming the largest shareholder of a bank already showing signs of difficulties. He seemed unable to keep away from the gamble of land speculation, and had now involved his brother-in-law, Alfred de Bathe Brandon, with himself in land at Tai Tapu, in which "they would double their money within a year", and which his brother George, in Sydney, was trying to sell for them.

At The Camp the most cheerful thing to happen since Kate's death ten months earlier was another wedding, that of Alice to a young solicitor, Mr William Francis Inder of Naseby. It was a small wedding, celebrated at The Camp by the Rev. Dr Stuart. It was May, and the cold weather was not

Alice Larnach about the time of her marriage to Walter Inder.

suitable for chiffon. The bride wore white serge trimmed with white fur, while Colleen and Gladys, the bridesmaids, kept warm in dresses of cream serge trimmed with beaver. Alice and her husband left to live in Naseby, and Larnach's relations with his children started to deteriorate rapidly.

His generosity to his children had been returned with selfishness and a belief that he should continue to provide for them perpetually, but slowly he was retaliating. In a letter to Donald he makes his intentions clear:

The perusal of your insolent and insulting letters left no doubt in my mind as to the course that I should take in the future in regard to you and your family, and that is to have nothing further to do with you. My treatment of you has been "brutal" has it? I suppose it was so when I sent you to England to make a good man of you? I suppose it was and has been all these years since, of struggling to keep you going? . . . I am done with you, I don't wish to know you or have any further communication with you. You may hold your present allowance until the end of January next, when it will be cancelled. [18]

His words belied his actions however. He created a trust for Violet and his three granddaughters, and continued to support Donald for another two years until Larnach's own difficulties rather than personal feelings put an end to the allowance. Donald was then finally forced to live on the many investments his father had already put in his name.

Colleen and Alice also felt the bitterness in his tone when Colleen wrote asking for money.

> Since you and Alice returned from England you have simply made use of me in every possible way. . . . No father could have been kinder or more indulgent to his children — too much so — and I have a fine example of the gratitude of some of you — pray what have you done with the share moneys which you took away from my keeping and control after you left home? . . . I cannot understand you requiring a promise from me that if you come home you will be treated fairly. If anyone has been treating you improperly when you have been home it is Miss Colleen Larnach herself, who for the last three years has been acting like a foolish child . . . and her sister Alice is no better . . . we will all be glad to have you home and it will rest with yourself to treat yourself as kindly as possible by acting wisely in future. P.S. I enclose two dividend documents. You will be required to write your name on the back. [19]

The postscript is again evidence of his soft heart.

In endeavouring to provide his children with every advantage, all Larnach had achieved were two indolent sons, who felt they were above earning a living. And his elder daughters, regardless of their father's happiness, were so concerned that Conny might inherit their father's money, they were incapable of friendly relations with her.

Chapter XIX

THE COLONIAL BANK

The Premier, John Ballance, died in the middle of 1893, and Richard Seddon, with the backing of Sir George Grey, was sworn in as prime minister of the colony. Joseph Ward became Colonial Treasurer, Minister of Customs, Postmaster General, Minister of Marine, Minister of Trade and Customs, and in the new year, minister of the newly created portfolio of Industries and Commerce. Described as "that heaven-born treasurer"[1] he was fêted where ever he went. But another title about to be added after his name was "Bankrupt". Ward, originally a successful businessman from Bluff, was heavily in debt to the Colonial Bank, a fact this now nationally prominent figure successfully concealed at the general election at the end of 1893.

Seddon, with many unreliable members in his party, needed a man whose friendship he could trust. Larnach was that man, and although reluctant to re-enter politics, Larnach was persuaded by Seddon to contest the Wakatipu seat. He polled badly, getting only 831 votes to Mr W. Fraser's 1191. He blamed his defeat on the editor of the *Wakatipu Mail*, who printed "letters containing unblushing falsehoods in reference to me and which I had no opportunity of denying before the poll took place."[2] But the real reason was that over the previous three years, he had changed his views on education policy. Previously he had suggested giving state aid to Catholic schools, but now, finding so many denominations clamouring for aid, he feared it would break down the national education system. In changing his mind, Larnach lost the Catholic vote.

His return to Parliament was only delayed a short time. A few months later, Vincent Pyke — whom Larnach had offended on his mining tour — died, leaving the Tuapeka seat vacant. Having lost two seats already, and with his recent appointment as a director of the rapidly declining Colonial

Bank, Larnach was not interested in standing a third time; but early in June the first of many telegrams arrived from Richard Seddon:

> I have received telegram from Mr R. Pyke [Vincent's son] in which he informs me that if you contest the Tuapeka seat that it will be in Government interest. I need scarcely say we are all very pleased indeed to hear the good news. Personally I should have been very much surprised and disappointed had it been otherwise, for I felt sure at the interview we had when I was enjoying your hospitality, the cobwebs of doubt were removed. My only regret being that we had not compared notes before the last General Election. The Hon. Mr Ward left by Steamer this afternoon for Oamaru and will be in Dunedin on Saturday. Kindly meet him when there and talk matters over. In the meantime I am doing my best to ascertain the wishes of the supporters of the Liberal Party in the Tuapeka district. It will be gratifying to you to know that so far as at present ascertained, the opinion of our supporters dominates in your favour. Kind regards to Mrs Larnach and yourself, R.J. Seddon. Wellington. [3]

Larnach telegraphed back,

> My friends should never have doubted my allegiance to the Party, which has remained firm since entering political warfare in 1875. If I can see my way to run will be in interests of Government, they would have my unflinching general support, am hesitating to declare for a few days to learn what measure support am likely to receive, am also planning how I can leave Dunedin and Home at present time, having many important matters requiring my attention personally. Am anxious to serve you and Government otherwise am not desirous for political warfare or to leave comfortable Home. Wire Ward I cannot be Dunedin tomorrow, but will be pleased to see him if he drives down here. [4]

Ward had only one day in Dunedin, and it was over an hour's journey from Dunedin to The Camp. Larnach's declining to meet Ward in Dunedin suggests a strained relationship between the two men. Larnach had become a director of the Colonial Bank two months earlier, and since then, the bank was threatening to stop payment on Ward's Farmers' Association cheques and urging the association to take its business elsewhere. [5] At this stage not even Seddon was aware of Ward's true financial difficulties, but soon the three men would be conspirators on a course of concealment.

However, Ward did not go to The Camp that day to talk finance, only to persuade. He was a courteous man with an easy charm, and obviously swayed Larnach to the Government's advantage, telling him that many farmers in the Tuapeka district whose vote his opponent, the aristocratic runholder Scobie Mackenzie, was dependent on were declaring in favour of Larnach. Playing on Larnach's vanity, he revealed that a large proportion of women would also support him.

Ward's visit resulted in Larnach telegraphing Seddon, "I will announce myself this afternoon although at great personal sacrifice and inconvenience. Shall do my best and relying on you and your colleagues utmost assistance have confidence in making good run." To Ward he telegraphed, "I am running this election for you," again stressing how inconvenient it was. But Seddon's reply must have raised his hopes that eventually he might receive the recognition he had always yearned for, a knighthood.

Your consenting to contest the Tuapeka seat gives my colleagues and myself very great pleasure indeed and you may rely upon one and all of us rendering you every assistance. You may further rest assured the great personal sacrifice and inconvenience which I know is entailed shall not go unacknowledged. I am not ungrateful old friend and in contesting the Tuapeka seat you have placed another good turn to your credit. . . . Good luck old friend. [6]

Seddon had always used favours, threats, cajolery and good fellowship to enlist his friends, and Larnach was fooled into believing him.

Encouraging telegrams arrived daily from Seddon, "The ball is at your feet, leave no stone unturned and your return is certain . . . the ammunition required duly prepared and will be sent first thing in the morning." (The ammunition referred to were innuendos that Larnach could use against his opponent Mr Scobie Mackenzie.) "When you were Minister of Mines the Goldfields were even better attended to, and your Mining Act of 1886 was the most perfect mining legislation ever passed . . . shoulder to shoulder we have fought in the past and together I sincerely hope we shall in the future be found doing our duty to New Zealand and in the old digging parlance and nothing is more expressive I wish you good luck . . . go on and prosper old friend." Ward also sent a nine-page telegram of encouragement.

Larnach narrowly won the seat from Scobie Mackenzie by fifty-four votes. It had been a bitter fight, with the two men exchanging accusations of equal vehemence. Seddon was delighted. "I assure you old friend that nothing will give myself and the Hon. Mr Ward greater pleasure than introducing you once again to Sir Maurice O'Rorke [the Speaker]. I hope Mrs Larnach has quite recovered from the effects of the election. By this time she will be able to write a book. I am looking forward with pleasure to hear her recount the experiences of the late contest." [7] The late Vincent Pyke's son also graciously conveyed his congratulations "on your being elected my father's successor." During his return from Lawrence after the contest, the new member for Tuapeka's euphoria at winning was dampened when the carriage overturned fording a swollen stream and he and Conny were tossed into the water, escaping wet but unharmed.

Exactly ten days after Ward's visit to Larnach, the Colonial Treasurer was faced with the alarming fact that the Bank of New Zealand was on the verge of bankruptcy, from which only the Government could save it. Both Ward and Seddon realised the gravity of the situation; it was Friday and the bank doubted it could open its doors on Monday without assistance. That afternoon a bill was drafted, and Ward, apprehensive enough about his own shaky finances, piloted it through the House. Finally at 4 a.m. on Saturday morning, the Bill was passed with the Governor waiting in readiness to give his assent. The Bill gave a state guarantee for a new share issue of £2 million. In return the bank's affairs were to be investigated by a parliamentary committee and the Government was given power to appoint the bank's president and auditor.[8] The bank retained the Government account and with a sigh of relief opened its doors on Monday morning, its trading role unchanged.

The Government had now became responsible for the liabilities, but when things improved, the shareholders would reap the profits. Larnach was critical of the report produced by the investigating committee:

If they had had the technical expert knowledge I think was necessary on a committee of that kind, they should . . . have had a glance at the one book which is the key of the whole business of the bank: I refer to the general ledger . . . the assets I allude to particularly are those under advances due to the bank . . . if the general ledger was shown to me I should be in a better position to say whether they were genuine or not.[9]

Events the next year would prove how right Larnach was in his criticism, and apparently his words were heeded.

Ward had praise heaped on him by the public for his quick action in avoiding disaster, but his idea of cheap loans from private banks for those wishing to settle on the land was now out of the question. It was Larnach he turned to for advice. In discussions before what would be called the Advances to Settlers Act was put to Parliament, Larnach convinced Ward that he could float a loan in London, at the cheap rate necessary to finance the scheme. He gave him a letter of introduction to Uncle Donald, and Ward went to London the following year, where to everyone's surprise the loan of £1.5 million at three per cent was over-subscribed, a total of £5.9 million being offered. It was later said that the Advances to Settlers Act was as important to New Zealand as Disraeli's purchase of Suez Canal shares had been to Britain.[10] It was the forerunner of what in 1913 would be called the State Advances Office. Ward never acknowledged Larnach's contribution, keeping the praise for himself, though Seddon did acknowledge it on Larnach's death. Seddon was not a man of original ideas,[11] and over the next four years Seddon bled Larnach's brains for financial advice, but the reward of any recognition for his help never eventuated.

Ward's triumph after his return from England with the over-subscribed loan was short-lived. Further unsound investments had been found which had been concealed by the Bank of New Zealand when the rushed band-aid had been applied twelve months earlier. With the approval of both sides of the House, the Government made available another £3 million on top of the £2 million already given, to shore up the tottering Bank of New Zealand. An Act was passed empowering the Bank to buy out the Colonial Bank, taking away the Colonial Bank's freedom to negotiate a merger between the two banks that had been underway since September 1894. Agreement had not been reached at that point, as both banks had liabilities to be worked out.

The reasons for the merger went back to the time when the Bank of New Zealand was given all Government business. The Colonial Bank had also tried to obtain a share of the Government account but was unsuccessful, so rather than be at a disadvantage to the Bank of New Zealand, it preferred to merge with it. The Bank of New Zealand was to buy out the Colonial Bank and by absorbing the Colonial Bank, the Bank of New Zealand would gain assets and be relieved of competition. However, when the Government stepped in and passed the Act, revelations of Ward's debt although only known to the two banks and kept highly secret, put the Bank of New Zealand in a powerful position to buy only the sound accounts of the Colonial, leaving it with all the doubtful and bad accounts, which included Ward's £89,382 debt.

The purchase of the Colonial Bank was carried out on 18 November 1895, and the bank handed over its books and cash that night. To his credit, Larnach took no part in the Bank of New Zealand crisis and stayed away from Parliament while the Act was being debated, but he was very against the compulsory merger, saying it put "directors [of the Colonial Bank] who are guarding shareholders interests . . . in an invidious and ridiculous position."[12]

News of Joseph Ward's dubious finances with the Colonial Bank, which terminally weakened the bank, [13] were surfacing in its negotiations with the Bank of New Zealand. In spite of the strictest confidentiality kept by both banks, who feared a run on the Colonial Bank should Ward's liability be revealed, speculation was growing and embarrassing questions were being asked by the Opposition. When the Bank of New Zealand and Banking Act of 1895 Amendment Bill was introduced on 27 October 1895, there was a clause, which Ward seconded, stating that lists of accounts need not be produced in any court proceedings following the merger, thereby concealing Ward's involvement. Ward would be severely criticised later for this; as Colonial Treasurer and managing director of a company heavily indebted to the Colonial Bank, he had officially connived at a transaction of potential benefit to a concern with which he was involved. Seddon was doing his utmost to try and hide the scandal from the House, but there would soon be a point beyond which Seddon could no longer protect Ward.

Larnach had returned to The Camp early in December and to add to his misfortunes, while travelling into Dunedin in his buggy with Conny and Douglas, an axle broke at Anderson's Bay. Conny and Douglas were not injured, but Larnach was catapulted onto the road, breaking several ribs and dislocating his shoulder. He lay in an armchair for about a fortnight because, as he said, "you cannot lie down in a bed with broken ribs and be comfortable." So he had plenty of time to contemplate his fortune once again filtering through his fingers as the Bank of New Zealand picked the eyes out of the Colonial Bank's assets. Although he was to lose £60,000 as a result of Seddon's Banking Act and Ward's huge debt, Larnach stood by his friends, showing no signs of complaint, resentment or rancour.

Larnach's tumbling fortune was not unique among well known businessmen in New Zealand at that time. Although he would have hated to be compared with the businessmen of Auckland, of whom he had little regard, two Auckland men in particular, Josiah Firth and Thomas Morrin, who were mostly responsible for the second crisis of the Bank of New Zealand, followed a similar but less honest pattern to Larnach in

Gladys, Douglas and Constance Larnach in 1893.

the making and losing of their fortunes. All men had been treated with great leniency by the banks, enticing them to borrow enormous sums. Both Firth and Morrin in an indirect way contributed to Larnach's downfall. Their huge unmarketable land tracts, which had been taken over by the Bank of New Zealand, became the enormous liability that had brought the Bank of New Zealand to its knees. Other well known and wealthy Auckland businessmen, such as Dr John Logan Campell and James Dilworth, also an investor in the Colonial Bank, suffered similar setbacks during the ten years of depression that had been the ruin of so many.

* * *

The court, with the approval of the shareholders, had appointed Messrs Ramsey, Vigers and Larnach as provisional liquidators of the Colonial Bank. In Parliament, the Opposition was stirring up a hornet's nest, ignoring that they too could get stung. In their eagerness to bring Ward down, they were clamouring for full information from the Colonial Bank about Ward's finances, disregarding the Bank of New Zealand's efforts to hide some large shady transactions of their own, and some relating to former members of the Opposition. Seddon was at a loss as to how to protect Ward, and Larnach warned him that as a liquidator of the Colonial Bank he would soon be forced to publish Ward's accounts unless the Bank of New Zealand took the accounts over, which would then mean that under the Amendment Bill to the Banking Act of 1895, they need not be disclosed. Giving the alternatives in a letter he wrote to Seddon on 11 January about Ward's dilemma, he said,

> I wish to God that you had consulted me in regard to much of this Cursed Bank legislation . . . but you know it was not for me to intrude myself by volunteering an opinion at the risk of being snubbed. The business so far is done and the question is what course should now be taken to make the best of it and so prevent a damnable scandal.

In my opinion the whole solution of the difficulty we have got into by too much legal advice and too little Practicable and Technical knowledge as to what was necessary, can only now be satisfactorily settled by acting under clause 18 of the agreement which means one of two alternatives — i.e. The purchasing bank . . . should now take over the account . . . which would take the whole out of the jurisdiction of both the Liquidators and the Courts. Now failing this course the other alternative — and I fear compulsory — is for the Liquidators to call upon the Bank of New Zealand — under the same clause 18 — to proceed forthwith to liquidate and realize [Ward's Farmers Association]. The immediate result being "the fat in the fire" and the reputation of everyone connected to the Party blasted and soiled for all time, and the credit of the Colony injured for a very long period. I feel heartily for you in this awkward business, but I am as innocent in connec-tion with the whole ramification as you are. Now is a very critical time for all of us. Pull yourself together, as you can, and be bold and prompt. There is no time for delay. I will do all I know and can to help. The Treasurer must remain Treasurer if possible or the cat is loose among our politics. . . . You have a hard task. Whatever you do it will make no difference to me or my loyalty. . . . You may show this letter to your colleagues then burn it. [14]

On the same day he wrote to Ward:

My anxiety has not ceased to worry me day and night since I saw you, and more especially as the anonymous correspondents and Leader writers who are daily becoming more numerous and bold, and insinuating more vocally at matters concerning liquidation . . . our side must make clear entries on the debit side of our political ledger, so that we can pay off every cent of spite and animosity that we may now have to give credit for with interest; and with the help of God — Compound Interest. . . . I have written to our friend

Seddon, there are only two courses to choose from. . . . The one is that a certain Institution must take over a certain Business, and a certain important piece of Money, Stamp and Paper would go with it. Then there would be nothing about it to go before the Court and the whole would be clean away from its old haunts. The other alternative means scandal, disparagement and entire loss of prestige to all of you and your party. The same will apply to the executive officers and Directors of both institutions; and to the institutions the brand of "crooked" will always remain as an indelible stain — i.e. The BNZ must be called upon at once, failing their accepting the first course here referred to, to liquidate and realise certain accounts, and the onus of bringing trouble upon everyone, including themselves, will rest entirely upon themselves. Our course is clearly laid down in clause 18 of the Agreement, as Liquidators, and I hope and trust that the responsibility of our having to act in this direction will not be thrown upon us for we will be helpless to do otherwise. If you had only insisted upon fulfilling your promises to me in 1894, you would not now be made a butt by a certain money shop. I cannot help saying to a certain extent "it serves you chaps right". You did not seem to know your real friends, and I was one of them. [15]

Seddon wrote to Larnach a few days later:

It is with pleasure that I acknowledge the receipt of your very nice letter of the 11th inst. In the first place I must congratulate you, Mr Ramsey, and Mr Vigers on having the confidence of the shareholders of the Colonial Bank, which was so fully demonstrated by the result of the voting at the late meeting. I am of the opinion that had your advice been acted upon sooner, the majority would have been much greater and probably a good deal of feeling and adverse criticism would have been avoided. It is unnecessary for me to tell you that the very name of bank, banking legislation, and banking troubles too numerous to mention, always creates with me an unpleasant sensation. I must confess I knew very little about such matters myself, and I should have been only too glad to have had the advantage of your sound advice and ripe experience in such matters; and had I to go through the same again — which God forbid — I should have broken through all rules and have invited your assistance. You say that you are afraid that had you volunteered your assistance, it might have been construed unwarranted. Nothing of the kind, old friend, and what prevented me doing it was the course you took in opposing the proposals. It is only by later events that I have been able to grasp the situation. I quite agree with you that smoother and better roads and easier might have been constructed, and there is no doubt whatever that the lawyers in this, as in other matters, have been to a great extent the cause of the difficulties. Now that we come to work the legislation that has been passed, and which was prepared by the banks themselves, one's common sense points out the absurdity, and in some instances the absolute impracticality, of the same. At the same time, the lawyers are not always to blame, because those who had bank knowledge and were interested in the legislation ought to have foreseen the difficulties which have since cropped up.

I am not chicken-hearted and am not afraid of a stiff fence with a water jump behind it and like yourself I fully believe that the bold course is the best, and believe this course is the best in the present case. Old Mick Houlihan used to say "The Lord afflicts his own first" and during the last six months I have been particularly favoured and begin to feel that I am a veritable political Job. No sooner do we get over one difficulty than another crops up. . . . If all goes well, I intend to be down in Dunedin at the opening of the Medical Conference and hope to have the pleasure of seeing you. It will be a relief to me to unbosom myself; for there are very few,

in delicate matters of this kind, that one can trust. Many thanks
old friend for your good wishes, with regards to Mrs Larnach and
Douglas, R.J. Seddon.[16]

For two months Larnach worked on the Colonial Bank as a liquidator,
until Mr Justice Williams suddenly reversed his decision and announced
that William Larnach, as a large shareholder, would no longer be eligible
as a liquidator of the Colonial Bank. "This of course involves no personal
imputation against Mr Larnach," he stated.[17] Larnach vented his fury at
this decision by publishing a four-page pamphlet. He felt the court had
gone too far in dealing with the bank matters. He pointed out it had not
had to close its doors through "reckless management, or speculations of its
Directors. The Colonial Bank with its uncalled capital at its back, could
have easily carried on its excellent business, with perhaps a little temporary inconvenience to its shareholders. . . . There were NO CREDITORS
CONCERNED, and it only remained for a prudent and careful
Liquidation to produce the best results for Shareholders."[18] It was, Larnach
believed, simply a matter of disposing of a number of properties to the best
advantage.

Within a few months this same judge refused to allow the sale of
Ward's personal assets and those of his company, which would have saved
the Colonial Bank shareholders £67,750.[19] (The 1996 value of these assets
is about $6 million.) The judge said that this would amount to "an offer to
buy off from bankruptcy and its consequences a man who ought not to
escape them. This is in effect an offer of hush money . . . that those who were
responsible for the management [of Ward's Farmers Association] should no
longer be permitted to roam at large through the business world. . . . Mr
Ward is hopelessly insolvent."[20]

Ward resigned as Colonial Treasurer on 16 June 1896, with speculation
that he may even surrender his seat in the House. When a second offer to
purchase Ward's estate, an offer that would have saved his many shareholders' monies, was again refused by Judge Williams, Ward resigned his
seat on 8 July 1897 and the next day was declared bankrupt.

Larnach and many others felt the *puisne* Judge Williams (in Larnach's clipping book, puisne is scored out and 'puny' substituted), had a political bias, preferring to drag Ward through the courts heedless of the cost to many small shareholders in Ward's Association. It had already been established that Ward's busy parliamentary life had led him to neglect his business affairs, and no evidence of fraud had been found. Ward and Larnach remained friends throughout all the upheavals of the 1890s. Both having the tenacity to endure setbacks, they recognised the abilities in each other. They were men of vision, which extended even to improving that smallest room in the house — Larnach with his methane mansion, and Ward as the first man in Bluff to have a "hush flush" lavatory.

Chapter XX

DISILLUSIONMENT

The Seddon and Ward families had spent many an evening with the Larnachs, singing round the piano together. But these pleasant gatherings were soon to come to an end as the continued decline in his income forced Larnach to put 45 Molesworth Street, next door to the Seddon residence, on the market. Larnach asked for advances on his policies from Commercial Union Insurance. He also tried unsuccessfully to interest the Hon. John McKenzie, Minister of Lands, to buy Moa Flat. Where he had been casual about collecting rents from his various properties on the Peninsula, he became more exacting. His attitude to his tenants and neighbours was less friendly. He scalded his hand badly, and claimed from the Scottish Metropolitan Insurance Company for two weeks partial disability.

During this time, Seddon relied on Larnach's opinion on matters as diverse as whether he would have the support of the nation if he went to London for the Queen's Jubilee, or what was Larnach's advice on the banking legislation — a continuing nightmare to Seddon. Larnach was constantly advising and drafting letters for Seddon to send to the colonial auditor of the Bank of New Zealand, so that Seddon would have a better idea of the real state of things. When the police force came under criticism, Seddon was reluctant to authorise an enquiry, but Larnach and many others thought otherwise: "Have great sympathy with you for numerous troubles, but difficulties must be settled or I will not return Wellington as member," wired Larnach to Seddon. A royal commission was set up to enquire into the state of the police force, but this was probably more a result of the efforts of the prohibitionists, who were pushing for an inquiry, than any threats of Larnach's.

When the appointment of chief justice was considered, senior *puisne*

Judge Williams, who had created so much financial hardship for both Larnach and Ward, was in line for the appointment, but Seddon had no desire to appoint him, neither did he want Sir Robert Stout. Seddon considered that after all the bitter disagreements between himself and Sir Robert Stout, they would be unable to work together. Larnach pointed out that Stout "had always been a friend of our side, and he has the Capacity and Energy to transcend the whole business in a satisfactory way for the whole country." [1] Stout was appointed chief justice in 1899.

The death in May, 1896, of his uncle Donald Larnach in London was not an occasion of sorrow for William, as might have been expected from such a once close relative. Nor was there any sympathy for his Aunt Jane.

Not many months after his uncle's death, Larnach received a begging letter from his own widowed sister Emily, pleading hardship. He replied,

> I received your letter on my return from the country and I must say I was not pleased with its tone. I am not to blame for your being in your present unfortunate position, nor for the position your loving Aunt Jane has taken by not sending you the allowance made by your late Uncle. I have helped all those belonging to me whenever in my power, you included, but I am sorry to say I am not in a position to continue to do so . . . I don't want any more begging letters my dear Emily. [2]

To a young nephew who wrote wanting work in New Zealand, he replied, "I enclose you a cheque for £5 which is all I can do for you, I have my own troubles to bear. . . . I return your letter to point out several words badly spelt, which ought not to be, and I advise you to try and improve your handwriting . . . and while you are young you had better shorten your name, take one Christian name instead of three."

The Larnach children were not without their own misfortunes. Alice's firstborn son had died before he was a year old. Colleen was still at odds with her father. She had written from Naseby to ask his permission to marry Alfred Inder, Alice's brother-in-law. Her father replied,

*This portrait of Alice, Gladys, Douglas and Colleen was taken by
Burton Brothers of Dunedin.*

Remember that marriage is a solemn obligation on the part of the
contracting parties, easily entered into but difficult to withdraw
from, therefore I want you to think well over what you propose
doing. . . . I have written to Mr Inder and told him similar, only further that I much prefer you to return Home and live with me . . .
however of this, you and he must now be the best judges.[3]

Colleen replied that her father's letter had not been "an altogether kind one" and, angry with her father, continued to stay in Naseby with her married sister Alice. The marriage did not take place, and without further money from her father she was eventually forced to return to The Camp, where her petulance added to the misery Conny was already enduring with William's growing querulousness.

Douglas's dreams of farming in the style of the English gentleman farmer were disappearing as his father's finances deteriorated, although his father had given him to understand that in compensation for all the money he had spent on Donald, Douglas would inherit The Camp. Douglas was now, at thirty-two, the bored, disgruntled telephonist at the telephone office, which had opened at The Camp in 1895. For each message Douglas received, he was paid 3d by the Post Office. In November of that same year Douglas also had a disagreement with his father, and he too sought refuge at Naseby with Alice for a while.

Donald, still struggling to make ends meet in Melbourne, was losing his sight. He received the news from his father that

> force of circumstances compel me to give you positive notice that I can no longer continue making you any allowance from my limited means. You have been a heavy drag on me for a great number of years and I have struggled to meet your wants and demands as few fathers would have done . . . I can now go on no longer . . . this notice will give you three clear months including this month.[4]

Donald's eldest daughter, Gretchen, a little younger than Gladys, had been in Dunedin for the last two years as a companion to Gladys after Kate's death, and the two girls boarded at the Dominican convent. Even the revered Mother Prioress did not escape Larnach's censure: "You will pardon me if I point out to you that, in my opinion, there is a want in your Institution of teaching girls method and tidiness. I allude to teaching girls to look after their clothes, so as always to be neat, and keeping their bedrooms the same. The two girls who have so recently returned home seem to have no idea of that."[5]

Gretchen Guise Larnach, William Larnach's granddaughter.

Gretchen was to refer in later life to the friction-filled, bitter, joyless atmosphere at The Camp in those years, years when she had been so unhappy she "could hardly bear to talk about them."

There were angry scenes between Colleen and her father, and between Alice and her father, when Alice visited The Camp, and their father had promised to disinherit them. According to Mr Sievwright, Larnach's solicitor, "He was a strong high-tempered man. It wasn't safe to contradict him. If I, as his adviser, contradicted him he would fire up and walk out of the room. I think the girls who lived in the house were frightened of their father. . . . I think Mr Larnach had a pretty strong hand over all members of his family." [6]

Gretchen was fifteen when she returned to Melbourne, to an equally unhappy home. Her father, Donald, was trying unsuccessfully to get the appointment of agent general in London for the State of Victoria, while his wife, Violet, was about to leave him permanently and return to England, and had boarded her three daughters at the Convent of Mercy, Mansfield, Melbourne. Sister Alacoque wrote,

Mrs Larnach is going to London and she heard such praise of our school that she brought her three children to leave them at school for twelve months, at the end of which time she hopes to send for them. They are very nice children, the youngest only five years. I suppose you know their grandfather W. Larnach. You will see by the programme of our Concert that Mrs Larnach is an operatic Singer, she hopes to be able to do wonders when she goes Home. [7]

In the election of December 1896 Larnach again contested and won the Tuapeka seat, but not without some explosive words between the editor of the *Tuapeka Times* and himself. The editor had accused Larnach of coarse language in criticising an editorial about Seddon, to which Larnach published this reply. "A vicious attack had been made by the editor upon the Premier, who was not present to defend himself, and which I there and then denounced in pungent and punitive Saxon." To Seddon he wrote,

I have fought a good many election contests, but the last just takes the cake from all that have gone before. In the recent encounter it was not myself that I was called upon to defend. It was you and your Banking Legislation . . . the things the Villain has said about you and Ward are the sole cause of my getting into hot water by indignantly defending you both in the strongest of justifiable language. [8]

The letter continued at great length, full of venom and wild accusations about the editor and the Opposition. This was quite unlike the Larnach of old who usually took criticism in his stride. An example of his growing irascibility shows in a letter to a firm requesting him to settle an overdue account. "Considering the time I have dealt with your firm, I look upon your memo as an indication of damned impertinence evidently emanating from some stomach-wormed individual . . . I hereby send you a cheque for £30. 2s. 3d. to keep the rumblings of your stomachs quiet, and their sphericity from caving in." [9]

Shortly before Seddon's departure for England to attend the celebra-
tions of Queen Victoria's sixty-year reign in 1897, he received a letter from
Larnach.

> Of course we cannot anticipate all that is to happen while you are
> in London, but I take it that certain "Honours" for Colonists who
> have distinguished themselves in their adopted country's service
> will be placed at your disposal or, at any rate you will have a say, or
> — You have only to mention it. . . . Now I was justly entitled to
> something better (than the CMG) for it was I who originated the
> idea . . . of the Loan of 1878. . . . Again I did great service to the
> Colony as Chairman of the Public Trust Commission . . . I have
> been twice a Minister of the Crown, holding many important
> Portfolios, and in all respect have frequently done good service to
> New Zealand. I place these few facts in writing for you as a
> reminder that I am entitled to some consideration, and leave
> myself in your hands. [10]

The letter fell on deaf ears; there was no pat on the back, no handle to his
name, no honorific, no reward for loyalty. Even so, Larnach took the rebuff,
if that is what it was, in reasonably good humour. In a letter to Seddon
some months later, he wrote,

> Now my old friend, as I believe you to be, but I don't know whether
> to be quite sure about it. . . . What about the Bank-auditorship? I
> shall feel that I have been treated scandalously indeed if it is not
> offered to me who is far and away the most fitted of any you can
> secure. After the "breach of promise" of the Auditor-Generalship,
> ditto the Public Trustee I want to know where am I? [11]

A miniscule mark of eminence came his way in June, when Larnach, as
New Zealand commissioner to the Brisbane Exhibition, left Dunedin
accompanied by Conny and Douglas for Queensland. "I don't go with very

Douglas John Larnach. He sent this portrait to his future wife
Margaret Ogilvie Culling about 1909.

much enthusiasm . . . because this Colony asks men of Experience and Capacity to undertake most responsible and important duties in its interests . . . and not only expects them to do the work for nothing, but for less. . . . I hope you will get your eyes opened and your heart enlarged by your travels," [12] he told Seddon.

The Larnachs were in Australia for three months, during which William complained it was "120 degrees in the shade and no cool clear water." While he was occupied as commissioner, and investigating the investment prospects of mining companies in Queensland, his wife Conny and son Douglas, far from the prying eyes of The Camp, enjoyed one another's company among the banana palms and the pineapple plants, under the tropical downpours and scorching sun, continuing a love affair which was the barely concealed subject of gossip for many years. Douglas was six years younger than Conny. Whether William ever realised their friendship had gone beyond the bounds of stepmother and stepson can only be conjecture, but it had become common knowledge among the family, and he was not an unobservant man.

Chapter XXI

RINGING DOWN THE CURTAIN

At 9 o'clock on the evening of 12 October 1898, Richard Seddon was called away from the debating chamber. Returning a short time later, he stood behind the vacant desk of William Larnach, and asked the Speaker "for an adjournment of the House." The difficulty he had in speaking and the emotion in his voice checked the usual inattentive undercurrent of chatter. Dead silence prevailed as he continued: "owing to the death of the member for Tuapeka under the most distressing circumstances, and I can say no more." Later he added, "Speaking as a friend, nothing has occurred since I have been in public life that has affected me so much, in fact it has quite unnerved me."[1]

The year had begun for Larnach with a bad attack of influenza, and his friend and medical adviser Dr Cahill had suggested a complete checkup, but Larnach kept procrastinating. Age had not diminished the vanity always simmering below the surface of Larnach's personality and, recovering from influenza, his spirits were not raised when a portrait of himself which he had commissioned, arrived from England. It had been painted by Ella Sievwright, to whom Larnach had sent a photograph of himself. She was a student at the Slade School of Art, and daughter of the solicitor in the firm Sievwright and Stout. When he received the painting, Larnach wrote in a letter to Ella, ". . . you have executed so cleverly from photographs sent to you . . . as a work of art it does you very great credit, but you must have misjudged me in regard to age, for you have made me much older looking than I am, however it is so many years since you have seen me, every excuse can be fairly made for you."[2]

Since returning from Australia, Larnach's parliamentary friends had noticed he had grown thinner, more withdrawn and preoccupied; he had lost his habitual cheerfulness and his characteristic mental and physical

William James Mudie Larnach towards the end of his life.

robustness. As chairman of the Public Accounts Committee and a member of the Goldfields Committee, two activities he enjoyed, it frequently appeared as if he was completely disinterested in them, as he often sat through a meeting without speaking.

Three weeks before he died, Larnach visited the gunsmith William Henry Tisdall in Lambton Quay. He told Tisdall he had been instructed to choose a revolver for a friend. The choice rested between two modern revolvers, one of which, after discussion with his friend, he would return to buy. He did so on 23 September. Mr Tisdall's suspicions were not aroused; he knew Larnach was a "good shot" and already had a large gun collection.

On the Sunday before his death, Larnach inquired of the assistant librarian at the parliamentary library, John James Costall, whether anyone was tampering with his mail. "Not while I am on duty," the librarian replied. On Wednesday, the afternoon of his death, Larnach collected the southern mail at 3 p.m. He was observed to appear upset by a letter he had received, and proceeded to walk up and down the library in an agitated manner. He then wrote several letters, one of which he asked the librarian to post to Dunedin; he put a late fee on it, stressing that he was most anxious that the letter would catch the mail for Dunedin. The librarian particularly observed that Larnach seemed absent-minded, depressed and disturbed, and couldn't help noticing Larnach's severe trembling when he handed him the letter. He was then seen about 4 p.m. entering committee room "J", situated almost over the lobby, and was heard to lock the door behind him.

Conny, who had come to Wellington for the Session, had noticed his increasing despondency that week, and had taken to sitting in the gallery reserved for ministers' wives. Was this the action of a guilty wife trying to prove her devotion? On the evening of 11 October, she had sat there till long after the supper adjournment. William had failed to return home for lunch or dinner that day. The next evening when Larnach had not appeared at home for dinner, she sent her brother Alfred down to the House to enquire of his whereabouts from Mr Mills, the Government Whip, who usually walked home with Larnach in the evenings. Mr Mills found a messenger who had seen Larnach go along to committee room "J" earlier in the afternoon. Mills found the door locked, and extensive knocking produced no response, so he sent for a carpenter to force the door open.

At the far end of the room, in the chairman's chair, William Larnach was sitting at a table. He had been dead for some hours. Resting on his lap lay his right hand still tightly clasping a revolver, proof of instantaneous death. His head was thrown back, revealing a gunshot wound to his left temple. Embedded in his brain was a bullet. That bullet had managed to propel Larnach into the annals of history more successfully than anything he had ever done in his lifetime.

* * *

Next morning the Premier spoke to the House with deep feeling about Larnach's death.

> When I announced last night to this House the sad intelligence, it caused such a sensation as I feel sure has never previously, and I hope may never again be occasioned. . . . I must ask honourable members not to judge our brother harshly. Those who have known him in the past and those who have known him during the last session, must have known that his health was failing, particularly during the last weeks.

Seddon then told of their long friendship, and recounted how when he, Seddon, as a young parliamentarian had suffered an accident on the West Coast, Larnach had paid to send a surgeon from Dunedin to treat him. He gave a short sketch of Larnach's political career, acknowledging Larnach's innovative concept in relation to the Advances to Settlers Act, successfully carried out by Joseph Ward, who at the time took full credit. Seddon called Larnach "the imperious man — the genial self-contained man — the man with a mind which was a master mind." He was magnanimous with his praise now that Larnach was dead, yet for some unknown reason had determinedly withheld any public acknowledgment of Larnach's loyalty during his life time. He then moved the following motion, "That this House desires to place on record its high sense of the distinguished services rendered to the Colony by the late Mr W.J.M. Larnach." The leader of the Opposition, Captain Russell, seconded this motion, and added,

> Daily we meet in parliamentary life in strife and joy, and jostle all uncaring of our neighbours perplexities. . . . Smart attack and reply succeed each other in endless occurrence, yet our feelings of kindliness and comradeship are as unending as our warfare, and

personal friendships are not weakened by political differences. So the abrupt termination of our dead friend's life came as an almost paralysing shock to every member of Parliament. Many of us have known him for two decades — ever genial, kindly, courageous, cheery.

The inquest was held that afternoon at the Metropolitan Hotel. After the jury had been sworn in, the coroner, Mr James Ashcroft, said it was seldom he had presided on a more painful occasion, having been a friend of Larnach's for thirty years. The last of several witnesses to be called was Larnach's brother-in-law, Alfred de Bathe Brandon; he gave no information that would throw any light on the occurrence, and his evidence was not taken. Inspector Pender of the Police Force said he had discovered no note, nor anything that would explain the more immediate reasons for the deceased to take his life. The coroner said he supposed there must have been an immediate cause, and while there was no evidence to show what it was, there was enough to show that the deceased was overwrought and suffering from disease and mental depression, and a verdict of suicide while of temporary unsound mind could be given. The jury accepted the verdict without retiring.

Douglas left The Camp immediately for Wellington, and arrangements were made for his father's body to be taken by the Government steamer *Hinemoa* to Dunedin. On its arrival there, crowds waited at the wharf. The seamen from the *Hinemoa* conveyed the coffin to the hearse, which was pulled by horses from Larnach's stables, among them one old favourite buggy horse of Larnach's called Traveller, which led the procession to the Northern Cemetery. Following the hearse were Douglas Larnach, Alfred de Bathe Brandon, and Larnach's son-in-law, W.F. Inder. Conny, Alice, Colleen and Gladys travelled in a mourning coach. Among the large numbers in the funeral procession were many now historic names in Dunedin history: Burt, Caughtrey, Fenwick, Fergus, Glendinning, Darcy Haggitt, Hallenstein, Hislop, Kempthorne, Macindoe, Rattray, Sew Hoy, Sievwright, Thomson, and many others too numerous to mention. When the procession arrived at the cemetery, a number of Peninsula settlers carried the coffin from the hearse to the graceful steepled family mausoleum, where he was interred with Eliza, Mary and Kate. Among the wreaths was a very handsome one from the miners of Kumara, which His Worship the Mayor of Dunedin, Mr E.B. Cargill, had been asked to place on the coffin. William Larnach was sixty-five, too private a man to reveal his anguish, too public a person to be left in peace. Any scandal lingering after the death of Larnach was not buried with his bones.

EPILOGUE

The crucial letter, the letter that so upset Larnach the afternoon of his death, was never found. Could it have been a letter from Douglas confirming his father's suspicions that his favoured son and his beloved young wife were indeed having an affair? Nor did the letter Larnach so anxiously posted to Dunedin that fateful day ever surface. Was it to Douglas? Nothing at all came to light that might have given a clue to his torment. He was no longer a wealthy man. Although he had lost heavily with the Colonial Bank, that had happened two years previously, and his letters written over the last six months of his life showed he was again playing the sharemarket, and continuing to build up his library by ordering books from Sydney and New York. He had remarked when Kate died, "money and business troubles are not much to me . . . but family troubles knock me over." Some trouble far greater than money had given him the determination and the deliberation to commit that fatal deed.

No will was found to be held by a solicitor. In an affidavit to the court, Alfred de Bathe Brandon describes how he, with Conny and Douglas, searched The Camp and the Wellington residence for a will, to no avail. To die intestate was a curious omission for a man who had so carefully planned every aspect of his life and death. Larnach was fully aware of the Public Trust's actions when there was no will. His widow would receive one third of his estate and the rest would be divided among his children. Perhaps this is the way he wanted his estate shared. However this was not to be, as a future court case would reveal. If Larnach had wanted revenge for the lack of love from his wife and unfilial behaviour of his son Douglas, he could not have planned more effectively the turn that events would take.

Straight after the funeral, Alfred de Bathe Brandon, long aware of the situation between Conny and Douglas, quickly organised Conny and her sister Annie to take a trip to England, hoping to avoid any further scandal. Donald did not arrive from Melbourne in time for the funeral, but went straight to Wellington to see Alfred de Bathe Brandon, who informed him that his father had died intestate and revealed that The Camp estate was in William Larnach's name, not left in trust to the children as promised, so a third of the estate would become Conny's.

Two weeks after the funeral Donald, Colleen and Alice, in the company of their solicitor Mr Saul Solomon, arrived at The Camp and demanded that Douglas, who was living there, hand over the keys of The Camp. They told him they were instituting court proceedings regarding the ownership of The Camp estate. Douglas maintained his father had always promised him the estate. Relations between the brothers and sisters deteriorated, and Gladys sided with Douglas.

On Conny's return from England nearly a year later, the court case commenced. Donald, Alice and Colleen were the plaintiffs against the trustees of the reversionary deed they had signed after Mary Alleyne's death in 1887, in which they claimed they had been misled by their father into signing away their inheritance to The Camp. If the Larnach children won their case, it would mean Conny would get nothing. Douglas, who had also signed the document, chose to stand apart from his brother and sisters, claiming the others were lying, that he and they knew full well what they were signing, that his father had never tried to conceal anything, and the only reason they went to court was to destroy the family honour. "I knew they were trying to do my stepmother out of every farthing they could, and I stood by her," he said.[1] He maintained that his father had always promised him The Camp, to balance the money that had been spent on Donald.

His loyalty was misplaced. The judge declared in Donald, Alice and Colleen's favour, which meant that as Douglas on his own admission had knowingly signed away his inheritance, he was now to receive nothing, and neither would Conny. Douglas then went to court himself, to set aside the verdict and join with his brother and sisters in agreeing they had all been deceived. But the judge — the same *puisne* Judge Williams Larnach had so disliked — ruled against Douglas, saying "he had been hoisted on his own petard", and went on to say if his father had wanted him to have The Camp, he would have made a will and left it to him.

The Camp plus £28,777 17s. 5d. worth of investments that were included in Mary Alleyne's marriage settlement, were made over to Donald, Alice, Colleen and Gladys, who had been too young at the time to sign the deed. The final distribution, after all debts and lawyers' fees for the court case had been paid, amounted to only £1,263 4s. 6d. That did not include jewellery, Mount Cargill land, sixty-two shares in the Round Hill Company, 200 shares in the Otago and Southland Company, or the sale of The Camp, all of which were sold later. The rest of the estate — an insurance policy taken out after the marriage settlement — was distributed according to the conditions under the Public Trustees Act for those dying intestate, which Larnach had helped formulate. Conny received a one third share of the insurance policy of £99 12s. 2d. amounting to £33 4s., the rest of the family receiving £13 5s. 8d. each, which was the only sum Douglas inherited.

*   *   *

Conny returned to live in Wellington with her sister Annie at 15 Hobson St, next to her brother at number 17, and opposite her sisters Fanny and Sarah. Her brother Alfred provided for her financially. She joined the Victoria League and became one of its most dedicated workers, and was recognised for her many good works in the community. Constance died in 1942.

Douglas also returned to Wellington and for some years lived just around the corner from Conny at 3 Pipitea St. In 1909 he married Margaret Ogilvie Culling of Dunedin. They had no children. Douglas died in Rotorua in 1949.

Colleen married Elliot Hume from Levin in 1902, and had one daughter, Colleen Jean (Pederson) and a son, Jack. After living some years in Canada, the Humes returned to Nelson, where Colleen died in 1954.

Constance de Bathe Larnach, widow of William Larnach.

Alice had one son, who died in infancy, then a daughter, Daphne (O'Donovan). Alice and Walter Inder separated not long after William's death. In 1903 she became postmistress at Weraroa, a suburb of Levin. This was a "non-classified" post office, which provided a small salary and accommodation, and hers was a position normally reserved for widows of post officers. She held this position until 1912, when she married Francis Joseph Devine. She died in Melbourne in 1942.

Gladys married Robert Aitken in January 1900, and died at the end of that year in childbirth, at the age of 22, just two years after her father's death.

After his father's death, Donald returned to Dunedin with his two elder daughters, Gretchen and Olive. His youngest daughter remained in England with her mother.

None of the family remained at The Camp after Douglas was ousted from it. For a short time a community of Dunedin nuns used it as holiday retreat, and in April 1900 the whole estate was put up for auction, but passed in at £10,000. On 15 October 1901 the property was transferred to Donald Guise Larnach. Within a year the stock and farming implements were sold, together with most of the furniture, but it was not until January 1906 that Donald sold the estate to the Government for £3,000, when it became a mental institution until 1918. It remained an empty forlorn sight for several years — a vandals' delight. It was sometimes used as a cabaret venue and in 1925 it was passed in at auction for £3,500. In 1927 it sold to Mr Jackson Purdie for £3,600 and was subsequently bought and sold several times by private owners, until 1967 when it was bought by the Barker family in whose ownership it still remains.

At the age of 50, in 1910, Donald Larnach committed suicide in Dunedin, shooting himself as his father had done. He left a note for Gretchen, then married to solicitor Percy Hjorring, stating that he wished his remains "to be taken out to sea and dumped overboard. Failing this, place them in the family vault. On no account have prayers read at my burial. I believe in a Creator, but I absolutely disbelieve in the Bible." He added in pencil, "The vault keys are in my hatbox. . . . Three sleepless nights, I am going mad." He was buried in the family vault.

One of the last of William Larnach's descendants to carry the ill-fated Larnach name was Gretchen's only child, Ivan Larnach Hjorring, who died tragically at the age of 27 in 1931. Gretchen died alone in her Dunedin home in 1954; she had been dead some days before her body was discovered. She left strict instructions in her will that on no account was she to be buried in the family vault.

*   *   *

The *Sydney Evening News* of 31 October 1898, in an obituary, wrote,

> William Larnach was a kind, big-hearted man, generous almost to
> a fault, and no more considerate employer of labour, skilled and
> unskilled, was ever known in New Zealand. Endowed with a great
> spirit of enterprise, for many years he gave employment to a large
> number of people in various undertakings, even after retiring from
> business pursuits and settling down upon his beautiful estate over-
> looking Dunedin Bay on one side and the Pacific Ocean on the
> other. By all classes he was greatly esteemed, and "it is a pity there
> were not a few more Larnachs in New Zealand" became quite a
> common expression, as indicating what a good employer and
> enterprising man he was.

Apart from his term as Minister of Mines, Larnach gained little satisfaction
from his political career, feeling his initiatives went unrecognised. Yet he
had achieved success in bringing down the Continuous Ministry of thirteen
years standing in 1877, as Colonial Treasurer floating the loan of 1878, and
as an efficient Minister of Mines. In his personal life, his remarkable enterprise and energy found scope in the building of his great dream, The Camp,
and its showcase dairy farm; in founding Guthrie and Larnach; in developing Moa Flat as a model station; in being a sought-after director on the
boards of numerous companies; all gave him great satisfaction, as did his
popularity with his working class constituents.

The deaths of his wives and daughter he bore with great stoicism. The
ten-year depression in New Zealand, which started in 1880, gave him huge
business worries; the setback and acrimony of the Agricultural Company,
the failure of Guthrie and Larnach, the debacle of the Colonial Bank — all
these he accepted philosophically. By far his greatest disappointment was
his family. There is no doubt Larnach spoilt his children, but this was tem-
pered by his dictatorial insistence that they conform to his ideas as to their

future. But the blow that tipped the balance must have been the betrayal by Douglas and Conny.

It is easy in hindsight to see why his business ventures failed, and where, at times, his integrity could be questioned. Yet this clever man, his enterprise and optimism so often marred by misfortune, deserves recognition for the part he played in Otago and New Zealand's history. As long as the castle stands bearing his name, William Larnach will be remembered. It will always be his greatest monument, and it is fitting that now, one hundred years after his death, the castle is again giving employment to people. Coachloads of tourists, school children and conference delegates wind up the scenic road to The Camp, and pay to enter the grounds to admire his masterpiece. They wander through the rooms and marvel at the workmanship, pause and gaze at his portrait, and imagine how life was for this man and his family. William Larnach would have enjoyed this interest in his castle; he would have approved of this successful tourist venture.

ENDNOTES

Abbreviations

ATL   Alexander Turnbull Library, Wellington

LFP   Larnach Family Papers, privately held

LLB   Larnach Letter Book, Larnach letter books are held as follows:
McNab Collection, Dunedin Public Library —
vol. 1 (3 Jul to 31 Aug 1882), vol. 2 (15 Aug 1884 to 10 Jul 1887),
vol. 3 (14 Jul 1889 to 17 Dec 1891), vol. 4 (30 Dec to 15 May 1896),
vol. 5 (6 Feb 1897 to 14 Mar 1898);
Otago Early Settlers Museum, Dunedin —
two volumes from 18 Sep 1893 to 16 Dec 1895 and 14 Mar to 6 Oct
1898; Hocken Library, Dunedin — all letter books held on microfilm.

ML   Mitchell Library, Sydney

NZPD   New Zealand Parliamentary Debates

Note: The source of a footnote is given in full the first time it appears. Thereafter an abbreviated entry is given.

Chapter I — A SCOTTISH HERITAGE

1 Brasch, C., *Present Company*, Blackwood and Janet Paul, Auckland, 1966.

2 Donaldson, J.E., *Caithness in the 18th Century*, The Moray Press, Edinburgh, n.d.

3 Cordiner, C., *Antiquities and Scenery of the North of Scotland*, Wick Library, 1780.

4 Prentice, M.D., *The Scottish in Australia*, A.E. Press, Melbourne, 1987.

5 "A Settler", *Sydney Morning Herald*, 16 Jan 1839.

6 *Sydney Gazette*, 1808.

7 Denholm, D., *The Colonial Australians*, Penguin Books, Sydney, 1979.

8 Ibid.

9 Sir Ralph Darling to the Earl of Bathhurst, Governor's Despatches, 15 Oct 1826, ML.

10 Cunningham, P., *Two Years in New South Wales*, ML, 1827.

11 Mudie, J., *The Felonry of New South Wales*, ML, 1837.

12 Ibid.

13 Ibid.

Chapter II — JOHN AND EMILY LARNACH

1   Whitfellow, E., "A History of Singleton", unpublished, held at Singleton Library, New South Wales.

2   Kingsley, H., *Across the Island Continent*, edited by Herbert Strang, Henry Froude & Hodder & Stoughton, London, n.d.

3   Clark, C.M.H., *A History of Australia*, vol. III, 1824-1851, Melbourne University Press, 1971.

4   Mudie, J., *The Felonry of New South Wales*.

5   Eyre, E.J., unpublished autobiography, ML.

6   Therry, R., *Reminiscences of Thirty Years Residence in New South Wales*, ML, 1863.

7   Ryan, J.T., *Reminiscences of Australia*, ML, 1835.

8   William Watt was a clever ex-convict who had been transported for fourteen years for forging documents, but was on probation and was now the editor of the *Sydney Gazette*. An anonymous pamphlet was published denouncing Mudie and Larnach, and Mudie was convinced that William Watt was the author. He hounded Watt through the courts on trumped-up charges, at the same time using the court as a platform to attack the administration of Governor Bourke. Watt was no sooner acquitted of these dubious charges when Mudie discovered a loophole to at last deprive Watt of his freedom. Mudie discovered Watt had breached his terms of probation, a fact that Governor Bourke had been aware of but had chosen to ignore. Watt's crime had been an affair with a woman, which had ended many months before Mudie even found out about it, or laid charges. The charges were heard at the police office. Mudie chose nine magistrates where three would have done, but these men were all opposed to Governor Bourke's humane attitude to convicts. Not only did they try Watt, but they tried to impeach everybody from the Governor to the lowliest officer in the Government service. When Bourke's prior knowledge of Watt's affair was exposed, the Governor was forced to remove Watt to the penal settlement of Port Macquarie. While the thought of transportation to Australia struck terror in the hearts of English convicts, Port Macquarie held even greater horror for those who had already experienced penal settlements in the colony. It was meant for incorrigible

prisoners and second offenders, and the sadistic punishments practised there made death the only desirable option. William Watt was found drowned within a week of his arrival.

Chapter III — YOUNG WILLIAM

1   In 1837, James Mudie appeared in London before the Convict's Transportation Committee, to give evidence of the lax state of the penal settlement under Sir Richard Bourke. Mudie was a sorry sight: he had become obsessed to the point of near insanity in his endeavour to paint Bourke as a man resorting to "political concealment, trickery and collusion with the convicts." His distorted thinking had become obvious to all. He described the colony as a "Pandemonium", neglecting to mention the hand he had had in making it so. Sir Robert Peel, from whom the constabulary received the nickname "peelers", said that Mudie "as a witness under examination had told such improbable tales, he could place no reliance on such evidence." Some of Mudie's evidence was ordered to be struck out by the committee, but enough remains to reveal his unbalanced mind.

2   Ullathorne, Bishop, Comments to Select Committee on Transportation, 1837-1838, (ii) Minutes.

3   Preshaw, G.O., *Banking Under Difficulties*, 1888, reprinted by Capper Press, Christchurch, in 1971.

4   Hughes, R., *The Fatal Shore*, Collins Harvill, London, 1987.

5   Speech by W.J.M. Larnach, 18 Aug 1888, LFP.

6   Holder, R.F., *Bank of New South Wales, A History*, vol. II, 1817-1893, Angus and Robertson, Sydney, 1970.

Chapter IV — THE GOLDFIELDS OF VICTORIA

1   Holder, R.F., *Bank of New South Wales, A History*.

2   Ibid.

3   Ibid.

4   Ibid.

5   Birchfield, L., *Like the Ark, The Story of Ararat*, A.E. Press, Melbourne, 1993.

6   Speech by W.J.M. Larnach, 18 Aug 1888, LFP.

7   *Ararat Advertiser*, 8 Oct 1857.

8   Speech by W.J.M. Larnach, 18 Aug 1888, LFP.

Chapter V — THE FRENCH CONNECTION

1   As a partner in shady land dealings, William Guise chose the right man. W.C. Wentworth is described as a "slouching copper-head mixture of Irish rage, English manipulation, and pure Australian brashness."* Just before the signing of the Treaty of Waitangi in New Zealand, in 1840, Wentworth came close to concluding the shrewdest and largest private land deal of that time. He and some associates conned eight Maori chiefs into selling them about a third of the South Island. The chiefs personally drew their individual moko on the document, which was signed on 15 February 1840 in Sydney, where they had travelled to obtain allies in their fight against the chief Te Rauparaha, who was claiming large areas of the South Island. Wentworth's plan was foiled when it was quashed by government order, as the deed had been signed just after the Treaty had taken place.

   * Hughes, R., *The Fatal Shore.*

2   Merrylees, C., *Brave Beginnings, A History of the Carrothool District, Victoria,* held at Wagga Wagga District Family History Society (Inc.), n.d.

3   Denholm, D., *The Colonial Australians*, Penguin Books, Sydney, 1979.

4   *The Goulburn Gazette*, Oct 1855.

5   Ibid. In the *Australian Book of Records* Mary Brownlow is recorded as the only woman to have breast-fed her infant while the hangman adjusted the noose around her neck. She is said to have handed the baby to a warden just before dropping to her death.

Chapter VI — GEELONG

1   Larnach to Hon. H. Miller, 21 Nov 1881, LLB.

2   Larnach to F.N. Dougal, LLB.

3   *Geelong Advertiser*, 15 Apr 1864.

4   In 1836 the Royal Geographical Society had accepted the offer of a young man, Captain George Grey, to survey the area on the Western Coast of Australia, the area the Larnachs proposed to take their sheep. This young captain would later become Sir George Grey, Governor of New Zealand, and, in 1877, Premier. Captain Grey's survey was short-lived. He and his party of twelve men were tossed into the surf, their ship broke up on rocks 400 km below the Exmouth Gulf, forcing them to make a perilous 480 km walk to Perth without food. Captain Grey's diaries tell of a great variety of terrain, impenetrable well-watered scrub, then fertile valleys backed by a chain of lofty mountains, followed by areas of blindingly white sand, with wide dry

river beds — the land becoming increasingly arid, with neither vegetation nor signs of animal life. He and his men were close to death from thirst and starvation which affected both their sight and hearing. Grey wrote that it was "as if my blood was being driven by a forcing pump through my veins." They at last came upon a muddy spring, and, though the mud was almost too thick to swallow, in some small degree it satisfied their hunger. One man in the party died before they finally reached Perth. This terrain and a considerable distance of unexplored land north was the route George Larnach intended to take.

Chapter VII — DUNEDIN

1   Johnson, D., *Dunedin*, Canterbury University Press, Christchurch, 1993.
2   Hawke, G.R., *The Thoroughbred Among Banks in New Zealand*, The National Bank, Wellington, 1997.
3   *Australian Dictionary of Biography*, vol. II.
4   Pinney, R., *Early Northern Otago Runs*, Collins, Auckland, 1981.
5   Webster, A.H.H., *Teviot Tapestry*, Otago Centennial Historical Publications, Dunedin, 1948.
6   Clarke, M., *Big Clarke*, Queensberry Hill Press, Victoria, 1980.
7   Ibid.
8   Ibid.
9   Webster, *Teviot Tapestry*.
10 Eliza Jane Larnach, to the children 5 May 1880, LFP

Chapter VIII — THE BANK OF OTAGO

1   Gore, R., "History of The National Bank", unpublished ms.
2   Ibid.
3   Larnach, to Miller, 1881, LLB.
4   Gore, "History of the National Bank".
5   Hawke, G.R., *The Thoroughbred Among Banks in New Zealand*.
6   Church, I., *Port Chalmers and its People*, Otago Heritage Books, Dunedin, 1994. One of the vessels owned by Guthrie and Larnach had a fascinating history. Built in Gavle, Sweden, in 1857 as the *Daniel Elfstrand Pehrsson*, she was afterwards sold to South American owners and named the *Don Juan*. Later, as the *Rosalia*, she was used to carry Chinese slaves, or 'coolies', from Macao to Peru, for which she was equipped with shackles and leg-irons and

fitted with two cannons on deck to keep order. In May 1874, she was purchased by Guthrie and Larnach to bring a cargo of timber from Puget Sound, after which she was sold to a Port Chalmers shipchandler, Captain Charles Clark, who intended to put her into the cattle trade between New Caledonia and the Pacific Islands. The ship was found to be so rotten that customs clearance was refused, and when Clark tried to leave the harbour, the ship was arrested. The Supreme Court ordered a new survey which condemned her as "totally unseaworthy". The ship was eventually cut up for useful timber in 1900.

7   Scott, D., *Fire on the Clay*, Southern Cross Books, 1979.
8   Gore, R., "History of the National Bank".
9   Ritchie, J.M., letter to George G. Russell, 5 Jul 1875, held at the Hocken Library, Dunedin.
10 Grief, S.W., and Hardwicke Knight, *Cutten*, Knight, Dunedin, 1979.
11 Dalziel, R., *Sir Julius Vogel, Business Politician*, University of Auckland Printing Services, 1986.

Chapter IX — THE CASTLE

1   "The second bath was eventually removed from the castle and bought by the well known criminal lawyer, Alfred Charles Hanlon. It was conveyed to his residence on a dray pulled by eight horses, but because of its weight, (one ton) could not be carried up the stairs. Not to be denied his handsome bath, Mr Hanlon had a shed built for it and used it for the cold storage of his apples." From Jenny Glue, granddaughter of Alfred Hanlon.
2   Larnach, Eliza Jane, letter to daughters, 26 Mar 1880, ATL.
3   *Southland Daily News*, 5 Jul 1950, article by F.G.W. Miller.
4   Eliza Jane Larnach, letter, 6 Apr 1880, ATL.
5   Information from the marriage settlement between William Larnach and Mary Cockburn Alleyne, 5 Jan 1882.
6   Undated newspaper cutting found in Donald Larnach's wallet, LFP.

Chapter X — IN A STEW OVER RABBITS

1   Hamer, D.A., "The Agricultural Company and New Zealand Politics, 1877-1886", *Historical Studies, Australia and New Zealand*, vol. 10, no.38, 1962.
2   Goodall, A.W., "William James Mudie Larnach 1833-1898. New Zealand Politician", unpublished thesis, B.A. Hons., Univeristy of Otago, 1981.

3   Olssen, E., *A History of Otago*, John McIndoe, Dunedin, 1984.

4   *Otago Daily Times*, 20 Dec 1875.

5   *Otago Daily Times*, 21 Aug 1875.

6   *Otago Daily Times*, 21 Dec 1875.

7   NZPD, vol. 20, 1876, p.15.

8   Rice, G.W., *The Oxford History of New Zealand*, 2nd edition, Oxford University Press, Auckland, 1992.

9   NZPD, vol. 22, 1876, p.460.

10 NZPD, vol. 22, 1876, p.570.

11 Rupertswood was extended to fifty rooms, with a large garden of terraced lawns stepping down to an artificial lake surrounded with exotic trees and shrubs. Weekends consisted of dinners, balls and sporting amusements, and the Victorian Coursing Club held their meetings on the Clarke's land. William Clarke was made a baronet for his services as president of the Melbourne Exhibition in 1880. Lady Clarke, in 1884, at a cricket match held at Rupertswood, burnt a bail used in a game between England and a local side, sealed the ashes in a cremation urn, and presented it to the English captain, Ivo Bligh, so instigating the great cricket trophy, "The Ashes", now held in the original urn at Lords.

12 Eliza Jane Larnach, letters to her daughter Kate, 18 Jun to 15 Jul, 1877, ATL.

Chapter XI — THE GODFATHER OF THE GREY GOVERNMENT

1   Wilson, T.G., *The Grey Government*, 1877-79, Auckland University College, Auckland, 1954.

2   NZPD, vol. 26, 1877, p.23.

3   Goodall, "William James Mudie Larnach 1833-1898".

4   NZPD, vol. 26, 1877, p.285.

5   Ibid., p.285.

6   Ibid., p.608.

7   LFP

8   Dalziel, *Sir Julius Vogel, Business Politician*.

9   NZPD, vol. 26, p.209.

10 Saunders, A., *A History of New Zealand*, vol. 2, Whitcombe & Tombs, Christchurch, 1899.

11 Ibid.

12 *Saturday Advertiser*, 18 Oct 1877.

13 Goodall, "William James Mudie Larnach 1833-1898".

14 *Otago Daily Times*, 5 Dec 1877.

15 Dalziel, *Sir Julius Vogel, Business Politician*.

16 Scott, *Fire on the Clay*.

Chapter XII — LONDON, A LOAN AND A LAND COMPANY

1 Grey Papers relating to the Agricultural Company, G.N.Z.MSS. 64, Grey/Vogel, 22 Apr 1878, Auckland Library.

2 Grey Papers, Larnach/Grey, 10 May 1878.

3 Dalziel, *Sir Julius Vogel, Business Politician*.

4 Goodall, "William James Mudie Larnach 1833-1898".

5 Larnach to Sir Penrose Julyan, 29 May, 30 Nov 1897, LLB.

6 James Walker Larnach, with his brother Herbert, when making a world tour in 1870, arrived at the Bluff, purchased horses and rode to Auckland, achieving what was said to have been the longest ride in the colony at that time. During one of Donald Guise's visits to Brambletye, James Larnach was seriously injured in a hunting accident when, after mounting his cousin Donald on his own hunter, he was thrown from the horse he was riding, suffering serious injuries from which he never recovered. Yet in spite of that, he achieved the great distinction of winning the English Derby on his own horse Jeddah, the greatest outsider ever to take the Epsom prize.

7 Seddon Family, MS Papers 1619-044, 17 Apr 1897, ATL.

8 Hamer, "The Agricultural Company and New Zealand Politics, 1877-1886".

9 Kynaston, D., *The City of London*, vol.1, 1815-1890, Chatto & Windus, London, 1994.

10 Dalziel, *Sir Julius Vogel, Business Politician*.

11 Hamer, "The Agricultural Company and New Zealand Politics, 1877-1886".

12 Dalziel, *Sir Julius Vogel, Business Politician*.

13 Hamer, "The Agricultural Company and New Zealand Politics, 1877-1886".

14 Saunders, *History of New Zealand*.

Chapter XIII — ELIZA

1 Eliza Jane Larnach, extracts from letters, ATL.

2 Information from Magdalene Wallscott, daughter of Emma Karetai.

3 National Maritime Museum, Greenwich, England.

4 Port Chalmers Museum, Dunedin.

5 Sinclair, K., *A History of New Zealand*, Penguin Books, Auckland, 1959.

6   Julius Vogel, MS Papers 2072, Larnach to Vogel, 17 Jun 1881, ATL.
7   Ibid., 22 Apr 1881.
8   Goodall, "William James Mudie Larnach 1833-1898".
9   *New Zealand Herald*, 3 Dec 1880.
10 Mary Alleyne to Larnach children, 17 Nov 1880, LFP.
11 Julia Hocken to Donald G. Larnach, 4 Dec 1880, LFP.
12 LFP.

Chapter XIV — A MARRIAGE OF CONVENIENCE

1   Larnach to Benjamin Petersen, 16 Jun 1882, LLB.
2   Larnach to Joseph Clarke, 21 Jan 1881, LLB.
3   Larnach to H. Driver, 6 Jul 1881, LLB.
4   Larnach to Uncle Donald, 8 Nov 1881, LLB.
5   Larnach to W. Dickson, 20 Dec 1881, LLB.
6   Larnach to Walshe, 5 Jan 1882, LLB.
7   *Otago Daily Times*, 16 Jan 1883.
8   Ibid.
9   *Otago Witness*, 17 Nov 1883.
10 *Evening Star*, 18 Jan 1883.

Chapter XV — THE MINISTER OF MINES

1   In 1883 legislation was passed removing defects in previous acts and enabling the company to at last collect its rates.
2   Dalziel, *Sir Julius Vogel, Business Politician*.
3   Julius Vogel to Mayne, ATL.
4   *Evening Herald*, 14 Jul 1884.
5   *Otago Witness*, 26 Jul 1884.
6   NZPD, vol. 51, 30 Jun 1885, p.252.
7   NZPD, vol. 56, 1886, p 681.
8   Larnach to son Donald, 16 Aug 1884, LFP.
9   Dalziel, *Sir Julius Vogel, Business Politician*.
10 Hamer, "The Agricultural Company and New Zealand Politics, 1877-1886".
11 Larnach to son Donald, 14 Sep 1884, LFP.
12 Reed, A.H., *Larnach and His Castle*, A.H. Reed, Wellington, 1951.
13 "This is Your Guide to Larnach's Castle", pamphlet.
14 Larnach to Petersen, 2 Jun 1886, LLB.

15 Larnach to Bethuene, 1 Feb 1886, LLB.

16 Larnach to uncle Donald, 29 Aug 1885, LLB.

17 Larnach to son Donald, 14 Sep 1884, LLB.

Chapter XVI — OF MINES AND MINERS

1 *Lyttelton Times*, 16 May 1885.

2 Oliver W.H., *The Story of New Zealand*, Faber, London, 1960.

3 *West Coast Times*, 14 Feb 1885.

4 *West Coast Times*, 16 Feb 1885.

5 Ibid.

6 *Timaru Herald*, 5 Jul 1887.

7 *Otago Daily Times*, 1 May 1885.

8 *Cromwell Argus*, 30 Mar 1885.

9 *Christchurch Press*, 24 Apr 1885.

10 Ibid.

11 Larnach to House of Assembly, 18 Aug 1888, LFP.

Chapter XVII — MISFORTUNES MULTIPLY

1 *Otago Witness*, 26 Jul 1886.

2 Professor Mainwaring Brown lost his life in 1888 exploring between Lake Manapouri and Doubtful Sound.

3 Untitled clipping, 12 Jul 1886, LFP.

4 Larnach to Petersen, 22 Sep 1886, LLB.

5 Larnach to Tyssen, 12 Sep 1886, LLB.

6 The *Press*, 9 May 1886.

7 Larnach to Sir Julius Von Haast, 11 Sep 1886, LLB.

8 Larnach to Amelia Larnach, 1 Mar 1887, LLB.

9 Ibid.

10 *Otago Witness*, 21 Sep 1899.

11 *Thames Examiner*, 22 May 1887.

Chapter XVIII — NEW BEGINNINGS

1 Goodall, "William James Mudie Larnach, 1833-1898".

2 Complimentary Dinner Pamphlet, 18 Aug 1888, LFP.

3 Larnach to M. Pym, 18 Aug 1889, LLB.

4 Ibid.
5 Larnach to M. Pym, 25 Aug 1890, LLB.
6 Larnach to Messrs. Kenyon and Hosking, 1 Nov 1890, LLB.
7 Ibid.
8 Larnach to P.K. McCaughan, 31 Dec 1890, LLB.
9 Larnach to M. Pym, 20 Oct 1890, LLB.
10 *Otago Witness*, 4 Dec 1890.
11 Ibid.
12 *Otago Witness*, 11 Dec 1890.
13 *Dictionary of New Zealand Biography*, vol. 1, 1769-1870, Allen and Unwin/Department of Internal Affairs, Wellington, 1990.
14 Larnach to Alfred be Bathe Brandon, 5 Jan 1891, LLB.
15 NZPD, 21-23 Sep, Session II, 1891, p.821
16 Larnach to Petersen, 5 Oct 1891, LLB.
17 N. Duggan to Colleen Larnach, 1 Aug 1891, LFP.
18 Larnach to Donald Guise Larnach, 6 Dec 1893, LLB.
19 Larnach to Colleen Larnach, 31 May 1896, LLB.

Chapter XIX — THE COLONIAL BANK

1 NZPD, 21-23 Sep 1891, Session II, 1891.
2 Larnach to Petersen, 5 Oct 1891, LLB.
3 Seddon to Larnach (telegram), 14 Jun 1894, LFP.
4 Larnach to Seddon (telegram), 15 Jun 1894, LFP.
5 Bassett, M., *Sir Joseph Ward, a Political Biography*, Auckland University Press, Auckland, 1993.
6 Seddon to Larnach, 20 Jun 1894, LFP.
7 Seddon to Larnch, 12 Jul 1894, LFP.
8 Gardner, W.J., "A Colonial Economy", in *Oxford History of New Zealand*, 2nd edition, Oxford University Press, Auckland, 1992.
9 NZPD, 3 Sep 1895, vol. 90, pp.1-13.
10 Oliver, *The Story of New Zealand*.
11 Burdon, R.M., *King Dick*, Whitcombe and Tombs, Christchurch, 1955.
12 NZPD, 3 Sep 1895, vol. 90, pp.1-13.
13 Bassett, *Sir Joseph Ward*.
14 Larnach to R.J. Seddon, 11 Jan 1896, LLB.
15 Larnach to Joseph Ward, 11 Jan 1896, LLB.
16 Seddon to Larnach, 27 Jan 1896, LFP.

17 "The Colonial Bank in Liquidation" by W.J.M. Larnach, 16 Mar 1896, LFP.
18 Ibid.
19 Information from Statistics N.Z., 1996. C.P.I. figures only go back to 1914, since then inflation has risen 50 times, i.e., £100 (1914) = $10,000 (1996).
20 Bassett, *Sir Joseph Ward*.

Chapter XX — DISILLUSIONMENT
1 Larnach to Seddon, 23 May 1897, LLB.
2 Larnach to Emily Gill, 13 Dec 1896, LLB.
3 Larnach to Colleen Larnach, 25 May 1895, LLB.
4 Larnach to Donald Guise Larnach, 7 May 1895, LLB.
5 Larnach to Mother Prioress, Dominican Convent, 25 Jan 1895, LLB.
6 *Otago Daily Times*, 19 Sep 1899.
7 Sister M. Alacoque to Rev. Newport in Gore, 15 May 1895, LFP.
8 Larnach to Seddon, 13 Dec 1896, LLB.
9 Larnach to John Edwards, 16 Jun 1898, LLB.
10 Larnach to Seddon, 17 Apr 1897, MS Papers 1619-044, Seddon Family, ATL.
11 Larnach to Seddon, 23 May 1897.
12 Ibid.

Chapter XXI — RINGING DOWN THE CURTAIN
1 *Auckland Weekly News*, 21 Oct 1898.
2 Larnach to Sievwright, 27 Jan 1898, LLB.

EPILOGUE
1 *Otago Daily Times*, 19 Sep 1899.

BIBLIOGRAPHY

PRIMARY SOURCES

Papers and correspondence

Grey papers relating to the Agricultural Company, G.N.Z. MSS 64 (2), Auckland
  Public Library.
Larnach, Eliza Jane, Letters, MS Papers-4894-1, ATL.
Larnach Family Papers, held privately.
Larnach, W.J.M., Letter Books, McNab Collection, Dunedin Public Library,
  Otago Early Settlers Museum, Dunedin, and all surviving letters are on
  microfilm at the Hocken Library, Dunedin.
Normanby-Carnavon Papers, ATL.
Seddon Family Papers, ATL.
Julius Vogel Papers, ATL.

Newspapers

Ararat Advertiser.
Argus (Melbourne).
Auckland Weekly News.
Bruce Herald.
Christchurch Press.
Cromwell Argus.
Evening Star (Dunedin).
Geelong Advertiser.
Goulborn Gazette.
Kumara Times.
Lyttelton Times.
New Zealand Herald.
Otago Daily Times.
Otago Witness.
Saturday Advertiser.

Southland Daily News.
Sydney Gazette.
Sydney Morning Herald.
Thames Examiner.
Timaru Herald.
West Coast Times.

SECONDARY SOURCES

Articles

Gardner, W.J., "A Colonial Economy", in *Oxford History of New Zealand*, 2nd
    edition, Oxford University Press, Auckland, 1992.

Hamer, D.A., "The Agricutural Company and New Zealand Politics, 1877-1886",
    Historical Studies, Australia and New Zealand, vol. 10, no. 38, 1962.

Kingsley, Henry, "A Thousand Mile Journey", *Macmillan's Magazine*, 1860.

Wilson, T.G., *The Grey Government*, 1877-1879.

Books

Augustine O.P., *Sister Mary, Star of the Sea*, St Dominic's Priory, Dunedin, 1970.

Bassett, M., *Sir Joseph Ward, a Political Biography*, Auckland University Press,
    Auckland, 1993.

Birchfield, L., *Like the Ark, the Story of Ararat*, A.E. Press, Melbourne, 1993.

Brasch, C., *Present Company*, Blackwood and Janet Paul, Auckland, 1966.

Burdon, R.M., *King Dick*, Whitcombe and Tombs, Christchurch, 1955.

Chappell, N.M., *Bankers Hundred, a History of the Bank of New Zealand*,
    1861-1961, Wellington, 1961.

Church, I., *Port Chalmers and its People*, Otago Heritage Books, Dunedin, 1994.

Clark, C.M.H., *A History of Australia*, vol. III, 1824-1851, Melbourne.

Clarke, M., *Big Clarke*, Queensberry Hill Press, Carlton, 1980.

Cordiner, C., *Antiquities and Scenery of the North of Scotland*, held at the Wick
    Library, Scotland, 1780.

Cunningham, P., *Two Years in New South Wales*, London, 1827.

Dalziel, R., *Sir Julius Vogel, Business Politician*, University of Auckland Printing
    Services, 1986.

Denholm, D., *The Colonial Australians*, Penguin Books, Sydney, 1979.

Donaldson, J.E., *Caithness in the Eighteenth Century*, The Moray Press, Edinburgh, n.d.

Dunn, W.H., and L.M. Richardson, *Sir Robert Stout, a Biography*, A.H & A.W. Reed, Auckland, 1961.

Greif, S.W., and Hardwicke Knight, *Cutten*, Knight, Dunedin, 1979.

Grey, Sir George, *Journals of Two Expeditions of Discovery in North, West and Western Australia, during the Years 1837, 38, 39*, 2 vols., London, 1841.

Harris, A., *Settlers and Convicts, or Recollections of Sixteen Years Labour in Australian Backwoods, 1848*, Melbourne, 1969.

Hawke, G.R., *The Thoroughbred Among Banks in New Zealand*, The National Bank, Wellington, 1997.

Holder, R.F., *Bank of New South Wales, A History*, vol. 1, 1817-1893, Angus and Robertson, Sydney, 1970.

Hughes, R., *The Fatal Shore*, Collins Harvill, London, 1987.

Johnson, D., *Dunedin, A Pictorial History*, Canterbury University Press, Christchurch, 1993.

Knight, H., *The Ordeal of William Larnach*, Allied Press, Dunedin, 1981.

Kynaston, D., *The City of London, A World of its Own, 1815-1890*, vol. 1, Chatto and Windus, London, 1994.

Larnach, W.J.M., *The Handbook Of New Zealand Mines*, Government Printer, Wellington, 1887.

McLintock, A.H., *The History of Otago*, Otago Centennial Historical Publications, Dunedin, 1949.

Mudie, James, *The Felonry of New South Wales*, London, 1837.

Mundy, G.C., *Our Antipodes, or Residence and Rambles in the Australian Colonies with a Glimpse of the Goldfields*, London, 1855.

Olssen, E., *A History of Otago*, John McIndoe, Dunedin, 1984.

Pinney, R., *Early Northern Otago Runs*, Collins, Auckland, 1981.

Prentis, M.D., *The Scottish in Australia*, A.E. Press, Melbourne, 1987.

Preshaw, G.O., *Banking Under Difficulties*, (original edition 1888), reprinted by Capper Press, Christchurch, 1971.

Reed, A.H., *Larnach and His Castle*, Wellington, 1951.

Reeves, W.P., *The Long White Cloud*, (original edition 1898), Viking edition, 1987.

Rice, G.W., *The Oxford History of New Zealand*, 2nd edition, Oxford University Press, Auckland, 1992.

Ryan. J.T., *Reminiscences of Australia*, 1835.

Saunders, A., *The History of New Zealand*, vol. 2, Whitcombe & Tombs, Christchurch, 1899.

Scott, D., *Fire on the Clay*, Southern Cross Books, 1979.

Sinclair, K., *A History of New Zealand*, Penguin Books, Auckland, 1959.

Stone, D.I., and Donald S. Garden, *Squatters and Settlers*, A.H. & A.W. Reed, Sydney, 1978.

Stone, R.C.J., *Makers of Fortune*, Auckland University Press, Auckland, 1973.

Stone, R.C.J., *James Dilworth*, Dilworth Trust Board, Auckland, 1995.

Strang, H., *Across the Island Continent*, Henry Frowde and Hodder & Stoughton, London, 1911.

Therry, R., *Reminiscences of Thirty Years Residence in New South Wales*, 1863.

Trollope, A., *Australia and New Zealand*, vol. 2, London, 1873.

Webster, A.H.H., *Teviot Tapestry, a History of the Roxburgh-Millers Flat District*, Otago Centennial Historical Publications, Dunedin, 1948.

Whitfield, E., *A History of Singleton*, Singleton Library, NSW.

Directories and Encyclopedias

Australian Dictionary of Biography, vol. 2, 1788-1850.

Cyclopedia Of New Zealand, Otago and Southland, The Cyclopedia Company, Christchurch, 1905.

Dictionary of New Zealand Biography, Guy H. Schofield (ed), 1940.

Dictionary of New Zealand Biography, vol. 1, Allen & Unwin/Department of Internal Affairs, Wellington, 1990.

Statistics N.Z.

Unpublished theses and manuscripts

Goodall A.W., "William James Mudie Larnach, 1833-1898", unpublished thesis for a B.A. Hons., University of Otago, Dunedin, 1981.

Gore, Ross, "History of the National Bank", unpublished MS held at the National Bank Archives, Wellington.

INDEX